MASSACRE AT WOODY POINT

D1808818
9780919531352

On March 22, 1803, the *Boston*, one of the finest American ships of her day to visit the Pacific Northwest, was attacked by hostile Indians in Nootka Sound. Led by the celebrated Chief Maquinna, the warriors overpowered and killed the unsuspecting crew and plundered the ship.

O N September 3, 1802, the American brig *Boston* left England bound for the Pacific Northwest on a trade mission. In addition to her captain, John Salter, she had a crew of 26, including a 19-year-old blacksmith named John R. Jewitt, who signed on in England as an armourer. This voyage was the first time young Jewitt had put to sea and, as we will see, it very nearly proved to be his last.

In addition to a rich cargo of fine English cloths, Dutch blankets, looking-glasses, beads, knives, razors, sugar, molasses and 20 hogsheads of rum, the *Boston* also carried 3,000 muskets and scores of pistols and fowling pieces. These items were to be traded with the natives of the Pacific Northwest for fine furs and skins, which would then be traded or sold in China.

After a voyage of 29 days, the *Boston* reached the island of St. Catherine, off the coast of Brazil, where she stopped to take on wood and water. Four days later the brig put to sea again, and on December 28 rounded the treacherous Cape Horn and headed for the calm waters of the Pacific Northwest.

On March 12, 1803, the *Boston* reached Woody Point in Nootka Sound. Once again needing wood and water, Captain Salter decided to put in here because the natives were friendlier than farther north. As an added precaution against hostilities, the ship proceeded about five miles north of the Indian village they had seen, dropping anchor about midnight in 12 fathoms of water close to the shore.

The next morning several natives, accompanied by their chief Maquinna, approached the *Boston* in a canoe. After assuring himself that the natives were not armed, Captain Salter welcomed them aboard. Maquinna likewise welcomed Salter and his crew to his country. Young Jewitt, who had never seen a native before, was particularly struck by the chief's appearance, describing him as "a man of dignified aspect, about six feet in height" and extremely straight and well proportioned. He had a large Roman nose — uncommon among his people — and with his eyebrows painted in exaggerated black arches, his complexion resembling weathered copper and his face and arms smeared with red paint, Maquinna presented an awesome appearance. His long black hair, which shone with oil, was fastened into a bunch on top of his head and was powdered all over with white down (the soft under plummage of birds). Maquinna wore a mantle of black sea-otter skins that reached to his knees and was fastened about his waist with a broad belt of native cloth, painted in many figures.

Maquinna had the bearing of an unquestioned leader; one who had had many dealings with Europeans. Indeed, this was not the first time Maquinna had welcomed white men to the area. In 1878 John Meares, a British fur trader, spent the summer at Nootka Sound

This drawing of the brig Boston *depicts the scene shortly after the massacre. Jewitt is shown on board the vessel surrounded by the murderers, while to the far left, natives in the boat had two of the severed heads mounted on poles.*

and, according to him, acquired a piece of land from Maquinna. During the Spanish occupation of Nootka Sound, Maquinna became a house guest and friend of Juan Francisco de la Bodega y Quadra. When Capt. George Vancouver and the *Discovery* visited the area, he also visited Maquinna's village, although Vancouver was apparently not impressed by the chief or his customs.

Nevertheless, Maquinna's intimacy with these explorers and the white traders who followed gave him a strong feeling of importance and self-esteem, and both he and his people enjoyed the wealth of European trade. Unfortunately, after the Spanish handed over Nootka Sound to the English in March, 1795, there were fewer visits to the area, especially after 1800. This declining trade affected the wealth and influence of Maquinna, and put a strain on his leadership. Thus, he was always pleased to see a trading vessel which made him, as chief, feel important once again.

Although the *Boston* had stopped only for wood and water, it not being the trading season in the area, Captain Salter invited Chief Maquinna to join him in his cabin for a glass of rum.

Over the next several days some of the crew went ashore filling water casks and cutting pine timbers for spars, while those who remained on board busied themselves with refitting and repairing the rigging and sails. During the same period the ship was visited daily by natives who brought fresh salmon which they traded for trinkets.

On March 15, Maquinna, accompanied by several sub-chiefs, again visited the *Boston.* Resplendent in their regal robes, they formed a distinguished group as they joined Captain Salter for dinner. Four days later Maquinna visited the ship alone to dine with Salter. Because of his past involvement with Europeans, Maquinna's understanding of the English language was sufficient for him to make himself understood, and he and Salter conversed for some time. Then, as the chief was about to leave the ship, Salter presented him with a doubled-barrelled fowling piece as a gift.

To this point, everything had been cordial and serene. The 27-man crew, although cautious of the natives, had never mistreated them. Likewise, Maquinna and his chiefs had always been graciously received and dined. Unfortunately, the friendship and respect shared by both sides was about to deteriorate rapidly.

By March 20 the *Boston* had taken aboard all the wood and water required and preparations were made to get underway. The next day Maquinna visited the ship again. As a present for Captain Salter he brought 18 wild ducks. He also carried the gun that had been given to him by the captain two days earlier. Showing it to Salter, Maquinna complained that one of the locks was "bad." Salter, offended by this suggestion, called him a liar. Cursing Maquinna for breaking it, Salter snatched the gun from the chief and threw it into his cabin.

It was now Maquinna's turn to be offended. He knew enough English to understand that he was being belittled and insulted by Salter. Jewitt, who had been called by the captain to see if the gun could be repaired, later wrote that while Salter was speaking, he saw Maquinna "repeatedly put his hand to his throat and rub it on his bosom,

FRONTIER DAYS IN BRITISH COLUMBIA

FRONT COVER:
Fort Victoria in 1846 with the Ss Beaver *in the harbour.*

PHOTO CREDITS

Sunfire Archives: 2, 5, 7 (bottom), 8, 9, 12, 18, 20 (all except lower right), 23 (bottom), 30, 34-34, 38, 43 (centre), 47 (bottom inset), 52, 53, 58, 59, 66 (inset), 85 (bottom), 86 (top), 91 (top left), 95 (top), 96 (top), 97, 99 (top right), 102, 104 (top), 108, 109, 110 (top & centre), 112 (top), 113, 114, 117, 134, 134-135, 135, 138 & 140.
Bill Maximick: 2-3, 6-7 & 118-119.
HBC./Manitoba Archives: Front cover, 10-11, 15 & 22.
B.C. Prov. Archives: 11 (bottom three), 13, 16, 17, 18-19, 20 (lower right), 23 (top), 25, 28, 29, 30 (top centre), 31, 34, 35, 36, 41, 42 (top), 46 (top), 48, 49, 50, 51, 55, 56 (bottom), 60-61, 62-63, 64-65, 69, 71, 74 (inset), 78 (top), 79 (inset), 81, 83 (top), 85 (top), 89, 91 (top right), 96 (bottom), 103, 105, 112 (bottom), 115 (top), 122, 125, 127, 130, 131, 132 & 133.
B.C. Government: 14 (top left), 67 & 70 (bottom).
Garnet Basque: 14 (all except top left), 42 (bottom & inset), 42 (top & bottom), 46 (bottom), 47 (main & top inset), 66 (main), 70 (top), 74-75, 75 (inset), 78 (bottom left & right), 79 (main), 107 (bottom right), 122-123, 123, 126 & 142.
National Archives: 26-27, 98-99, 99 (top) & 107 (bottom left).
J. Stevenson: 30 (all except top centre).
Terry McLean: 39.
Vancouver Public Library: 56 (top) & 137.
Nelson Museum: 64 (inset).
N. Robertson: 82-83, 83 (bottom), 86 (bottom) & 87.
Richard James: 90-91, 94 & 95 (bottom).
Victoria City Archives: 101.
National Film Board: 104 (bottom).
Joan Goddard: 106-107, 110 (bottom) & 111.
Paul Grignon: 115 (bottom)
R. Keene: 139 & 143.

SUNFIRE PUBLICATIONS LIMITED
P.O. BOX 3399,
LANGLEY, B.C. V3A 4R7

PRINTING HISTORY
First Printing — April, 1993

PRODUCTION CREDITS
Design & Layout — Garnet Basque
Printing — Colorcraft Ltd., Hong Kong

Canadian Cataloguing in Publication Data
Main entry under title:

Frontier days in British Columbia

ISBN 0-919531-35-0

1. Frontier and pioneer life — Alberta.
2. Alberta — History. 3. Alberta, District of (Alta.)
I. Basque, Garnet
FC3661.F76 1992   971.23'02   C92-091471-3
F1078.F76 1992

COPYRIGHT © 1993 SUNFIRE PUBLICATIONS LIMITED

No part of this book may be reproduced or transmitted in any form by any means, electronically or mechanically, including photocopying and recording, or by an information storage or retrieval system, without permission in writing from the publisher. Exception is given to reviewers who may quote brief passages for the printed or electronic media.

(Above) A pen and ink portrait of John R. Jewitt made some years after his escape from Maquinna. (Facing pages) "Greeting the Discovery." This original painting by artist Bill Maximick depicts Kwakuitl natives welcoming Captain Vancouver to their Cape Mudge village in 1792. Later, Vancouver and his crew were greeted by Chief Maquinna at Friendly Cove, Nootka Sound.

which he afterwards told me was to keep down his heart which was rising into his throat and choking him." Although Maquinna uttered not a word, he was obviously furious when he left the ship after the incident.

Enraged by this insult to their chief, the angry villagers assembled on the beach, where one embittered warrior leaped to the centre of the gathering and began a wild oration. For 20 years now they had suffered insult at the hands of white men who "rode out of the moon in their great canoes." His own father had been killed by an English captain. The Spaniards had tortured and killed many of their people, including Chief Callicum, when all they wanted to do was to trade in peace. This latest indignity was a sign that now was the time to appease the spirits of the tribe's dead with the blood of the white man.

On the eventful day of March 22, as was customary, some natives brought salmon to trade. Around noon, Maquinna and a considerable number of his chiefs visited the ship, but they gave no indication of the treachery that had been planned. In fact, Maquinna, his face covered in an ugly wooden mask, appeared to be in remarkably good humour, for as his natives danced about the ship, he entertained the crew with a variety of tricks and gestures. Everything appeared normal. Maquinna displayed no sign of anger; in fact, he seemed to have forgotten the incident entirely. Then during a casual conversation with Captain Salter, he asked when the ship would be sailing.

When Salter replied that they were planing to leave the next day, Maquinna said; "You love salmon — much in Friendly Cove, why not go there and catch some?"

Chief Callicum, left, and Maquinna, right. Callicum was murdered, apparently without any justification, by the Spanish explorer Jose Martinez. This murder, combined with the insult by Captain Salter, is probably what precipitated the massacre.

Salter, who obviously suspected nothing, thought this was a good idea, and after dinner sent Mr. Delouissa and a nine-man fishing party to Friendly Cove. The first part of the plan had worked, Maquinna having unsuspectingly divided the crew. However, although the remaining 15 crewmen were outnumbered, Maquinna's warriors waited until most of them were busy hoisting a long boat before making their move. Overpowered with deadly swiftness, the men never had a chance. In the scuffle, Captain Salter was thrown overboard where he was quickly killed by natives waiting in canoes.

Jewitt was working below decks when he heared the commotion and rushed up the stairs. As he peered out he was grabbed by the hair by a native with murderous intent. Fortunately for Jewitt, his hair was short, and the ribbon with which it was tied slipped. As he fell from the Indian's grasp, however, the warrior struck at him with an axe cutting a deep gash in his forehead and rendering him unconscious.

Meanwhile, the natives broke into the weapons lockers and, having obtained muskets, headed ashore after the fishing party. Like those on board, they were quickly killed and beheaded.

After regaining consciousness, the wounded and bleeding Jewitt was ordered above deck by Maquinna. There he faced a grisly scene: 25 bloody heads, severed from their bodies, were arranged in a ghastly row on the blood-drenched deck. One by one they were taken to the terrified Jewitt for identification.

Encircled by knife-wielding warriors who were anxious to kill the only surviving witness, Jewitt expected death at any moment. But Maquinna had watched the blacksmith aboard ship and felt his services would be useful to the village. Offered a choice between death or slavery, Jewitt chose slavery. He was then ordered to sail the *Boston* into Friendly Cove, which he was able to accomplish with the assistance of the natives. After it was driven ashore, Jewitt was taken to the village where 500 warriors had gathered to celebrate their success. Once again the natives harangued their chief for the death of Jewitt. But Maquinna persisted that he would be useful in making weapons for them and he was to live. Maquinna, fearful that an attempt might be made to kill the prisoner at night, then had him taken to his own house where he slept with him and his son.

Around midnight there was a commotion outside and Jewitt again feared for his life. But the warrior had come for another reason. While wandering about the ship's hold he had been struck by someone in the dark. There must be another survivor. Maquinna explained this latest development to Jewitt, stating that this person would be killed in the morning.

As Jewitt lay there, still suffering from the injury that had completely swelled one eye shut, he thought long and hard about who the last survivor might be. After a time he concluded that it must be John Thompson, for he could not recall having seen his severed head with the others. Jewitt then devised a plan to save Thompson's life. Since Thompson was an older man, Jewitt claimed that he was his father and begged Maquinna to spare him. This plea, plus the fact that Thompson was a sailmaker, a trade which could also benefit the natives, was sufficient to spare his life.

On March 24 and 25 the natives stripped the vessel

of sails and rigging. Cutting away the spars and masts, they rendered the once mighty ship as complete a wreck as possible. During the same time some muskets, ammunition, cloth and other valuables were deposited at the chief's house.

The next day two ships were observed in the distance. This greatly excited the natives who feared their treachery was about to be discovered. As a result, a number of them began firing muskets at the ships, which were well out of range. As a result the ships, which Jewitt later learned were the *Mary* and *Juno,* realizing the natives were hostile, turned and sailed away.

On April 18, a lone warrior, prowling the deck of the *Boston* with a blazing torch, accidentally allowed sparks to fall into the hold where they quickly ignited. Jewitt and Thompson were greatly depressed as they watched their last link with civilization go up in flames. The natives, too, were saddened by the lost, for, although some of the cargo had been removed, most of it was destroyed in the fire.

For the next two years Jewitt resigned himself to the situation and tried to make the best of it. He learned to eat whale blubber covered with train oil, a most unpleasant meal that was highly relished by the Indians. He learned their language and in the course of a few months could converse with them. He made ornaments for the wives and children of the chiefs. As a result, Maquinna became fond of him and treated him well. Thompson, on the other hand, was antagonistic from the start. He considered slavery at the hands of these heathens, which he despised, worst than death itself. As a result he was disliked not only by Maquinna, upon whom his very life depended, but all the other natives as well. Once Thompson was very nearly shot by Maquinna.

The incident occurred when Thompson was attempting to put oil in the lamps in their room. As he did this, some boys, including Maquinna's son, began to tease him. At one point Maquinna's son pulled at Thompson's trousers, causing him to spill the oil. This so infuriated Thompson that he struck the boy and knocked him down. By the time Jewitt learned what had happened and rushed to the scene, he found Thompson, his chest bared, standing in front of Maquinna and a loaded musket, daring him to fire. Although Maquinna was greatly agitated, Jewitt was able to calm him by begging that his father not be killed.

Maquinna never forgave Thompson for this insult, and threatened to kill him many times. The natives also considered this insult unforgivable and wanted him tortured to death. Despite this constant threat, and the fact that his life had only been spared by the timely intervention of Jewitt, Thompson's attitude towards the natives did not moderate.

One part of Indian life which continually upset Jewitt was their eating habits and lack of personal hygiene. Not only was he disgusted by their practice of eating whale meat that was offensively putrid, but he found their practice of eating vermin from their head and clothes something less than desirable. Thompson, on the other hand, seemed to get a particular lift from the situation. He particularly relished watching as they stretched their gar-

(Above) "Nootka Lighthouse," an original painting by artist Bill Maximick of Friendly Cove, Nootka Sound as it appears today. (Right) Friendly Cove as it appeared when visited by Capt. George Vancouver. The massacre of the Boston's *crew occurred not far from here.*

ments over the cooking pots so the heat could set the little critters in motion!

On occasion Jewitt and Thompson were forced to stand guard over Maquinna. Sometimes he needed protection from neighbouring tribes who claimed that since the destruction of the *Boston* no ships came to trade with them. On other occasions, his life was threatened by his own warriors who blamed food shortages and other village problems on their chief. During these times Jewitt and Thompson were armed and stood guard over him day and night. Of course, it was in their own best interest to make sure that no harm came to Maquinna, for he was

FRONTIER DAYS IN BRITISH COLUMBIA

7

This engraving shows the interior of a house in Nootka Sound in 1784. Often several families shared these houses, each room partitioned only by planks. Because the interior was used for gutting and drying fish, and meals were cooked on an open fire in the centre, there was always a nasty stench. Smoke from the fire escaped through holes in the roof.

frequently the only thing that stood between them and death.

Jewitt took advantage of his relationship with Maquinna to inform him about the mistreatment he and Thompson had received from some of the natives, especially those from visiting tribes. This displeased Maquinna and he told them that if they were mistreated by visiting natives they would be justified in killing them. It was not long before Thompson took him up on the offer.

One day while washing his clothes and some of Maquinna's blankets at a pond, Thompson was approached by several Wickinninish braves who soon began to insult him in the customary manner. Then one of them walked on the clean blanket spread on the grass. Thompson threatened the Indian with death if he did it again, but, having done similar acts with impunity in the past, he boldly walked over the blanket a second time. Without further warning, Thompson withdrew his cutlass and in one swift motion neatly severed the man's head from his shoulders. While the other Indians ran off in terror, Thompson picked up the bloody head and dirty blanket and went to see Maquinna. He must have been relieved when the chief highly commended his action. From that point on, the two slaves commanded a little

more respect among the natives.

By midsummer of 1805, no fewer than seven vessels had passed along the coast, yet none had been inclined to visit Nootka. It looked like Jewitt and Thompson were destined to be slaves for life. At one point months before, Maquinna had said as much, and told Jewitt it was time for him to marry and settle down to their customs. When Jewitt tried to protest, Maquinna said that unless he married, both he and Thompson would be killed.

Forced with that choice, Jewitt took a 17-year-old princess as his wife. After a few months, however, Maquinna told Jewitt that if he was unhappy with his wife he could send her back to her father, which he promptly did. Single again, and once more permitted to wear European clothes, Jewitt felt relieved. Nevertheless, both he and Thompson longed for freedom.

Finally, on July 19, 1805, a vessel appeared in the harbour. Suppressing their great joy, the two men tried to appeared unconcerned while Maquinna and his chiefs held a council over what to do. Some suggested that Jewitt and Thompson should be killed and the destruction of the *Boston* blamed on other tribes. The more moderate felt that sending the captives 15 miles into the woods until the ship left would be sufficient. A few even suggested releasing them, but Maquinna was against this if at all possible.

It had been over two years since a trading vessel had visited their village, and Maquinna wanted desperately to go aboard. His chiefs, however, were against this, certain that he would be killed by the captain in retribution for the *Boston*. Maquinna then went to Jewitt, who he trusted by this time, and asked his opinion.

Jewitt was well aware that he and Thompson would never be released voluntarily by the natives: their only hope was to be exchanged for Maquinna. To accomplish this it was imperative that he convince Maquinna to visit the ship. It is not surprising, therefore, that Jewitt did everything possible to assure Maquinna that the captain had no reason to harm him. Maquinna, craving to go aboard, was easy to convince. This state of mind might help explain why he asked Jewitt to write a letter of introduction to the captain!

Jewitt then wrote a note explaining that he was one of two survivors of the *Boston*, and that warriors led by Maquinna had murdered the other crew members. He then asked the captain of the ship to seize the chief and hold him in exchange for himself and Thompson.

When the letter was completed, Maquinna asked Jewitt what he had written. Jewitt replied that he had told the captain how kind the chief had treated him, and how he wanted the chief to receive the same treatment.

Maquinna then pointed to Jewitt's signature on the bottom, turned to stare him straight in the face, and bluntly asked: "John, you no lie?"

Jewitt later wrote that he had never felt such apprehension in his life as that very moment while Maquinna studied him intently. Realizing that the slightest sign of treachery would mean instant death, Jewitt gathered as much courage as he could and asked: "Why do you ask me such a question, Tyee, have you ever known me to lie?"

After more tense moments, Maquinna told the other natives "John no lie," and despite their protestations, he and several natives were soon paddling out to the ship.

Meanwhile, Maquinna was unaware that Capt. Samuel Hill and the *Lydia* had come to Friendly Cove in hopes of finding the survivors of the *Boston*. They had sailed from Nahwitti on July 11, 1805, and as they navigated into Nootka Sound, Captain Hill had observed six cannons mounted in front of the Indian village. So, when Maquinna handed Captain Hill his "letter of introduction," he was unaware that his part in the massacre had already been suspected.

After reading the note, Hill invited Maquinna into his cabin for some biscuits and rum, while discretely signalling for five or six armed men. Maquinna was then taken prisoner and placed in irons. Although greatly surprised and terrified by these actions, Maquinna made no attempt to escape. The chief was then told to have his warriors return to the village and free the white men.

At first the villagers were greatly agitated by fears that Maquinna might be killed. But Jewitt was able to calm them through assurances that no harm would come to their chief if he and Thompson were freed. However, upon reaching the safety of the ship, Jewitt asked the captain not to release Maquinna until all of the remaining property of the *Boston* was returned. This was promptly done, upon which Maquinna was released unharmed. The *Lydia* then set sail up the coast. After nearly two and a half years in captivity, Jewitt and Thompson had been freed at last.

This drawing shows John Jewitt working his forge under Chief Maquinna's watchful eye after his capture. For two and a half years Jewitt and Thompson were slaves to Maquinna. During that time they were never sure what would come first, rescue or death.

THE FIRST FORT LANGLEY

They had three months to build a fort before winter came — and they did, despite heat, cold, illness and threats of annihilation from hostile Indians.

EARLY on the morning of June 27, 1827, a party of 25 men, in two canoes, left Fort Vancouver, on the lower Columbia River, and headed north into wild country. That evening they camped on the banks of the Cowlitz River, near present-day Longview, Washington. From there they followed a system of waterways to Puget Sound and their ultimate destination, the Fraser River.

The party consisted of Chief Factor James McMillan, three clerks, Francois Annance, Donald Manson and George Barnston, and 21 workmen, including carpenters, cooks, blacksmiths and hunters. Their goal was to establish and maintain a new Hudson's Bay Company (HBC) fort in the midst of dense coastal forest.

Their choice of a site on the Fraser was important, for they were selecting a transfer point between the coast and interior. The HBC needed a position to fall back on in the event United States territorial expansion forced the company from its posts on the lower Columbia, as indeed happened later. HBC governor George Simpson hoped that the Fraser would become a new route for the conveyance of furs from the interior to the company's ocean-going vessels. The Fraser would also be vital for transporting supplies from ships to the inland posts. In addition, American traders, derisively dubbed "Yankee pedlars," were operating along the Pacific coast up to the Russian base of Sitka, Alaska: Simpson wanted to cut into this trade and maintain a British presence in the Pacific Northwest.

At the head of the Fraser River expedition was Chief Factor James McMillan, a man that Govenor Simpson had once described as "fit for any Service requiring physical strength, firmness of mind and good management & provided he has no occasion to meddle with Pen & Ink in the use of which he is deficient. . . ."

After buying three horses and some canoes from Indians along the way, the party was met by the HBC schooner *Cadboro*, which took them up the Fraser. Progress upriver was slow. Although the crew constantly took soundings, they still ran into a few shoals before reaching the spot which McMillan, on a previous expedition, had mentally selected as a good site.

The site first chosen, on July 27, appeared desirable until it was realised that ships could not come to within 300 yards of the shore. Thus the *Cadboro* sailed downstream to an alternate location they had spotted on their way in. Here, on July 30, according to the journal:

"The schooner was brought close to the shore and the horses landed by slinging them off to the bank. The poor animals appeared to rejoice heartily in their liberation. Our men at noon were all busily employed clearing the ground for the establishment. In the evening all came on board to sleep, a precaution considered necessary until we are better assured of the friendly disposition of the natives."

(Above) This 1958 HBC calendar illustration by Franklin Arbuckle, shows Governor Douglas about to leave Fort Langley after proclaiming the Colony of British Columbia.
(Opposite page, left) Chief Factor James McMillan picked the first Fort Langley site on an exploration trip in 1824 and returned three years later.
(Opposite page, centre) Donald Manson was an HBC clerk in 1827 when he accompanied James McMillan.
(Opposite page, right) Chief Trader Archibald McDonald succeeded James McMillan as head of the first Fort Langley.

This sketch of Fort Langley first appeared in Harper's Weekly *on October 9, 1858.*

From break of day until after dark the men toiled by cutting pickets for palisades, squaring timbers for bastions, sawing planks for houses and stores, as well as the laborious task of clearing land. Watching the men constantly were some 40 to 50 natives. Although the natives were essentially friendly, they would not hesitate to steal any construction tools or supplies left unattended. However, when Shaskia, the friendly chief of the Cowichans, joined the white men, he warned that there were hostile tribes in the area that promised to destroy any fort that was built.

The first evidence of this hostility surfaced on October 10 when the Indians set fire to the forest, forcing the workers to run from the flames. The blaze burned fiercely all next day. However, instead of frightening the white men away, they doubled their efforts to get the fort completed, and by August 15 the first log bastion was finished, except for its bark roof. A week later the pickets for the palisade, that would encircle the post, were cut and ready, and men were busy digging a trench around the enclosure to hold them.

Excavations made at a later Fort Langley site indicated such trenches varied from one-and-one-half to five feet wide and three or four feet deep. The logs, squared on the sides so that they fitted together, more or less, were dropped into the trench and secured by planks joining them near the top and bottom. The ends of the posts were charred beforehand, a crude means of protecting them against damage from water or insects.

The workers prepared their logs in a sawpit, an excavation in which they erected a crude trestle. One man in the pit and another on the trestle operated a two-man handsaw, "squaring" the trunks for use in building and cutting planks out of the larger ones.

The men worked hard under the summer sun, with illness and accident taking their toll. In early August, Abraham Vincent was out of action "with venereal... under a course of mercury." On August 25, Simon "Plomondeau, one of our best men, is unable to work, on account of a swelling in his hand and arm, which have been severely injured by the use of the axe." Six days later, James Baker "got himself severely hurt in carrying logs. An attempt was made to bleed him but he sickened at the touch of the Lancet and the vein in consequence would not run." Another man, described as having "fits," required five of his companions to leave work to hold him down. He, too, was subjected to bleeding. It may not have helped his condition, but it probably rendered him weak enough to be left unsupervised.

By the end of August, the second bastion was completed. A week later, on September 8, McMillan noted in the journal: "Picketting (sic) of the fort was completed and the gates hung. The rectangle inside is 40 yds. by 45; the two bastions 12 ft. square each, built of 8-inch logs and having a lower and upper flooring, the latter of which is to be occupied by our artillery. The Tout ensemble must have a formidable enough appearance to the eyes of the Indians, especially those here who have seen nothing of the kind before."

With the palisades up, the construction of living

quarters inside the walls began. First came the store-houses, built so speedily that by mid-September "our outfit was landed from the *Cadboro,* and stowed away." On Tuesday, September 18, the *Cadboro* departed, firing a three-gun salute to the new fort as it did so. From the bastion, the fort answered with a three-gun salute of its own. That evening, friendly Indians reported that the vessel was safely out of the river.

Silence and darkness settled over the tiny enclosure, now left to rely on its own devises. Inside, McMillan and his band were now on their own. Their nearest HBC neighbours, some 300 miles away — either southward at Fort Vancouver, or northeast at Kamloops — were both too distant to render any assistance in case of trouble.

But McMillan and his men were not to remain alone for long. As word of the new post spread, crowds of Indians from Vancouver Island, Howe Sound, Burrard's Inlet, Juan de Fuca and other points soon came "to spy and pry and argue over barter prices."

As the days drew on, the men busied themselves with the task of getting houses built before the cold weather came. By Saturday, September 22, the shell of the first building was ready and it received "a good Bark covering." Two days later, McMillan wrote that "the wintering House gets on apace and promises to make snug and comfortable quarters. It is 30 ft. long, by 15 Broad. . ." with rooms for himself, Manson and Annance, each with a fireplace. After these HBC "gentlemen" were housed, a second building was begun for the "servants." By mid-October every man of the fort had a roof over his head, while timber was still being brought in and prepared for further building. A salmon-drying shed was also up, a structure as necessary as the houses because dried fish was a diet staple in winter. There was probably also a shed for canoe repair and storage.

Now came the building of a gallery inside the palisade. In case of attack it would be a sheltered location

from which to fire upon marauders. It was reached by a ladder; stairs were a refinement which came later. Five of the men had built the first section of the gallery by the end of October and at intervals during the next month they strengthened it "with a Breastwork of Plank 2 inches thick. . .to render them more secure from shot."

Pierre Charles was the group's leading hunter. One October day he left the fort and returned with "six beaver and a red deer," the deer meat a welcome change from a steady diet of fish. Charles and others continued to go hunting despite the torrents of rain that poured down throughout the final weeks of October. Meanwhile, inside the fort, stumps were being removed and timber processed to provide such amenities as benches to sit on and barrels for stores.

Little work was done on November 1, All Souls Day, but after this rare holiday the men were hard at it again. One man was doing carpentry, another mending clothes, two were clearing trees outside the palisade to give the fort a clear view along the river. The others were occupied in the endless task of drying winter provisions, squaring timber, chopping firewood, burning stumps and visiting trap lines.

Then a series of misfortunes struck. The three horses, which had more than earned their keep as haulers of logs, died one after another in a space of 10 days; one in a quagmire, one by drowning and one through illness. Some of the dried salmon stocks mildewed and spoiled. The chimney in Annance's room collapsed and had to be rebuilt, taking time and labour away from other tasks. The kitchen chimney, too, needed repairs.

Information is sparse as to how the men built their chimneys without bricks, but one can deduce the process by collecting information from other posts. Photographs of old stone posts from Fort Reliance, Northwest Territories, show a wooden framework plastered over with a clay mixture. Used as an inner coating, the

This photo of the only remaining original building at Fort Langley was taken prior to 1931.

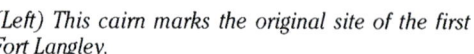

(Left) This cairn marks the original site of the first Fort Langley.

(Above) The Big House, Fort Langley, in 1976.

(Above right) Each August 3, Fort Langley celebrates the arrival of the fur brigades as people dressed in period costumes re-enact the event. This is the Big Boat's arrival at Fort Langley on August 3, 1987.

(Right) Dressed in period costume, this man is preparing his musket for firing a salute upon the arrival of the fur brigade on August 3, 1986.

(Opposite page) Although this painting by Newton Brett depicts the building of Fort Victoria in 1843, it clearly shows typical construction techniques employed at Fort Langley.

(Below) The Storehouse at Fort Langley in 1985. It is the only original building to survive to the present day. The others have been reconstructed.

This drawing of the interior of Fort Langley was done by E. Mallandain in 1858.

clay would bake hard and protect the frame from sparks or flame. The bottom part of the chimney was made from local stone; other photos from other places show chimneys made entirely from stones.

John Work's journal of 1833 describes the building of a chimney: "...the foundation has to be sunk 8 feet below the flooring, and requires a great quantity of stones to fill it up...the clay for the mortar has to be brought a considerable distance...Burning shells into lime is a tedious job...."

A Fort Langley journal entry, dated December 1, 1828, by Archibald McDonald, McMillan's successor, reads: "Two (men) have been securing the Chimney of the New House with Bark as our heavy rains here are destructive to anything of that kind. Brick would be the thing."

Piecing together such fragments suggests that the first Fort Langley chimneys were built according to a formula that worked at interior posts, using local stone and a wooden framework, with a mixture of clay, lime and dried grass as mortar. Building a chimney in the coastal rain forest, however, was a different matter from building one in the comparatively dry interior. The heavy autumn rains probably caused the structure to become unstable and require rebuilding and waterproofing.

Hence the exterior covering of cedar bark. Its waterproofing qualities are indicated by the fact that the natives used it for canoes and rain capes, and by a later note in the Fort Langley journal that reads, "Converted one of our Bark Canoes into a wood shed."

The monotony of daily routine was broken by a major celebration on Monday, November 26. Notes the journal, "This morning a Flag Staff was cut and prepared, and in the afternoon erected in the South East corner of the Fort. . . . Mr. Annance officiated in baptising the establishment, and the men were regaled in celebration of the event. Our two hunters came home at night, having been alarmed at the firing which took place on the Occasion." The fort was named in honour of Thomas Langley, a HBC director.

By mid-December the river was frozen, but winter did not stop construction at Fort Langley. More buildings were added and the gallery steadily made its way around the inside of the palisade; a year later it would boast a stairway.

Christmas week saw a diversion with the visit of a party from Fort Vancouver and there was feasting, singing, toasts and merriment. Between Christmas and New Year's, Pierre Charles led his hunters out and brought back 1,600 pounds of bear and deer meat, so there was good fare to see the New Year in. "Everyone in high glee," reported the journal on January 1, 1828. But tragedy followed. On their return trip to Fort Vancouver, the visitors were ambushed and killed.

This led to fears that the fort itself would be attacked, and the community kept a constant vigil. Snug in its little fort, however, the residents survived its first winter. The threatened attack did not come.

In mid-March several of the men went to Fort Vancouver with the Fort Langley accounts. McMillan was proud of the fact that, in addition to erecting the post, he had succeeded in trading 1,182 skins. Of these, 683 were large beaver, 228 were small beaver and 269 were land otters. When the men returned, the *Cadboro* was unloading mail and fresh supplies at the fort's fine new wharf.

That spring a building, 44x24 feet, the most ambitious yet, was begun. A brisk trade in skins and sturgeon was going on, although the men's attempts to fashion nets to catch sturgeon for themselves met with initial failures.

By mid-June, when the *Cadboro* made a second visit, the new house was complete to the point where it was being clad in cedar bark, and soon another building was under way. On Friday, August 25, the season's first salmon-salting was undertaken. A blacksmith's shop was built. With more space for storage, goods were rearranged.

The journal makes little mention of women at the fort, but it was by no means an all-male establishment. Possible some of the men brought their wives along, while others took "country wives" from nearby Indian tribes. B.A. McKelvie, in *Fort Langley: Outpost of Empire*, states there were 11 women at the post during the summer of 1828. On the morning of July 28, one unnamed woman made Fort Langley history, giving birth to the first white child, a boy that was given the name Louis Langley.

Potatoes had been planted in the spring of 1828, and by September the men had completed two cellars to house them, probably pits with roofed sheds on top. In

October and November the bumper crop was harvested — all dug and stored by November 15, an event celebrated with drinks all 'round and a dance at night. With plenty of dried potatoes and dried fish in the storehouses, the winter food supply was assured.

It was decided that autumn to enlarge the fort, which meant more chopping, trimming and squaring of logs. Despite heavy rains, the stockades were extended on the sides and the southeast bastion was moved to its new position. "This much is done," noted the fort journal, "without making any imprudent breach in the Garrison."

By the end of November the enclosure was complete and the bastion cannon re-installed. Meanwhile, the man who had taken on the role of blacksmith was busy turning out barrels, latches and hinges for doors and cupboards. On December 2, he and his assistant "contrived to make 12 small Axes today — his first trial at work of this Kind."

The major event at Fort Langley in 1828 occurred about 8 p.m. on October 11. As the skirl of bagpipes filled the air, a "fleet of canoes emerged from the semi-darkness and swept to a magnificent landing at the little wharf," wrote McKelvie. "Out of the leading craft stepped the small, but dignified figure of a man of importance. McMillan knew him instantly. It was Governor Simpson himself! With him came Dr. Hamlyn and two men who were to play important roles in the future development of Fort Langley: Archibald McDonald and James Murray Yale." They were accompanied by 20 men. Each year, on Brigade Days, this historic event is recreated at Fort Langley.

It was the final phase of Simpson's famous dash down the Fraser River, the canoe trip that proved to him the impracticability of that river as a fur brigade route. It might have meant the end for the little fort built in the face of so much, but McDonald, who now took over for McMillan, developed a thriving export trade in salmon and roof shingles.

During Fort Langley's first decade, 14,651 beaver skins were collected. Of these, no less than 10,330 were prime pelts. But furs were not the only valuable crop at Fort Langley — salmon was plentiful. In 1829, 7,544 salmon, weighing an average of six pounds each, had been traded from the Indians for less than a halfpenny each! McDonald immediately realized the potential profit in a salmon fishery and began to experiment with brine curing and exporting. Coopers were eventually provided to construct barrels, and before long salmon from Fort Langley was being shipped all over the world.

In 1837, the long-feared attack from the ferocious Yucultas finally materialized. "The Yucultas came in great numbers," wrote McKelvie. "Each long canoe bore at least 20 warriors, and there were scores of canoes.

Chief Trader James Murray Yale developed the manufacturer of isinglass at the third Fort Langley.

Word of their approach was conveyed to the fort. The alarm was sounded. Men hastened to bastions and galleries. The cannon in the blockhouses were loaded with grape, swivel guns on the walls were packed with musket balls and small shot. The Kwantlens, and their allies the Musqueams and the Katzies, retreated before the invaders, and hid in the forest fringe."

Just before dusk the Yuculta armada nosed around the bend and shot diagonally across the Fraser "to within range of the death-crammed guns of the fort. Patiently the gunners awaited the word. It came at last, and from the bastions and galleries death and destruction poured upon the close-packed canoes.

"The carnage was terrific. Canoes were blasted right out of the river; others splintered and sank; dead and dying mixed in the reddened, muddy waters. Then from the forests burst the Kwantlens with knives and spears. They and their allies started the work of butchery."

According to tradition, few if any Yucultas warriors escaped. The total number killed will never be known, but Kwantlen leaders have claimed the number was several thousand. In any event, the battle destroyed the Yuculta power, and they were never a serious threat again.

Meanwhile, with the additional room required for cooperage and fish-curing, Fort Langley was becoming crowded and inconvenient. In addition, according to author Robie L. Reid, the first Fort Langley "had been hurriedly constructed by unskilled workmen, with few tools. It deteriorated rapidly, and by 1839 rebuilding was necessary." By this time, James Yale had taken over from McDonald. Under his guidance another phase of the fishery industry had developed into the manufacture of isinglass, made from the float bladder of sturgeons. Each year some 600 pounds were exported.

Since the original fort had outlived its usefulness, in 1839 Yale selected a new location upriver that was more suitable for agriculture. Once again his men toiled in clearing land and erecting the palisades. When the stockade was completed, the heavy buildings from the old fort were torn down and moved to the new site. On June 25, 1839, the move was completed. So ended the story of the little settlement painstakingly hacked out of the wilderness in 1827.

Today, no trace remains of the first Fort Langley constructed by James McMillan and his little band of adventurers. Only a historic cairn, not far from Derby Reach Park, marks its passing. Other reminders of that period are Barnston Island, named after George Barnston, and McMillan Island, opposite the current Fort Langley, named after James McMillan.

Pioneer Ships of British Columbia

From 1849 to 1854, the *Harpooner, Cowlitz, Norman Morison, Tory* and *Princess Royal* brought more than 500 people to Vancouver Island — immigrants, miners and labourers — all sent to colonize and build a new land.

IT was on March 15, 1843 that James Douglas came ashore with a small group of men from the little steamer *Beaver* on the southern tip of Vancouver Island, where, on behalf of the Hudson's Bay Company (HBC), he set about building the fur-trading post which would in due course develop into the city of Victoria.

Like other HBC posts, Camosack, as Fort Victoria was first called, was rough, rugged and isolated. By 1845 there were only three HBC vessels providing service between London and its primitive outposts in the Pacific Northwest — the *Vancouver, Cowlitz* and *Columbia.* The first of these to enter the harbour of Fort Victoria directly from England was the *Vancouver* in 1845. These vessels made yearly voyages, bringing outfits 12 months in advance, which enabled Fort Victoria to have on hand a one or two years' supply of provisions.

For a time in 1846 it appeared that the boundary dispute between Britain and the United States would plunge the region into open warfare, and to prepare for that possibility, six British warships were anchored in the area. But the dispute was amicably settled, although England had to relinquish all claim to what is now the states of Washington and Oregon. This forced the HBC to move its headquarters from Fort Vancouver, in Oregon, to Fort Victoria.

With the threat of war ended, Fort Victoria enjoyed two years of quiet, steady development, during which time several HBC farms were started. In 1849, however, aroused by fears of further American takeovers, the HBC tried to acquire control of all territory north of the 49th parallel and west of the Rocky Mountains. However Lord

(Above) A painting of the Princess Royal, *the ship that brought settlers to Nanaimo in 1854.*
(Below) The historic side-wheeler Beaver, *(1835-1888), was the first steamship on the Pacific coast.*

Grey, speaking for the British government, considered that proposal excessive, and in the end the HBC settled for Vancouver Island.

Thus, on January 13, 1849, Vancouver Island was ceded to the HBC "at the rather reasonable annual rent of seven shillings. In return, the Company agreed to bring out colonists and sell them land at a fair price, using the proceeds (less 10 percent for the HBC) to improve the colony; if no colony had been established within five years, then the British Government could resume control of the Island."

To fulfil their obligations, the HBC began advertising in the English newspapers for settlers. Glowing promises of what they might expect included free homes, food and tools. The reward for such services "being land to the regal extent of 25 acres to labourers, and 50 acres to tradesmen, payable at the expiration of the term."

In addition to settlers, the HBC was in desperate need of coal miners to work the coal deposits that had

been discovered at Fort Rupert in 1835. It had taken the HBC 14 years since the discovery to locate its first buyer, the Pacific Mail Steamship Company, and the HBC did not consider the untrained Indians qualified to conduct the mining.

The advertisements caught the attention of Capt. Walter Colquhoun Grant, who applied for the position of surveyor in the colony. When accepted, he sold his commission as Captain and, at his own expense, assembled eight agriculturists and colonist with all their belongings and prepared to sail. The vessel which would transport them was the barque, *Harpooner*.

Answering the call for miners, meanwhile, were John Muir Sr., Overman; his four sons John, Andrew, Robert and Michael; his nephews John McGregor and Archibald Muir, and miner John Smith. With their wives and children, this party waited impatiently at Irvine, Ayshire, on the west Scottish coast for word to head for London. In late November they were finally summoned, and on

November 29, 1848, they first laid eyes on the puny vessel they would call home for the next six months.

Altogether, the *Harpooner* carried 26 passengers; 21 men, three women and two small children. In addition to the eight men of the Muir party, Captain Grant and his party, passengers included a cooper named Flett, a surgeon named Benson, a blacksmith named Walker, and two carpenters named Tolmie and Yates.

On November 30, the *Harpooner* cleared the Thames Estuary and sailed into France's stormy Bay of Biscay. From there she sailed south to near the Cape Verde Islands before heading diagonally across the South Atlantic to the South American coast. After rounding Cape Horn in the dead of winter, she sailed north into the calm waters of the Pacific. In comparison to the other vessels which would follow, the *Harpooner's* voyage was not rough, young Andrew Muir describing it as mainly tedious.

On June 1, 1849, the *Harpooner* lay at anchor in Victoria Harbour. After a careful examination of the country, Captain Grant choose Sooke Harbour as what he regarded as the most favourable spot. Flett was sent to San Juan to make barrels for the HBC's salt fish and salt pork, and the others were likewise soon employed in their occupations. All except the Muir party. Eager to begin work and dreaming of the fortunes to be made, they were told that there was no ship to transport them to Fort Rupert, more than 200 miles to the north. They spent the next three months digging wells, blasting rocks and doing odd jobs. Finally, in late August, they boarded the *Mary Dare* for the journey to Fort Rupert.

(Above left) John Muir headed a large group of coal miners that came to the west coast on the Harpooner *in 1849.*
(Above right) Agnes Hunter Bayley (1839-1931) came around the Horn on the Tory *in 1850 at the at of 11.*
(Bottom left) Andrew Hunter (1812-84), father of Agnes Hunter, arrived on Vancouver Island as a passenger on the Tory *in 1851.*
(Bottom right) John Helmcken had to tend the sick and dying on his visit to the west coast aboard the Norman Morison *in 1849.*

The next vessel to transport settlers to Vancouver Island was the *Norman Morison*. Built in Mouleim, Burma, in 1846, the 513-ton vessel was purchased by the HBC to serve as an annual supply ship to the Northwest coast two years later.

On her maiden voyage to the Pacific Coast she carried 80 passengers, mostly coal miners and labourer — settlers under contract to the HBC — and a cargo that included three puncheons of Scotch whisky for Captain Grant. A few of the men had brought wives, but none had children, which proved fortunate as their voyage was not to be a pleasant one.

Leaving Gravesend, east of London, in October, 1849, the ship was held up by severe storms in the English Channel. After encountering more storms in the Bay of Biscay, they sailed into calm waters for a while.

Unfortunately, the respite from the weather was followed by a more serious problem; sickness. Smallpox dogged them as they sailed across the Atlantic, but, thanks to the care of the young doctor on board, John S. Helmecken, only two passengers died. Even with the epidemic over, however, there was to be no peace. More illness followed, and their rounding of Cape Horn was a rough one. Gale force winds, hail, and storms assailed them, and huge waves threatened to engulf the ship. Eventually, in late January, they made it round the Cape and headed into the tranquillity of the Pacific. It was to take them another three months to reach Fort Victoria, however, for as they approached the fort they were delayed by calms in the Strait of Juan de Fuca. Bereft of winds, the *Norman Morison* drifted up and down the Strait with the tides and current.

When they finally approached the whitewashed fort, they experienced another delay. After Dr. Helmecken reported the cases of smallpox that had occurred, as well as outbreaks of scarlet and rheumatic fevers, the ship was quarantined off Esquimalt Harbour for three weeks. Adding to the passenger's gloom, they had asked Pilot Sangster for news of home. His astonished reply that the *Norman Morison* was the mail boat was not well received.

Finally, on March 24, 1850, the immigrants were allowed ashore, their arrival more than doubling the white population of Vancouver Island. The *Norman Morison* then sailed for Fort Rupert where she landed the remainder of her passengers, the little company of English miners who were to work there along with the Muirs. The *Norman Morison* stayed on the coast for six months, visiting other HBC forts up the coast, delivering mail and supplies. She even went as far north as Sitka, Alaska, before returning to England.

A short time later, the barque *Cowlitz* sailed in from England with nine passengers. Hamilton Moffatt and Samuel Robertson, two Scots, were to be HBC clerks. The rest were labourers for the HBC's farms. A small ship, the *Cowlitz* was to serve a special purpose. She was to remain on the coast to carry mail and goods between the isolated forts, to trade with the Indians, and to be Chief Factor Douglas' eyes and ears, roaming the coast on the lookout for any disturbances or signs of American penetration.

1851 saw the arrival of three groups of immigrants. In October the *Norman Morison,* making her second trip to Vancouver Island, brought 35 passengers. Among them were the Marwick brothers, the Irvines and the Sibistones.

Another vessel, the *Tory,* had taken on passengers at the London Docks in September, 1850. But one delay after another kept her at anchor until November, when she sailed north to the Orkneys to pick up farm labourers.

The *Tory* was beset by storms off France, and endured a horrible rounding of Cape Horn. Her sails froze and she was driven within 250 miles of the Antarctic Circle before reaching the calm of the Pacific. The passengers were spared illness, but suffered from abominable food, having only mouldy bread and wormy cheese by the time they reached the Pacific.

Charles Bayley, the ship's schoolmaster, who came out with his parents, described their arrival:

"The entrance to the Straits of Juan de Fuca was a welcome sight after such a long passage. . .with a fair wind we made all sail and anchored in Royal Roads on the 6th of May 1851. . .the scene that presented itself was grand. Mountains on the main land capped with snow. . . around us verdure most luxuriant, it being spring time. . . . The ship was surrounded by myriads of canoes filled with Indians in all sorts of dress. . .and many of them in a nude state, which to the eyes of our passengers was anything but agreeable. One lady burst into tears at the sight. . . . After moving the ship into Victoria. . .we scattered for a stroll together picking wild flowers."

Unfortunately, the *Tory's* arrival was marked by tragedy. Charles Fish, who had arrived in Fort Victoria earlier, had written such glowing reports of his new life that his brothers had decided to join him. As the *Tory* neared the fort, it was the HBC custom to fire two shots to announce their arrival. On shore, Charles had the honour of firing the answering salute. Tragically, the cannon misfired, burning his arm so badly it had to be amputated, and Charles died within a few days. His brothers, however, remained in Fort Victoria, and were important in the early life of the city.

One of the most important arrivals on the *Tory* was Capt. Edward Langford, the newly-appointed manager of one of the farms. As Captain Langford came ashore, all eyes were on his wife, decked out in the latest London fashions, and their five pretty daughters. Not long after their arrival, Mrs. Langford gave birth to a boy, the first white child born on Vancouver Island.

Aboard, also, were blacksmiths, sheepherders, tailors, miners, carpenters and farmers; skilled workers that Douglas desperately needed. They were housed in tents until they were parcelled out to the half dozen farm sites or to the little community growing up outside the fort

gates. Soon they settled into their new life and began the task of building their homes and planting gardens.

The *Tory* had also brought books, and a small library was established at Fort Victoria.

About 40 of the *Tory's* passengers sailed north to the coal mines of Fort Rupert. In the ship's hold, under the command of mining engineer Andrew Hunter, was a large steam engine. It was the first large piece of mechanical equipment to come into the Pacific Northwest, and was meant for the development of the coal works. But the coal was not of the quantity and quality needed for the new steamships and the engine remained in its crates for two years.

A short time later, the *Pekin* sailed from Scotland. However, when she reached the mouth of the Columbia River, the crew and passengers disembarked, refusing to go further. They considered the ship unseaworthy and were soon proved right, as she broke up on the sand bars, leaving them stranded. The passengers then made their way to Fort Vancouver where they remained until the HBC sent the *Mary Dare* to pick them up. Delivered straight to Fort Rupert, her illustrious passengers included the Dunsmuir party, destined for fame and fortune.

In 1852 a small group came out in the *Harpooner. They were* the only colonists to arrive that year. It was not until 1853 that the little colony was again inundated. On January 16, in her third crossing, the *Norman Morison* brought out 200 passengers. Most of these were families; 37 married couples with 47 children between them. The most famous passengers in this group were farm managers Kenneth McKenzie and Thomas Skinner. Among the craftsmen were bricklayers, carpenters and a gunsmith. In addition to her usual supplies and mail, the *Norman Morison* also brought more books for the library.

In April, 1855, the barque *Collinda,* contracted by the HBC to bring out 212 colonists, docked after a voyage plagued by problems that would have far-reaching consequences for the HBC.

The dilemma originated with Captain Mills. First, he was suspected of selling the passengers' food rations for those of inferior quality, and pocketing the difference. He then made amorous advances to a young woman passenger who spurned his attention, and the passengers had to protect her. When he fought a duel with the ship's doctor, tension became so high that the ship was forced to dock at Valpariso, Chile. Here, many of the passengers took advantage of the situation and left the ship. Meanwhile, Captain Mills was taken to court and found guilty of numerous offenses. To pay his fines, he breached and sold the cargo, an almost unheard of deed.

When the *Collinda* reached San Francisco, more people abandoned ship, so that by the time she finally reached Victoria on April 14, 1854, there was only a remnant of the original group still aboard, although some of the *Collinda's* passengers trickled into Victoria and Nanaimo over the next few months. As for Captain Mills, he had been promptly arrested and put in jail.

The *Collinda* incident proved to be a major setback for the HBC. Word of her distressful journey reached Scotland about the same time as the ship docked at Victoria, and the effect was immediate. Not only was the

(Above) This watercolour by Lieut. Panter-Downs depicts the coaling station of Nanaimo, on Vancouver Island, in 1859.
(Opposite page) On March 15, 1843, James Douglas established Fort Victoria for the Hudson's Bay Company. This painting depicts the completed fort in 1846 and shows the Ss Beaver *in the harbour.*
(Below) An old coloured postcard of Nanaimo Harbour, destination point for many of the early pioneers of British Columbia.

Nanaimo Harbour and Bastion, British Columbia.

HBC unable to obtain replacements, but long-term migration plans were also severely jeopardized. After a few months, the HBC gave up trying to hire Scottish miners and began to search in England, where they managed to sign over 100 individuals to contracts. But when news of the *Collinda* reached England, many of those who had already signed, defected.

Replacements were hard to come by, and the harried HBC was forced to accept many individuals who could not provide references. The HBC in London became nervous, and the whole immigration policy was put under review.

Seven and a half months after the *Collinda's* belated arrival in Victoria, a party of 120, including 23 miners, embarked on the *Princess Royal*, a fine new ship replacing the *Norman Morison*. Her journey from England was a relatively fast one, taking just under six months. Nevertheless, the voyage was "a gloomy history of deaths, misery and dissatisfaction." There were an unconscionable number of deaths, especially among the children, and the body of one infant was discarded over the side with no more ceremony than if it had been a dead cat. When the *Princess Royal* docked at Esquimalt in November, 1854, 75 passengers were speedily transferred to the steamer *Beaver* and schooner *Recovery* for the short trip to Nanaimo. These included the last of the contracted workers.

The *Collinda* incident was only part of the problem. Although the colonizing system was expensive, and it was not flourishing. After five years of colonization there was still less than 500 people on Vancouver Island, so the HBC governors decided to stop sending immigrants, hoping that disillusioned prospectors from California would drift north. Four years later, the Fraser River gold rush attracted over 30,000 people to Fort Victoria, and the colony has never looked back.

Many of these first immigrants made lasting contributions to the building of British Columbia. John Flett spent five years trading with the Indians. He returned to Scotland in 1854 married, and returned to Vancouver Island the following year. He then turned to farming and opened up the Cowichan Valley north of Victoria. His descendants still live on the old homestead. The McKenzies' Craigflower Manor still stands, but not as a farmstead in the wilderness west of Victoria. Today it is a museum, its fields all highways and condominiums.

After mining for coal at Fort Rupert and Nanaimo, the Muirs purchased Grant's farm and founded the town of Sooke. They introduced logging, saw-milling and shipbuilding to the colony, and exported their products around the world. There is still a sawmill at Sooke today.

After exploring the northern tip of Vancouver Island and putting a road through to the west coast of the Island, Andrew Hunter was transferred to the Nanaimo coal mines. For over 30 years he ran the machinery that kept Nanaimo coal pouring into ships and homes from Alaska to San Diego. The Nanaimo coal deposits were worked for 100 years, and there is talk of reviving them again.

Dr. Helmecken married the daughter of Gov. James Douglas and was Victoria's much beloved doctor for many years. His home, too, is now a museum. Like many of the early pioneers who combined two or three professions, Helmecken went into politics, sitting on early councils with pioneers John Yates, John Muir and Charles Bayley.

Bayley began his new life as a school teacher, then served as coroner. He later went on to build Victoria's first hotel and, later still, between gold mining ventures, became a colonial Member of Parliament and Speaker of the colony's Legislative House. He, with other merchants like Yates and the Fish brothers, was a diligent reformer for independence and growth for their fledging new home.

The most spectacular story surely belongs to the Dunsmuir party from the ill-fated *Pekin*. Robert Dunsmuir built a fortune in coal and railways and his oldest son James became Premier of B.C. His daughters married into the British aristocracy and American bluebloods. Robert Dunsmuir's massive Craigdarroch Castle in Victoria is now a major tourist attraction, only to be outdone in grandeur by his son's Hatley Park Castle, now the Royal Roads Military Academy.

As for the ships that transported these early pioneers, fate was not as kind. The *Harpooner* is yet untraced, lost to B.C. history after its two historic voyages here. The *Cowlitz* returned to England after its 1851 voyage and was sold for £3,250. The *Norman Morison*, after its third trip to Victoria, was sold in 1854. Working out of England as a trade ship, she disappeared on a tea-trading mission between Australia and India in 1866. No wreckage or report of her was ever registered. The *Tory* met a similar fate. After leaving the west coast she returned by way of Honolulu and Shanghai, carrying tea to England. She then immediately sailed for Australia where she was lost off the rocky east coast near Sydney, in 1853. The last of the pioneer ships, the *Princess Royal*, lasted the longest. She worked as a trade ship out of Hudson's Bay until driven ashore by a storm in 1885. The beached ship was lived in by Algonquin Indians for many years, until it was finally burned by accident.

Today, the descendants of these early pioneers still carry on the memories and traditions of the past. John Muir's great-granddaughter, Florence Muir Acreman, is well known in the Sooke area for her knowledge of local history. Alf Flett, following his great-grandfather's interest in politics, has served as an alderman and is active in Vancouver Island affairs. With a lifelong interest in local history and 30 years as a member of the Native Sons of B.C., he is now serving his second term as Chief Factor of Nanaimo's Post No. 3.

The Hunter family's younger generation have grown up on stories of the "olden days." William Hunter, the oldest family member, served as an alderman in Nanaimo where most of the family is yet based. His cousin, May Dension, is very active in the Native Daughters Society of B.C. and was head of this group in 1987-88.

Dr. John Helmecken's great-grandson, Ainsley Helmecken, founded the city of Victoria's archives department in 1966 and retired only six years ago. Frail health has not yet dampened his interest in preserving the past.

WILLIAM DUNCAN:
MISSIONARY TO THE TSIMSHIAN

On October 1, 1857, a 25-year-old missionary landed at Fort Simpson, an isolated Hudson's Bay Company fort on the northwestern coast of B.C. Surrounding the post were nine different tribes of Indians with a population of 2,300. Duncan, who was the first missionary they had ever seen, dedicated the remainder of his life improving their living conditions.

Port Simpson in 1884. When William Duncan landed here in 1857, it was an isolated HBC outpost consisting of a few buildings and a thick stockade of logs armed with cannons. Outsite the walls, over 2,000 natives lived in crude houses.

Built in 1834 near the beach of a sheltered bay, east of Dixon's Entrance, the Hudson's Bay Company's (HBC) Fort Simpson was located not far from the boundary of what was then Russian territory. "The walls of the fort consisted of palisades, 32 feet high, built of trunks of trees over two feet in diameter driven into the ground, and solidly riveted together. The double-gate was iron-bound and bolted, and in it was a smaller gate, similarly protected, at which a sentinel or doorkeeper was stationed night and day, and through which, under the rules of the company, not more than two Indians at any one time were admitted, so great was the fear of the inmates of the Fort of the savagery of the Indians."

When the fort was first constructed, there was no Indian village close by. The Tsimshian Indians were then located at Metlakatla, some 17 miles southeast of the fort. However, they had been induced to take down their houses and rebuild them in the immediate vicinity of the post. Thus, by 1857, there were nine tribes with a combined population of 2,300 living in 140 houses outside the fort's walls. Built on poles along the beach, 15 or 20 feet above high tide, the Indian houses were all one room, one story, windowless structures.

That was the cluttered view that greeted 23-year-old William Duncan as the *Otter* dropped anchor in the harbour late in the evening of Monday, October 1, 1857. A husky, five-foot-seven-inch young man with pink cheeks,

WILLIAM DUNCAN
1832-1918

blue eyes and brown hair and beard, Duncan would be the first missionary among the Tsimshian Indians.

Born at Beverley, in Yorkshire, England, in 1832, Duncan had demonstrated a Christian upbringing at an early age. At nine he joined the town choir, in which he remained active until his voice changed at the age of 16. In addition to his regular education, young Duncan had received a year's instruction in penmanship in a private institution. This may have proved helpful in his obtaining a position with a large tannery when he was only 15 years old. Duncan's first duties were producing the company's bills and invoices. However, he rose quickly to bookkeeper and was soon entrusted with the books and cash of the company. At the age of 17 he became a commercial traveller, representing the firm in seven or eight countries.

Duncan seemed destined to rise through the ranks of the company, but a stormy, drizzly evening in December, 1853, changed the course of his life. At the invitation of a friend, Duncan attended a quarterly missionary meeting in St. John's Church in Beverley. By the time the service was over, Duncan, who was the only young man present, had determined that he would become a missionary.

In 1854 he was accepted by the Church Missionary Society (CMS) and for the next two years attended Highbury College. There Duncan progressed so rapidly that it was felt that he might, after another year's study, be sent as an instructor to a higher educational institution run by the CMS in India. But fate, in the form of Capt. J.C. Prevost, intervened.

A commander in the British Navy, Prevost had returned to England in the spring of 1856 after a four year's cruise policing the waters of British Columbia. A religious man who had seen that drunkenness and prostitution were rampant at Fort Simpson, Prevost informed the CMS about the savages that lived in the region and suggested that it would be an ideal location for a new mission. The CMS were interested, but lacked the necessary funds for such purpose. However, they suggested Captain Prevost use their journal, *The Christian Missionary Intelligencer*, to appeal for funds from the public. This he did and $2,500 was raised within a month. Next they needed a proper missionary to send, but meeting after meeting failed to find the right man for the job.

Then one day Prevost advised the CMS that he would be returning to the Pacific coast in a fortnight, and that he had obtained the permission of the Admiralty to transport any missionary the CMS might wish to send. Once again the committee gathered, but were again having no success, until someone thought of Duncan. Immediately, they all realized that he was their man, but would he go?

Duncan accepted the posting without hesitation. The same evening he purchased a complete outfit, including a

These two watercolour paintings of Metlakatla were made by Lady Dufferin in 1876. Metlakatla was the principal home of the Tsimshian Indians before they left it for Fort Simpson. The Indians returned in 1862 and constructed a number of comfortable modern dwellings and a large wooden church. They left for good in 1887. The church burned to the ground in 1900.

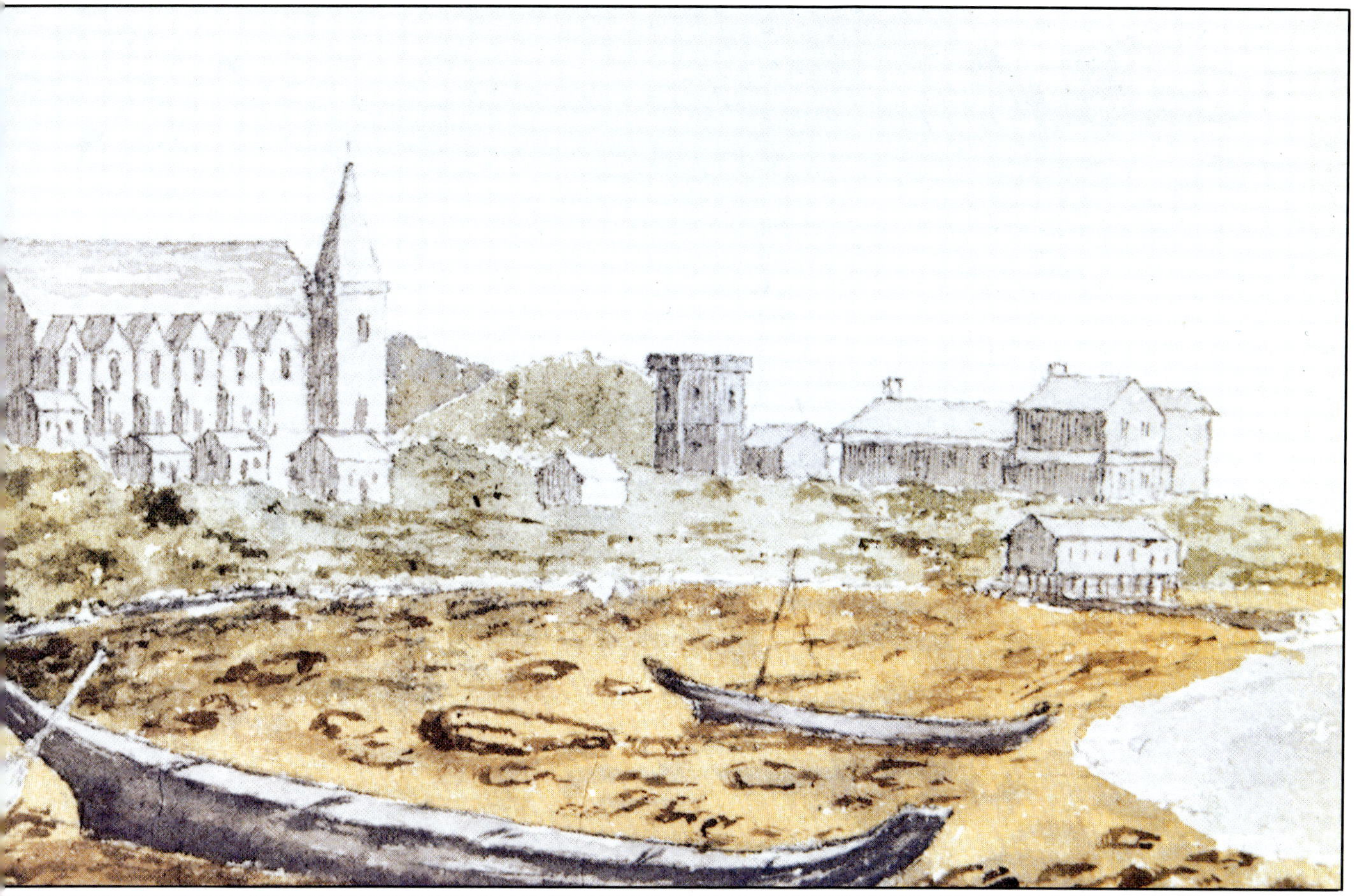

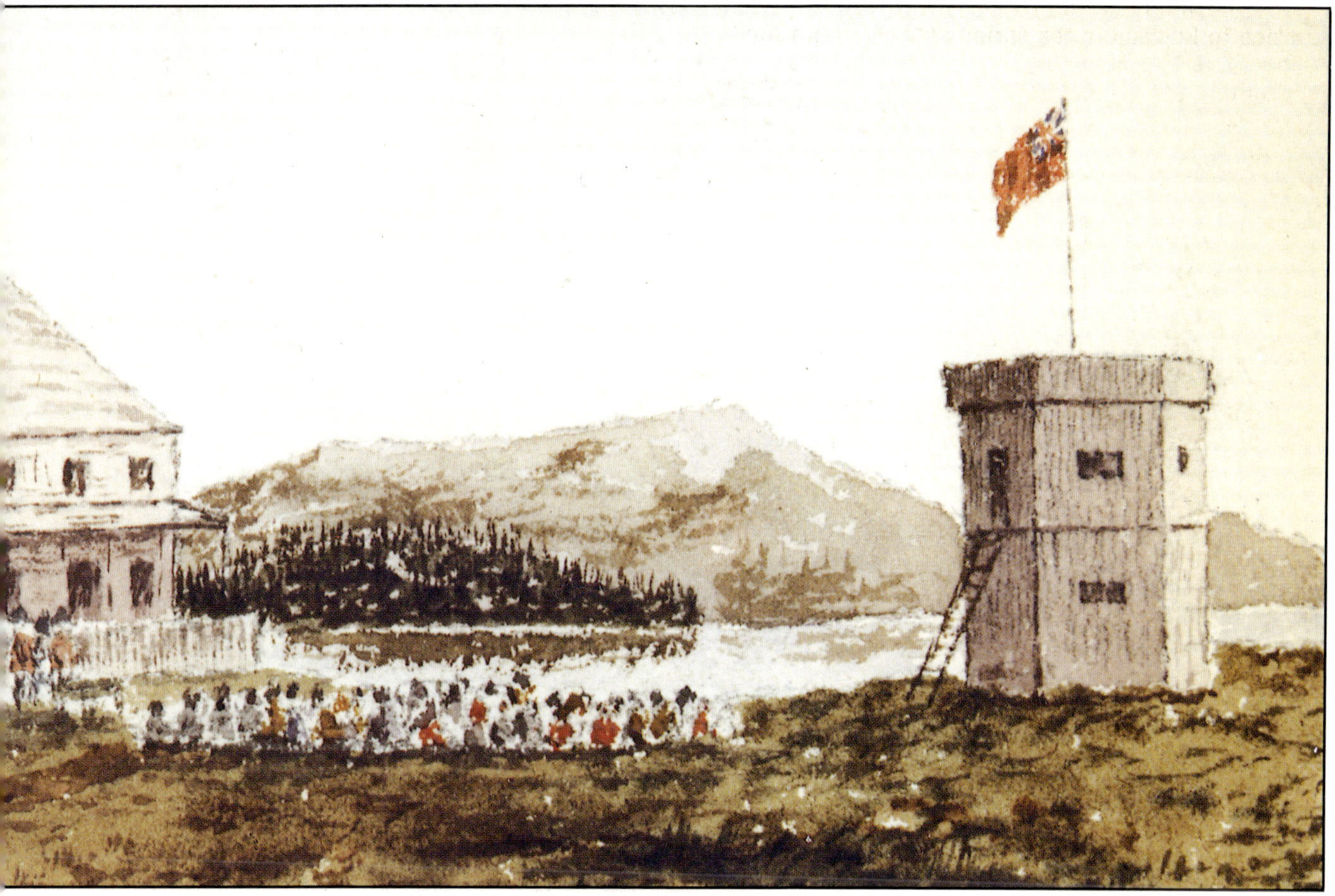

shovel, axe, saw, rake and hoe, for he expected to work hard physically as well as spiritually. On December 23, 1856, he boarded HMS *Satellite,* a newly-commissioned steam frigate, for the six-month voyage around Cape Horn to the North Pacific Coast.

On June 13, 1857, as the *Satellite* rounded Cape Flattery and started down the Strait of Juan de Fuca, eight Indians paddled a big canoe alongside the ship. This was Duncan's first look at the people with whom he would spend the rest of his life. He mused over their appearance but admired the craftsmanship of the canoe as the *Satellite* towed it astern and headed for Esquimalt.

Duncan spent the summer of 1857 in Fort Victoria, then an insignificant hamlet of less than 200 inhabitants, where he was shocked by the grubby, sprawling Indian camps around the post. Initially, Governor Douglas would not give Duncan his consent to travel aboard a HBC ship to Fort Simpson. Douglas felt that the CMS had made a serious mistake in sending a missionary to the Indians at Fort Simpson. Douglas was convinced it meant certain death and he tried to persuade the young missionary to remain in Victoria. But Duncan would have none of it; he wanted to remain only long enough to learn the Tsimshian language. While there, however, he also found time to organized the first choir at Christ Church and to teach a Sunday School class.

Duncan left Victoria on the *Otter* on September 15. As they approached Fort Rupert, at the north end of Vancouver Island, Duncan saw the bodies of three dismembered Haida Indians on the beach of an island.

Their deaths had been the result of an assault by Kwakiutls intent on avenging a raid in which one of their chiefs had been killed and four members of their tribe had been taken prisoner.

Finally, on the evening of October 1, the *Otter* reached Fort Simpson. The little steamship's whistle brought canoes alongside and Duncan was taken to the beach where Factor McNeill met him and escorted him to quarters where he would live for the next four years. The young missionary noted that the fort had been newly whitewashed and was armed at the bastions with cannons. Inside the stockade "were located the company's store and its immense warehouse, where thousands of

(Above) The native band in front of the church at Old Metlakatla.

(Below) Natives building a canoe at Old Metlakatla.

valuable furs, obtained by barter from the Indians at ridiculously low prices, were kept, the captain's residence, where the mess-room for the officers was located, a second building for the second officer and visitors, where Mr. Duncan, soon after his arrival, was installed in two small rooms. There was also a carpenter shop, a blacksmith's shop, and a large building, containing five rooms, for the garrison of the Fort, which, besides the three officers, consisted of twenty workmen, mostly French Canadians. They were all married to, or at least living with, Indian women, and four of the families were stowed

(Left) The jail and courthouse at Old Metlakatla.
(Below) William Duncan in his study at New Metlakatla, Alaska. This building is now a museum.

(Above left) This painting of William Duncan hangs on the wall of Duncan's former residence, which has been converted to a museum, in New Metlakatla, Alaska.
(Above centre) This middle-aged photo of William Duncan was taken at New Metlakatla.
(Above right) A young dancer in full native dress at New Metlakatla.
(Opposite page) A general view of Old Metlakatla in the 1880s.
(Below) The only way into New Metlakatla is by ship or float plane.
(Below, inset) William Duncan's former residence is now a museum at New Metlakatla.

away in one room, each family living in one corner, and doing its cooking at the common fireplace in the centre of the room."

Duncan's first task was to learn the Tsimshian language. An Indian named Clah was suggested as his teacher, but he understood no English. So, making use of "Chinook" jargon, Duncan taught him English while Clah taught Tsimshian in return. Progress was intolerable slow at first, Duncan relating how he often spent half a day obtaining the proper words for a single idea. In all, it took eight months of assiduous study before Duncan had a sufficient knowledge of the language to give the Indians a sermon in their native tongue. On June 13, 1858, he was ready. One by one, he attended the houses of the chiefs of the nine tribes, repeating his sermon before a total of 800 to 900 quiet, well-behaved and impressed natives.

Legaic, the head chief, was so impressed by the sermon that he offered his house to be used as a school. Duncan accepted and immediately held school; the children attended each morning, the adults each afternoon. Twenty-six children were in attendance the first day, the numbers steadily rising. Only 15 adults responded for the afternoon session, however, and Duncan reasoned it took more courage for them to attend.

During the summer Duncan decided to erect a school building, employing the Indians as willing labourers. The site chosen was on a hill near where the Methodist Church was later erected. Unfortunately, after an old man died, probably of heart trouble, the suspicious Indians were not anxious to return to the site. This delayed the project until September 16, when, with a new location, work was resumed. Within a few days the framework was in position, and by November 17 the school was ready, opening day seeing 140 children and 50 adults attending.

In December, Duncan learned that an Indian woman had been beating her slave. Fearing the girl would be slain, Duncan persuaded the woman to stop. The remorseful woman explained that she had been abused by her husband, and this was her only way to even the score.

In December, Chief Legaic asked Duncan to close the school for the month because of his daughter's "gone to the moon" ceremony which initiated young girls into womanhood. Despite warnings that the medicine-men might shoot the children if he did not, the feisty little missionary refused. However, only about 80 students attended the next day, the rest being undoubtedly aware of what was to happen.

All went well in the morning, but in the afternoon, just as school was about to commence, Duncan noticed several Indians approaching the school in single file. Led by Legaic, they all had war paint on, some even wore masks. When the Indians entered the room, the children all scampered outdoors. Duncan, appearing undaunted, simply folded his arms and stood firm.

At first Legaic merely scolded Duncan for refusing his request. However, as the other Indians began to taunt Legaic, who was considerably intoxicated, he drew a knife. As he threatened Duncan, another Indian named Cushwaht encouraged him by saying: "Kill him. Cut his head off. Give it to me, and I will kick it on the beach!"

Just as it appeared he might be slain, Duncan suddenly noticed Legaic's frenzied eyes shift beyond him. Turning, Duncan saw Clah, who had entered the school, standing behind him with his hand under his blanket. Fearing Clah was reaching for a pistol under his cloak, Legaic sheathed his knife and, grunting insults at Clah, backed off, followed by his medicine men.

In spite of further threats from Legaic, the school persevered. The children loved to hear Duncan play his concertina, and they sang with him. He even bought a canoe so that his pupils could reach the school when high tides flooded the trails. In March, Duncan closed the school to allow his pupils to fish with their parents for oolichan on the Nass River.

In June of 1859, an old chief, Neewklakkahnoosh, urged Duncan to encourage the Indians to move to a new location where they could live in peace. At their ancient home of Metlakatla, he said, they could settle along the sheltered beaches.

More violence in the fall reinforced the resolve of the young missionary to relocate his people in a better land. Cushwaht, known as a bad man, had sent his wife to the

fort to get salve for his wounded leg. When she was turned back, the drunken man smashed the school door with an axe and broke all the windows. Later, in Cushwaht's house, his sister and another woman were shot to death. Rum brought in from Victoria set off another round of fights and still more people were killed. On December 29, gunfire near the school sent Duncan and his pupils scurrying for the safety of the woods. The volatile Cushwaht was on the warpath again, proclaiming he had not received his fair share of goods from a potlatch, He sought revenge by shooting at the potlatchers, who returned his fire. Fortunately, the Indians were all too drunk to hit their targets.

In the spring of 1860, Duncan had a respite from his regular routine when he visited the fishing camps on the Nass River. There, 5,000 Indians had gathered to reap the oolichan harvest. The little fish could be smoked or pickled in salt brine for food. It also provided oil which they burned as candles.

Travelling by canoe and camping along the river gave Duncan an opportunity to get away from Fort Simpson for a lengthy time. Along the banks of the river people were growing potatoes and smoking salmon. As gifts, Duncan handed out gunpowder to the chiefs and presented their wives with soap. In one village a problem arose when two wives tried to claim the gift. As Duncan handed the soap to one of the women, he stated that he did not approve of a man having two wives. The recipient of the gift agreed most vociferously, and said that her husband should dismiss his second wife.

Duncan's plans for the move to Metlakatla quickened when a canoe arrived from Victoria with news that a smallpox epidemic had killed 30 Indians. The Fort Simpson Indians became alarmed and Duncan said they could look upon the threat as a warning from God — that it was now time to vacate the evil fort. Soon Duncan was leading a small flotilla of canoes in the direction of Metlakatla. An advance party that had already paddled to the promised land was busy clearing bush, building shelters, and planting potatoes. At an overnight camp, Duncan's group sang and prayed. On the afternoon of May 28, 1862, they arrived at Metlakatla and, despite a drenching rain, immediately started to work.

Within a few days a fleet of canoes brought two chiefs and 300 tribesmen to Metlakatla; they reported that people were dying from the plague at Fort Simpson. Among the arrivals was the chastened Legaic, who begged Duncan to baptize himself and his family.

Early in July, the plague came to the new village and Duncan moved quickly to inoculate his people so that only five died in comparison to 500 at Fort Simpson. Duncan noted with satisfaction that the medicine men lost face, for it was the white man's vaccine that had saved the settlement.

That summer the villagers recovered a blood-splattered whaleboat from the sea and discovered the remains of two dead miners who had been returning from the Stikine River gold rush. A partner who had escaped the slaughter claimed that four Tsimshians had been the killers. When miners in another canoe were attacked and robbed, Governor Douglas ordered two

gunboats into the area. On Dundas Island, the bluejackets had a shoot-out with Indians, but they captured two suspects and held some men as hostages.

When Captain Richards of the gunboat *Hecate* visited Metlakatla, he admired the restrained behaviour of the people and gave them a tour of his ship. The sailors collected money for Duncan's mission and provided plum pudding for the children.

Duncan laid down firm rules for the Metlakatlans: they were not to drink liquors or give away their belongings at potlatches; they were required to send their children to school, attend religious instruction and be clean, industrious and peaceful. Duncan oversaw the building of 30 houses and a combined church and school. In October, he harvested the first crop of potatoes from his garden. He obtained a grant from Governor Douglas for building materials and now asked for money to buy a schooner. It was needed to transport furs, salted and smoked fish, dried berries and oolichan grease to the Victoria market. Douglas praised the new settlement for its abstinence from liquor and granted $1,000 towards the schooner and uniforms for the Indian constables.

On New Year's day a council of 20 elders, for the church, and 20 constables, to maintain order, was chosen.

During the first winter, the new community was attacked by hungry wolves. After they had killed a slave girl in the woods, Duncan patrolled the village at night with a sword, for he feared that the ravenous animals would also kill the deer and goats in the expanding herd.

When Bishop Hill of Victoria visited Metlakatla, he advised Duncan that he favoured the elaborate rituals of "high church" Anglicanism. But Duncan opposed this as sheer popery that would have no meaning for the Tsimshians. He also refused ordination; he had not had a "call," he told the bishop. This disagreement formed the basis for an ongoing controversy between the combative little Yorkshireman and his superiors.

Meanwhile, as Duncan tightened his hold over Metlakatla, many of the Tsimshians became dissatisfied, for they wanted more freedom to act on their own. However, despite their complaints and his many responsibilities, Duncan found time to build a playground for the children and to organize sports. After a fund-raising journey to England, he returned with a weaving machine and instruments for a brass band which soon became the hallmark of Metlakatla.

In 1874, services were held in the new church which seated 1,200 worshippers. The largest church north of San Francisco, the imposing edifice had cost $12,000. The community was growing and prospering now, and in 1880, the women manufactured blankets on their new looms and made their own shawls and skirts. The new sawmill turned out lumber for houses, a cannery began operation, and, under Duncan's guidance, Metlakatla soon became a world-famous showplace.

By this time, Metlakatla had divided into factions; 200 for William Ridley, the new Bishop of Caledonia, and 800 for the feisty Duncan. Ridley was a pugnacious man who would not hesitate in knocking a Tsimshian down when he thought the man impudent. Duncan and his followers thought the bishop, with his fine robes, acted too much like a medicine man. Adding to the tension was the fact that Duncan opposed communion. He said it reminded him of the barbaric ritual in which the "cannibals" pretended to eat human flesh. The situation turned nasty when some of the bishop's adherents fired at Robert Tomlinson while he was in his canoe. The incident prompted Duncan's trusted assistant to reflect; "I know that they never intended to hit me, but they were scaring the tar out of me."

The struggle between Duncan and the self-righteous bishop continued for four years. During the same time, Duncan was battling the province over Indian rights, particularly land tenure. The attorney-general said that Metlakatla belonged to the Queen, not the Indians. When the Dominion government in Ottawa did not back the Tsimshians, a bitter Duncan contemplated moving the Metlakatlans to Alaska and soon set up a meeting with Pres. Grover Cleveland in Washington, D.C. Reporting on the controversy, the United States press stated that the dominion and provincial governments in Canada had acted in a shameful manner. This attack stirred up wounded pride and defensive postures in the Canadian newspapers.

Following discussions with the Americans, Duncan made an irrevocable decision to lead his Tsimshian charges to Alaska. Accepting a large 36-star flag in Philadelphia's Independence Hall, he vowed to become an American citizen.

After sending out advance parties from old Metlakatla to the untamed land in the north, the Tsimshians left their homes in a flotilla of 50 canoes, and over the next 10 days, craft of all shapes and sizes carried 800 men, women and children with all their possessions over 70 miles of water to their new home in Alaska. The little cannery steamer *Princess Louise* and the missionary boat *Glad Tidings* towed the strings of canoes to Annette Island, the chosen place for the new colony.

As winter approached, and under great hardship, the Metlakatlans prepared the land for another model village by building roads, houses, a church, and cannery. Some of the boys were sent to Sitka for schooling.

In 1888, they celebrated July 4 in style, hoisting the American flag and firing a salute from a small cannon. The brass band played and the children sang. Soon 60 Tlingits joined the Tsimshian to increase the population of the village.

After some settling-in time, many of the Tsimshian pointed out that New Metlakatla was not a communal organization because the Metlakatla Company, which owned the sawmill and cannery, consisted for the most part of Duncan himself. They accused him of mixing business accounts with charitable donations in his bookkeeping. Then too, he controlled the Benevolent Fund and refused to give the Indians grants or even interest-free loans. Although a few voiced suspicions that he was using the money for his own personal use, the missionary paid little attention to the incipient rebellion.

Despite the problems, the cannery and sawmill prospered, houses and boats were built, a breakwater and wharf were constructed and the gardens thrived.

In March, 1891, Annette Island was formally reserved by Congress for the Metlakatlans as a special Indian reserve separate from the general reservation system. Still unable to trust the Indians to take over business responsibilities, the old missionary's workload became heavier and he still retained the bad habit of juggling the books, but never in his favour. Duncan was not after personal gain, but thought in terms of the ultimate good of the whole community. Refusing to delegate authority, he tried to do everything himself, working day and night, and soon paid the price for his dedication. Duncan did not grow old gracefully, but became bitter and irascible. He quarrelled with his old Tsimshian supporters and became unfriendly with politicians who could have done so much for him and his flock.

Walking to the post office on the afternoon of August 27, 1918, the weary old man suffered a stroke. Although nursed by an Indian women, early on the morning of August 30, the church bell rang out the message that the colourful and controversial leader of the Metlakatlans had died. At the funeral, the choir sang songs written in Tsimshian by Duncan. The little Yorkshire missionary was buried beside his church near a clump of trees.

In spite of unrest before and after the death of their leader, New Metlakatla became the outstanding native community of Alaska, the only Indian reservation in that state. The town runs its own affairs and it self-supporting; the council owns a modern fishing fleet and cannery, and leases sawmill and timber to outside interests.

In the summer of 1988, I flew to Metlakatla in an Otter seaplane from Ketchikan, Alaska, only about a 10-minute flight away. There I found that Father Duncan's house was now a museum containing many memorabilia of his days as leader of the Metlakatlans. The plane's passengers were driven to the Tsimshian long house in a small Grayline bus. Our guide was a pretty, young Indian woman who also coaches Little League baseball. We feasted on fried bread and salmon with both dry and moist seaweed, while the Indians, in their colourful costumes, danced for us.

New Metlakatla, with a population of 1,500, has a Middle School and a Junior-Senior High School and there is a large activity centre with racquet ball courts and a modern Olympic-size pool. Our guide pointed out the dental clinic and the police department. She said that 50 new units of handicapped housing were underway, built on posts because of the muskeg.

At the wharf, a Japanese ship was loading cans of salmon and lumber. The ships came three times each month. "They often load herring roe," said our attractive Tsimshian guide.

I asked her if there was still communication with Old Metlakatla near Prince Rupert. "Yes," she replied. "I believe there are about 250 still living there. I visited my relatives a few weeks ago."

As the plane flew us back to Ketchikan, I reflected that, because of the early aggressive leadership of Duncan, and in spite of his stubborn and dictatorial ways in the later stages, the Metlakatlans had achieved a unique place in the history of Indians on the west coast of North America.

THE STRANGE CONCLUSION OF THE FRASER CANYON WAR

The first newspaper headline claimed that 45 miners had been massacred by Indians in the Fraser Canyon. According to the report, the Indians, carrying a white flag, pretended to come in peace. That night, while the unsuspecting miners slept, they were treacherously murdered and their bodies horrible mutilated. But what really happened in August, 1858?

FROM the very moment that the Thompson River Indians first discovered gold in their country, sometime around 1855, it was inevitable that a violent confrontation would develop between the native inhabitants of what now constitutes southern British Columbia and American gold seekers from below the 49th parallel. By rights the Indians claimed the gold as their own, and as the first trickle of foreign miners began to filter in, the natives made it perfectly clear that they would not tolerate any challenge to their authority within the bounds of their territories. As one contemporary correspondent stated it in the August 4 issue of the London *Times*, the proud, independent tribes of the Fraser and Thompson rivers were "a trial to the temper of. . .men who used to shoot all Indians as vermin in California in 1848 and 1849." Accordingly, as the Fraser River gold rush gained momentum in the spring of 1858 and some 25,000 men prepared to leave San Francisco for the New Eldorado, they were warned by the San Francisco *Bulletin* on June 7, 1858, that the native inhabitants of the British possessions were "very different beings from the Digger tribes of California. . .fierce, war-like, and expert with weapons. . . . The miners must prepare for a war with the savages. They will have to work with a shovel in one hand and a rifle in the other."

The anticipated collision occurred in the second week of August, 1858, when the headless, bullet-ridden bodies of miners drifted down through the Fraser Canyon, and hundreds of gold seekers retreated down river towards the safety of Yale for fear of Indian outrages. Donald Fraser, correspondent for

(Above) This scene, "Sunday Morning in the Mines," was painted by Charles Nahl, an early day miner in the Mother Lode Country of California, in 1872. Although it is a typical scene of an early California mining camp, since most of the first miners on the Fraser River were also from California, it is not unlike the earliest mining scenes here as well. The painting is particularly interesting as it is really two paintings in one. The left half depicts the rowdy element among the miners celebrating after work or on pay days, while the right half shows the ones who relaxed by reading or writing.
(Left) This painting by Hinds depicts an early Cariboo miner panning for gold.
(Right) The old HBC post of Fort Yale sprang back to life when gold was discovered nearby in the Fraser River.

FRONTIER DAYS IN BRITISH COLUMBIA
35

An Indian chief's grave at Chapman's Bar. Such were the scenes that the miners met as they proceeded up the canyon.

the London *Times,* stated on October 27: "Altogether four headless trunks came down from the upper waters, and were picked up by miners between Fort Yale and Fort Hope. The sight naturally roused the inhabitants to action, and a fellow named Graham, a Californian, burning to distinguish himself, raised a company of volunteers to fight the Indians. His plan was very simple. He was to commence killing the Indians at the nearest village (Spuzzum), just beyond Fort Yale, and keep killing as he went up the river as far as the Forks (Lytton), 90 miles. No investigation, no discretion, no segregation of the guilty from the innocent. It was to be an exterminating raid."

One of four rifle companies that departed from Yale on the morning of August 18, Graham's group, the Whatcom Guards, travelled together with another volunteer company led by a man referred to as Captain Galloway. These two companies, totalling 40 men, apparently followed the old Indian trail that led to the west side of the canyon to Spuzzum, eight miles above. Two other companies, led by "captains" Snyder and Centras and totalling 133 men, travelled towards the same destination by way of the old Hudson's Bay Company (HBC) brigade trail, Douglas Portage.

According to the September 1 issue of the Victoria *Gazette,* shortly after leaving Yale, Harry Snyder called the latter two companies to a halt and made a brief address. He stated the course that he intended to pursue, "and under which he would only consent to lead them." This was "to endeavor to affect a peace with the Indians by peaceable means if possible, and only as a last resource to use force." Another Californian, Snyder's motivation for this approach was strictly practical: as the

river was only now beginning to drop and expose the auriferous bars, the object was "to enable the men to get up the river as soon as possible." If total war was made on the Indians, "they had it in their power to prevent all canoes from ascending the river, as well as preventing any men from going over the trail.... True, they could be driven out — but it would take time and money to effect it." The men of the French Company, together with those of his own Pike Guards, supported Captain Snyder's proposal by a unanimous vote.

As they neared the abandoned village of Spuzzum later the same day, captains Snyder and Centras, together with their interpreter, advanced towards some Indians that had been observing them from a safe distance. After making signs of peace, a chief approached the three men and led them aside for about two miles, whereupon, reported the Victoria *Gazette,* some 70 Indians appeared from amongst the gulches and ravines.

"Capt. Snyder explained to them that he had come up to make peace with them — to punish those who had shot and robbed the whites, and as this tribe had not been engaged in the troubles, to merely give them notice that the white men were in arms and determined not to be further molested; that whilst they would punish those who did wrong, in return he would guarantee that on a white man's molesting them, he should be likewise punished, on their informing him, or any of the miners." Possibly mistaking Snyder as an agent of the respected British authorities, the natives willingly gave their consent, and peace was established.

Meanwhile, Graham and Galloway were approaching Spuzzum, still with the avowed intention of exterminating every Indian they met en route. Interpreter William Yates, a clerk in the employment of the HBC at Fort Yale, was one of the men that Snyder now rushed forward to the village in order to apprise the parties of the peace.

Yates later wrote: "We told Captain Graham that we were sent from Captain Sneider (sic) to tell him there was no attack to be made on the Indians. Sneider came up at dusk, and told Graham to wait and not to be so rash as he was endangering the lives of white men by doing so."

That evening, according to the correspondent for the Victoria *Gazette*, the captains of the four companies held a consultation "as to the course to be pursued — Captain Graham and Galloway avowing their intention to make it a 'war to the knife,' on men, women and children. The matter was left to all the men there — some 500 in number — who by an almost unanimous vote adopted Capt. Snyder's plan, and gave him nine cheers."

From this point on the *Gazette* correspondent's story may well be part of an intentional coverup, and not to be relied upon. Neither are his dates reliable, as for example he states in his account of September 1 that the rifle companies left Yale on August 17, whereas on August 24, the *Gazette* published a letter from Snyder, dated at Yale, 6 p.m., August 17, stating "There was no company left here to-day as anticipated. . . ."

In spite of the enthusiasm with which the miners rallied to Snyder's plan, Graham remained obstinate in his intention to wage a war of extermination on the Indians, and the most that Captain Snyder could extricate from him was a promise to remain in the rear while the others went on ahead and attempted to come to a peaceful understanding with the Indians. Consequently, Snyder was quite dismayed the following morning, when upon going to ferry his men across the Fraser, he observed that Graham's party had already crossed over ahead of him and were proceeding up the canyon in advance.

As interpreter Yates recalled the incident, "Captain Sneider saw him and called to him to halt and he kept still going on. He sent me with a party of 25 men to follow him up and ask him what he meant by not sticking to his promise. He told the head of my party to tell our Captain Sneider that he was on his way to hell and he hoped that he would be following him."

At this point, as Graham's Whatcom Guards proceeded up the Indian trail that had now crossed to the east side of the canyon, Snyder crossed the Fraser at Chapman's Bar, two miles above Spuzzum, intending to continue along the old HBC brigade trail known as Anderson's road, and intercept Graham's party at Boston Bar, where the two trails met.

A young miner from Oregon, J.C. Lual, left a brief account that helps to shed a little light on events as they actually transpired at this time. Lual, who had been at work on Chapman's Bar since the end of May, stated: "We had. . .no trouble with the Indians in no shape or form. . . . Then the toughs came from Frisco, the long shore men, coal men and such like. Then all kinds of stories was told about men floating down the river with their heads cut off. . . . Every tale that was told got bigger. . . . These fellows got in so thick on us and trouble commenced. . .said the only way to do was to clean them (the Indians) out as we went along and destroy what they had and make them apply for a treaty."

As the "advance guard" from Graham's party proceeded upriver from Chapman's Bar, Lual and Chapman

decided to go up and see what they were doing. After travelling about a mile or so they discovered that 10 or 12 of the miners had a lone Indian cornered on the bank of the river. According to Lual's account, "they tried to make sign to the Indian to lay down his gun, he had an old flint lock gun and a pistol. He shook his head. . . . Chapman said cover him with the guns and two of us will go down and disarm him. He turned around to me and said come on Charley and a gun cracked out of the crowd, and the Indian fell and as he rose (again) the Indian fired his gun into the crowd and shot one of our party right through the stomach with an ounce ball."

The scene of our story now shifts to Victoria, where thousands of newly arrived gold seekers were anxiously following events as they appeared in the local press. Ironically, communications being what they were in those days, Captain Snyder had already completed his march to the Forks and successfully concluded what he grandiloquently referred to as peace treaties with the Thompson Indians when a distressing rumour reached Victoria: Captain Graham's party had been treacherously massacred by the Indians. Consequently, a general Indian war was imminent.

Under the heading "MASSACRE OF FORTY-FIVE MINERS BY INDIANS," the August 25 issue of the Victoria *Gazette* published a graphic account to the effect that after making peace with the Indians at China Bar, Snyder had proceeded forward after leaving a letter with the chief there to deliver to Graham. When the letter arrived, so the story went, "The Indians hoisted a white flag and showed Graham the letter from Snyder. The party apprehending no danger, camped for the night. Near midnite (sic) the Indians attacked the camp, and. . .butchered all the men except two, who made their escape. . . . One of them. . .saw the Indians horribly mutilate 38 bodies and cast them into the river. . . . On Sunday morning twelve bodies were picked up above Fort Yale. . . . Four others were subsequently found below Fort Hope, decapitated and otherwise mutilated."

That same evening the record was allegedly set straight when a courier for Wells-Fargo Express arrived from the goldfields with the following account, published in the August 26 issue of the *Gazette*.

"A party of Indians who had been out on a 'war-hunt' returned to the rancheria about eleven o'clock at night, and seeing a company of whites encamped near their huts, fired upon them without giving any notice of their presence. Before the fire was returned or repeated, the friendly Indians gave a signal, and succeeded in preventing further hostilities; then full explanation was made, and the newly arrived Indians signified their willingness to abide by the treaty, and regret at the firing, and the whites were pacified. Capt. Graham and his first lieutenant were both killed outright, and one or two of his company wounded."

Although the above version of the story seems much more plausible, it too is apparently nothing more than a "fable which found its way into the papers." At least that was the opinion of Donald Fraser, the *Times* correspondent who accompanied Governor Douglas on his journey to Yale to investigate the matter. Fraser's account,

A post card showing a group of Indians fishing at Yale.

undoubtedly the closest to the truth, states that Graham's party went into camp "one fine night," when one of the party, upon "hearing a rustling in the bushes, cried out 'Indians!'. . . . On the first alarm the Major (Graham). . . jumped up and fumbled with his revolver. A shot immediately followed and the doughty Major fell to rise no more. By this time his Lieutenant got upon his legs; another shot, and he too fell dead. The camp was now a scene of ludicrous confusion; some fired right, some fired left, and some fired 'all round,' and some ran away. . . . There were no Indians in the case."

This last account is corroborated by Charley Lual, the miner from Chapman's Bar, who wrote that "while they were camped out at night they built a big fire and had two men on watch. . .while they were walking around the fire, one man waked up and thinking them (the sentries) to be Indians. . .he hollered Indians, and the result was firing commenced and two of their own men killed."

It is likely that this shameful incident occurred on the night of August 20, 1858, somewhere in the vicinity of Hell's Gate. William Yates, the interpreter, was camped near Spuzzum on his return to Yale when survivors of the "massacre" came "running by us like wild animals" in the night. He wrote:

"About 2 o'clock we heard parties rushing down singing out that they were murdered. . .by Indians. . . . Some of Captain Graham's men rushed right through where our own men were lying. . .and said that the Indians had been shooting at them and that a great many of their men had got balls in them and were lying up there. We found one or two dead bodies in the morning. We thought it was not Indians but that it was their own party that got in a panic some way and started shooting in the night. . . . There may have been 15 or 20 shot to death or wounded. Some of the men came into Yale with bullet wounds from five-shooters or dragoon pistol balls. . .not by Indian guns at all."

Correspondents later explained the origin of the false rumour of an Indian massacre that reached Victoria. The first to flee the scene of carnage, an Irishman, "was so horrible frightened that he never pulled foot until he got to Yale, where he told a tale which harrowed the feelings of that refined population to a degree of intensity altogether indescribable. The Indians had massacred the whole party but him, and had then mutilated the bodies of these Christian men in a manner too horrible to mention."

The man's panic was so infectious it created a "general impression. . .that the Indians were coming down the river in large bodies that night to attack the place." Early next morning the residents of Yale "sent a deputation with the Irishman's tale down to Fort Hope, where the same scene was re-enacted. . .and the deputation, now charged with the united suffrages of the good citizens of Yale and Hope, started off without delay. . .for Victoria with a most piteous cry for help."

In covering the subsequent government inquiry into the affair, Fraser reported: "The important question of 'Who Killed Major Graham and his lieutenant' is still unanswered. . . . The unlucky major being a 'politician' and not a sodger handled his pistol so clumsily (it appears) that he shot himself by accident. . . . The lieutenant was killed by one of the stray shots of his own men, which were discharged 'all around'." As the account which appeared in the London *Times* concluded: "Their fate looks like a just retribution."

The Gold Escorts Of 1861 & 1863

Conceived in 1858 and inaugurated in 1861, the gold escort proved to be a financial fiasco, saddling a young and struggling colony with losses of $80,000.

Using historical photos as a guide, artist Terry McLean painted this interpretation of the gold escort leaving Barkerville in 1863.

GOLD has been justifiably called the "pioneer" of civilization because it led men into the wilderness, across unknown seas, over wide prairies and desert plains. It has been pointed out that every gold rush was the beginning of new states and countries; that the discovery of gold in some far-off locality did more to populate the land than the most energetic efforts of immigration agents or government officials.

The vast expanse of fur-trading territory known as New Caledonia held an abundance of this golden wealth. Yet, while it was readily available in numerous creeks and rivers, it lay undetected and undisturbed. But all that was about to change.

It is ironic that the first discovery of this noble metal, which put British Columbia on the map and opened her vast hinterland to exploration and settlement, cannot be credited to a specific individual. It is believed, however, that the Thompson River Indians used iron spoons and other primitive tools to mine gold as early as 1852. This discovery, however, was suppressed by the Hudson's Bay Company (HBC) who feared that the news would spark a rush of settlers into the area and ruin their fur-trading monopoly. But the existence of gold could not be concealed forever.

In 1855, gold was discovered near Fort Colville, at the mouth of the Pend d'Oreille River, and a small rush followed. The invasion had begun, and there would be no stopping it. In April, 1856, prospectors who had continued north were earning from $10 to $40 a day. In July, 1857, Governor Douglas advised the authorities back in England that gold had lured prospectors to the watershed of the Thompson River, and that their efforts had been rewarded.

Spurred by rumours of a new "gold excitement," a small band of prospectors sailed from San Francisco on March 12, 1858, reaching Fort Hope 10 days later. Ascending the Fraser, they discovered rich pay on Hill's Bar, about a mile-and-a-half below Fort Yale. When news of this discovery reached the Puget Sound area, it generated such intense excitement that mills shut down, soldiers deserted their posts and sailors abandoned their ships.

A similar frenzy developed in California when, on April 3, confirmation reached San Francisco. With the California gold rush in decline, thousands of hopeful prospectors now swarmed north. The vanguard of these, arriving on the sidewheel steamer *Commodore*, docked in Victoria on April 25, 1858. After the *Commodore* and her 300 miners, came the *Golden Gate*, with 15, and the *Constitution* with 140. In May, the *Panama, Commodore* and *Pacific* delivered another 1,262 miners, while 7,149 more were landed by 21 different vessels in June, and a further 6,278 in July.

Fort Victoria, then only an isolated HBC outpost, did not have hotels to accommodate such a mass of people, and as early as May, most were spending their nights in the streets and bushes. Innumerable tents covered the ground as far as the eye could see, while the sound of hammer and axe was heard in every direction. Within a space of six weeks some 225 shops, stores and shanties had been constructed, as the lure of gold converted Fort Victoria from a small outpost to a booming city virtually overnight.

On July 19, 1858, during a reception of the International Boundary Commission in Victoria, Gov. James Douglas was called upon to say a few words to the large gathering of miners who had attended the proceedings. Douglas feared that the majority of foreigners might harbour "anti-British" sentiments. He was also undoubtedly aware that, in addition to the industrious, law-abiding, hard-working miners, the motley throng included individuals of every trade and profession, as well as gamblers, loafers, thieves and ruffians.

Possibly in an attempt to establish British authority and imbed law-and-order right from the start, Douglas stated, among other things, his intention of providing armed escorts for the miners in transporting their gold from the mines.

"The miner," he began, "who acts in submission to the laws, and pays the Queen's dues like an honest man, shall be protected in person and property; and as soon as good and trusted men are found, measures shall be taken for the conveyance and escort of gold from the mines to this place. Every miner will give in his own sack and his own weight and have it addressed and sealed in

his presence, and get a receipt for a sack said to contain so much gold dust. It will be deposited in the public treasury at Victoria and delivered to the owner upon production of the deposit receipt. There will be a charge made for the expense of conveyance, but that will be a small matter to the security of your property."

Apparently, finding "good and trusted men" posed a problem for Douglas, for when he wrote to Sir E.B. Lytton that October, he remarked that, although the venture had been authorized by the Home Authorities, he had not been able to establish the gold escort owing to an inability to obtain trustworthy officers.

Finally, in July, 1861, three years after Douglas had first suggested it, the colonial government was ready to put his gold escort into operation. Details of the venture appeared in the July 9 issue of the Victoria *Colonist:*

"The Hispano-American or military treasure escort system, which has been adopted so successfully in Australia, is soon to be put in motion in British Columbia. Mr. Treasurer Gosset, after two years agitation, has succeeded in one of his pet hobbies by getting the machinery of a Gold Escort in working order. As we understand it, the route of the escort will be from New Westminster to the Forks of Quesnelle River [Quesnelle Forks], via Port Douglas and Cayoosh [Lillooet]. Ex-Justice Elwyn of Cayoosh, will have charge of the route from Cayoosh to the Forks of Quesnelle; and will be accompanied by a sergeant and four soldiers of the Royal Sappers and Miners mounted. The time occupied in going from Cayoosh to the Forks of Quesnelle and back, is estimated at eighteen days on the average. This is considerably longer than desirable; but owing to the state of the trail, and the want of the relays of horses on the route, it is held next to impossible to do better this season without incurring a much larger expense than circumstances will warrant. The escort from Cayoosh to Douglas [on Harrison Lake] will be under the charge of Mr. [Philip] Hankin and two mounted policemen. The travelling time between those two points is set down at thirty-six hours. Whether Mr. Hankin is to continue on to New Westminster from Douglas or not, or whether the water escort will be given to some one else, we are not sure."

The escort was comprised of about nine men. Although each man was mounted and thoroughly armed, they were not uniformed and wore only normal street clothes. Although not a large force, it would have been sure lunacy for anyone, other than a determined gang of outlaws, to attack this heavily-armed force. This meant that the threat of robbery was virtually non-existent. Despite this, however, the government would not hold itself responsible for any loss of gold entrusted to its care. Perhaps Douglas still had not acquired the "good and trusted men" he desired, and the government feared that the very escort meant to guard the gold might abscond with it. Whatever the reason for a refusal of a guarantee, and despite the obvious need for the safe transport of gold dust from the mines, the venture was doomed to failure before it even began.

The fee to be charged for transporting the gold was calculated on a sliding scale per troy ounce, depending on the distance it was to be carried. According to the

This is supposed to be the only surviving photograph of the gold escort, but its authenticity has to be questioned. First, it is labeled as having been taken in 1862; but there was only an escort in 1861 and 1863. It could not have been taken in 1861, because Barkerville, seen in the background, did not exist that year. That means it must have been taken in 1863. However, the gold escort contained uniformed men in 1863, and these men appear to be in normal street clothes. Thus, this may not be a photo of the gold escort at all.

Colonist the rates were as follows: From Quesnelle Forks to Lillooet, 8¢; to Port Douglas, 10¢; and to New Westminster, 12¢. From Williams Lake to Lillooet the charge was 6¢ an ounce; to Douglas, 8¢; and to New Westminster, 10¢. From Lillooet to Douglas cost 4¢; to New Westminster, 6¢. Finally, the charge from Douglas to New Westminster was 3¢.

The *Colonist* seemed to have mixed feelings about the escort. Although the newspaper acknowledged the low transportation fee, it suggested these rates were designed to monopolize "the whole carrying trade." However, the *Colonist* still doubted whether the government gold escort could compete with the express companies, which were much faster.

In concluding their article on the gold escort, the *Colonist* added: "Regarding the escort in a profit or loss light, we believe it will prove considerable loss directly; but the savings in the transmission of gold, letters, and papers will in all probability make it indirectly profitable to the country. At any rate it is an experiment worth a trial. If it should not prove what its promoters imagine it will become, the quicker it is superseded the better. But to make it a really useful institution there ought this year to be a weekly escort between the Forks of Quesnelle and Cayoosh, and next year a semi-weekly or daily. It cannot be very long before private enterprise will put on a weekly or daily line of passenger trains and coaches to Cariboo, and except the Gold Escort is equally enterprising, it will be a useless institution."

When the *Colonist* next wrote about the escort, on July 27, its opinion seemed to have soured somewhat. "The Gold Escort is a government speculation like a post office, and like the latter, we presume, the bills will be strongly marked on the loss side of the ledger. Fortunately Government neither claims the monopoly to carry all the letters nor all the gold. A most satisfying reflection indeed. Were it otherwise, we would never hear from

Cariboo, nor see any of the yellow metal, except at long intervals, like 'angels visits few and far between.' The exact time to be occupied in the trip from the Forks of Quesnelle to New Westminster remains as much a matter of speculation as John Revelations or when the millennium will be ushered in. Dates and punctuality are cardinal points in a commercial education, in which we are to be instructed 'from time to time by the proper officers,' so far as they relate to the movements of the Gold Escort."

Perhaps the reason for the newspaper's jaundiced attitude was because it had learned that the government would not be held accountable for any loss. "We can scarcely apprehend the reason for this exception," complained the *Colonist*. "We had acquired an impression that one of the chief reasons why the speculation was started was in order to guarantee to the miners 'certainty' in the transmission of their dust. But the refusal of Government to take all responsibility and insure against loss, militates considerably against the feeling in favor of the Escort, or even its success. Such extreme caution is far too common, in all our government schemes, and till sufficient courage is scared up to take occasional responsibility, the very best measures will have to languish."

Despite the controversy, in August, 1861, amid high expectations, the first trip of the gold escort wound its way along the Harrison Trail from Port Douglas to Lillooet, where it collected a paltry $10,000 in dust. A second trip made later that summer extended as far as Williams Creek. But the miners, suspicious of a government that would not guarantee its shipments, would not support it. Only when Elwyn offered his personal guarantee, which he was not empowered to do, was the escort able to obtain a consignment of $30,000. The third and final trip of the season proved as dismal a failure as the previous two; the escort travelled only as far as Lillooet and returned with only a trifling $10,000.

The experiment thus proved a dismal failure.

(Above) Picturesque Port Douglas, with Douglas Lake in the background. The gold escort travelled from here, via the Harrison-Lillooet Trail to Lillooet, then on to Quesnel Forks. When Barkerville became established, it became the terminus for the short-lived gold escort.
(Below) Looking south across shallow Douglas Lake from the abandoned town-site of Port Douglas in August, 1986.
(Below, inset) This historic cairn was erected at Port Douglas by the Agassiz-Harrison Board of Trade in 1960. It reads: "In 1858, the start of the Cariboo Trail ran from here to Lillooet on the bank of the Fraser River. This gold rush town was the jumping off place for thousands until 1863-65 when the Fraser Canyon Road turned traffic through Yale."

Although the rates charged were far below what ought to have been charged for the service, the miners had no confidence in an escort that would not guarantee against losses. At the end of the season, the escort had cost the struggling colony $30,000, while the total receipts were only $300. During the same period the Dietz and Nelson's Express had transported $103,037.

A merchant from Port Douglas expressed some of the reasons for the escort's lacklustre showing in a letter published in the *Colonist* on August 26: "At the present time the Escort makes

(Top) Because of the conditions of the trails, the gold escort of 1861 travelled only on horseback. By the time the second gold escort was formed, in 1863, roads had been improved to allow the addition of a wagon. This scenario depicts the 1863 gold escort leaving Barkerville.

(Centre) The town of Seaton, on Seaton Lake, was on the old Harrison-Lillooet Trail about mid-way from Port Douglas to Lillooet. This view, c1906, is a coloured postcard.

(Bottom) The remains of Quesnelle Forks in 1987. Established in 1859, this was the first town to be erected in the Cariboo region. In 1861 it became the terminus for the first gold escort. When the gold escort was re-established in 1863, Barkerville had been founded and it became the new terminus.

the trip from Lillooet to Douglas in 40 hours, (very good) but here comes the delay. Instead of at once turning back to Lillooet with the mails they are obliged to go down to New Westminster, and there in all probability have to stop three or four days, or even a week, waiting for a steamer. When they do get back to Douglas they find the express, who have their agents on all the steamers, have made a trip from Lillooet to Douglas, whilst the Escort have been dawdling away their time at New Westminster, and the Escort horses eating their heads off on the road. This will never do. Why do not the Government have a person on the steamer to take charge of the treasure from Douglas to New Westminster, meeting the Escort at Douglas on their return from Lillooet? One man would be sufficient. The Government have already spent 90 per cent of the cost; surely it is bad policy to bosh the thing for the remainder. I cannot understand such false economy, if the Escort is to be carried on let it be done well or left alone.

"The merchants like the idea of having their treasure carried by an armed Government force, but their business will not let them wait a fortnight for the Escort whilst the express makes the trip once a week. The Escort to pay expenses must be an express as well as an Escort, and cannot be allowed to go ahead in the same manner as most Government things do in this Colony — per ex.: the Wagon Road on the second portage.

"In conclusion, I have only to say that the merchants have made a determination to send no gold by the Escort till they can show they are able to make the trip from Douglas to Lillooet once a week."

In contemplating the necessity of a gold escort, Douglas ignored the efforts of already established express companies. Granted, these companies were in their infancies when Douglas first announced his project in 1858. But by the time the first escort began operations, the system was well established.

The first of these was established by W.J. (Billy) Ballou, an experienced expressman from California, in June, 1858. The service operated initially from Victoria to Yale, then was extended to Lytton, and eventually, to Kamloops. Ballou carried not only gold and valuable parcels, but provided a postal service, carrying letters and newspapers. In the early days the service was very crude, with the main means of transport being a canoe or an Indian's back.

In 1859, when steamboat communication became more regular, Jeffrey's Express entered the competition, but without making any marked change in the system. In November, 1861, Jeffrey's Express was taken over by F.J. Barnard, who at once began a more earnest and efficient system. At first, Barnard walked the 670-mile round trip from Yale to Williams Creek, carrying letters and papers on his back. In 1862, Barnard established a sort of "pony express," that is, he led a horse loaded with express over the same route.

Ballou and Barnard competed against each other for the express business until 1862. In July of that year, the mail contract was awarded to Barnard. This spelled the death knell to Ballou's operation, and that October, a bankrupt Ballou withdrew from the competition.

Meanwhile, no attempt was made to revive the gold escort in 1862. Most miners trusted their gold to the efficiency and relative safety of Barnard's Express or Dietz and Nelson's Express. To protect their valuable cargo, the coaches were provided with burglar-proof safes, having combination locks, the combination of which was known only to the agent at the terminal. In addition, gold shipments were protected by a guard with a Winchester rifle. Although no one actually believed that one armed guard could protect the stage against a determined robber, it is nonetheless remarkable that during 1864-65 some $4,619,000 in gold was safely carried, and the first robbery of a stage on the Cariboo Road did not occur until 1885. It is all the more remarkable when one considers that the armed guard had been dispensed with long before that.

Despite this remarkable record, some miners still would not trust their gold to the express companies. These individuals chose instead to keep it close at hand, either hidden under the floor of their cabins or buried under the roots of trees. Some even carried it back and forth to their claims each day. Then, when leaving the goldfields, these miners carried the gold with them. This was inherently risky, however, and in the spring of 1863, three miners paid the ultimate price.

Near Quesnelle Forks the three miners were ambushed and murdered and their $12,000 in gold stolen. Although this incident might very well have been prevented if the men had trusted their gold to the express companies, it nevertheless created an uproar in Victoria and a demand to reinstate the gold escort. In addition to this incident, both the Bank of British Columbia and Macdonald's Bank had recently established branches on Williams Creek. It was expected that the greater part of the gold recovered from creeks like Williams, Lightning, Cunningham, Keithley, Antler and others would be funnelled through these two banks, and thereby provide the new gold escort with a source of treasure to transport. These factors provided Douglas with an opportunity to revive his folly.

Oddly enough, the Colonist, which had been one of the loudest critics of the 1861 escort, came out strongly in support of its re-establishment. On May 18, 1863, it wrote: "The duty of the Government in the matter is plain. They should regard its establishment as equally necessary for the development of the country with the system of roads which they are establishing. Roads are useless unless property of all kinds can be safely transmitted over them at all times. These conditions are not fulfilled, and cannot be, by the British Columbia roads, without an efficient gold escort. Having this, there could be no doubt but a vast increase of traffic of every description would take place between the mines and the lower country, and the revenue of the Government, consequently, be very much greater than could otherwise be hoped for. The Executive of British Columbia cannot, therefore, without neglecting an obvious duty, refuse to entertain the project which they have been so long and so often asked to be carried out."

When those interested in re-establishing the gold escort first approached the government, they were told the government lacked the funds to undertake the project. However, when a businessman offered the government $50,000, the government refused, claiming it had "no authority to borrow or pledge the credit of the country. . . ." The government did suggest that "if the Imperial Government authorized the additional loan of $250,000," it would proceed with the project. However, after this loan was approved, the government decided it had better uses for the money.

"This is very strange conduct, to say the least," complained the *Colonist.* "It may be possible to explain it satisfactorily; but till it is so explained, it assumes the character of a temporizing policy, designed to postpone from time to time the reasonable expectations of the public, till the summer is spent, the mining season closed, and agitation hopeless. It is as difficult to discover why there should be any hesitation on the part of the Government to take so small a responsibility as the establishment at once of a Gold Escort."

As demands and pressure for the gold escort increased, however, the government finally relented, and on May 21 the *Colonist* announced that a "Gold Escort will ere long not only be *un fait accompli,* but, we hope, one of the lasting institutions of the colony.

However, not everyone was in favour of re-establishing the escort. On June 1 the *Colonist* published a letter from a rather irate citizen of Yale who was totally against it. "Allow me to submit, that it is madness on the part of the Government to suppose that the miners will allow their gold to pass from their hands into the hands of persons they know not of, to any considerable extent; and that your calculation that $2,750,000 will be carried down this season by Escort, is wide of the mark. To do this in four trips, as proposed, they will have to carry $687,000 per trip. If you took off a 0 you would be nearer the mark."

This letter writer, identified only by the initials B.J.T., went on to state that the escort, "if continued for four months, whether they make monthly or fortnightly trips, will result in a loss of at least $20,000. If 54 men are employed, and 15 are put on, the loss will be $50,000, of which Vancouver Island will pay not one cent, and British Columbia the whole. This sort of legislation will do more to separate the two colonies and tend to keep them dissatisfied than the united efforts of the *Columbian* and the host of growlers around New Westminster.

"Mr. Humphry is at my elbow, and says he can get you a bet of $500, that the Government Escort will not carry treasure enough in all the season, the percentage of which will be sufficient to pay the expenses of one trip."

Two days later the *Colonist* published the names of some of the men who had been appointed to the gold escort. It was to be headed by Captain Hind, with Thomas Elwyn his second-in-command. Also in the group were Captain Torens, Captain Stuart, and "Messrs. Wakeman, Guest, Getliffe, Bentley and A. Skinner."

On June 6 the members of the gold escort assembled on Victoria's Beacon Hill, where they were inspected by Governor Douglas. This time the escort was uniformed, although their attire was rather plain, consisting "of

black foraging cap, grey shirt, cords, high boots and spurs."

On the evening of June 8, 1863, the gold escort, with its "Van and horses," left Victoria on the *Otter.* To offer the second escort a greater chance of success than that enjoyed by the first, the shipping fees were increased dramatically to 50¢ an ounce. Despite the fiasco of the 1861 escort, however, the government still insisted that " . . . no guarantee against loss was to be given."

From New Westminster the gold convoy made its way to Port Douglas, then along the Harrison Trail to Lillooet, eventually reaching Williams Lake five weeks later. They left Williams Creek on July 15 "with about $50,000 in gold dust." While this was the largest amount carried to date, it was less than half what the express companies transported during the same period. During the same time, Mr. Diller, owner of the famous Diller Claim, came down with $75,000, preferring, despite the dangers, his own guardianship rather than trust a government escort that would not accept responsibility for loss. The cost of the first trip of 1863 had been $12,000, while the receipts totalled only $1,250.

In writing about the arrival of the gold escort in its July 27 edition, the *Colonist* said that Captain Nind was "very sanguine of the future success of the undertaking. He met with a most encouraging reception from all quarters, and is of the opinion that next trip he will bring a considerable quantity of gold down, and the trip after that as much as they can carry. Two parties on the creek sent down a considerable quantity of their dust, merely to encourage the enterprise, although they stated they could get a larger return for it up here. Those who had gold to lend were getting various rates of interest from 5 to 20 per cent, per month.

"Capt. Nind thinks he brought down one-third of the gold then available on the creek."

On the second trip, the escort guarded gold valued at about $95,000, of which $70,000 was the property of the Bank of British Columbia. Costs for the second trip was again $12,000, while the revenue nearly tripled to $3,000. The third trip resulted in the transport of $78,000, of which $63,000 belonged to the Bank of B.C. Unfortunately, Macdonald's Bank, which handled as much gold as the Bank of B.C., refused to patronize the Gold Escort. Yet, the escort was not failing for lack of gold to transport as, during the same period, Barnard's Express was averaging about $100,000 a week. On the fourth and final trip, the gold escort straggled along in two sections with only $68,000.

When the scheme had been first discussed, it was estimated that the cost of operations for 1863 would total $44,000, while the earnings were estimated at $55,000. However, when the season was over, it was learned that the costs had risen to $60,000, while the total earnings were a paltry $6,000. The gold escorts of 1861 and 1863 had proved to be complete fiascos, saddling a young and struggling colony with losses of about $80,000. The people complained bitterly at this tremendous loss in a venture for which there was no great demand or need. So, without further fanfare, the escort was permanently disbanded.

JEAN CAUX
The Man They Called "Cataline."

Despite operating the biggest and most efficient pack trains, this famous packer boasted that in 54 years he never lost a pound of cargo. Only one shipment in his care ever went astray — two pounds of Limburger cheese discarded by "mistake."

JEAN Caux was undoubtedly one of the greatest packers in the Canadian west. He was of Basque origin and was born in Oloron, in the province of Bearn in southwestern France. This great freighter, whose years of continuous packing (from 1858 to 1912, a total of 54 years) exceeded that of all his contemporaries, is one of the hardest to trace in respect to his operations before arriving in the province.

The precise date Caux arrived in British Columbia is uncertain. However, early in June of 1858, 60 men and 400 pack horses and mules arrived in Lytton with supplies from Walla Walla, Oregon territory. Among them was a Spanish-American named Alvarez with a string of mules. Caux could well have been one of the men in Alvarez' employ. At least he must have had Mexican pack train experience. The entire nomenclature used in his outfit was that used by Mexican muleteers. The man in charge was the *corregidor;* his second in command, the *secundo;* the load was the *cargo;* the saddle, *aparejo;* the *manta,* a heavy piece of canvas to wrap around the load; and the whole load was covered with a waterproof *sobre jalama.* There are well over 50 of these Spanish-Mexican words to describe the various pieces of rigging used.

(Above) This undated photo of Caux was taken when he was a young man.
(Right) This display honouring the famous packer is located near Hazelton.
(Opposite page) The Skeena River at Old Hazelton, where Caux spent his final years. The top inset is St. Peters Anglican Church on Hazelton's Government Street.
The bottom inset is a postcard view of Ashcroft, which once served as Cataline's headquarters.

When Caux first arrived in British Columbia he spoke only pure Bearnaise. In Bearn, only the educated men spoke French, and since Caux was totally uneducated, he spoke very little French and knew no Spanish. This problem was somewhat alleviated a short time after his arrival in Yale when Joe Castillou happened on the scene. Castillou, also born in southwestern France, was the only one who could understand and communicate with Caux, and they soon became friends and business partners. During one of those early conversations, Caux told Castillou he was born at Oloron "near Catalonia." Thus Caux obtained the name Catalonia, which later became simply Cataline.

Joe Castillou's son, Judge Henry Castillou, of Williams Lake, remembered working on their pack trains. Each outfit had between 63 and 66 animals, and they had four such outfits. Henry recalled that each outfit consisted of "six men, counting the cook, and it was, oh, during that later period that I came into the picture. When they were short of men I had to. . .if the cook didn't come up, why, I had to cook. If the head wrangler didn't come I had to wrangle. If one of the packers got drunk I had to be a packer."

The pack trains started about 2 A.M. each day and travelled until about two or three in the afternoon, with rest periods in between. This schedule allowed they to beat the heat of the day and avoid most of the flies that would make the mules so difficult to handle. The distance travelled each day varied according to the terrain, but it was usually somewhere between 15 and 25 miles. When the mules were unloaded they ambled off to feed. Each mule always carried the same packs day after day. They became so well trained that when the *corregidor* rang the signal bell, the mules would immediately go to their own packs, like a cow to its stall, without fail.

These amicable animals could carry ponderous loads, from 250 to 300 pounds, walk with ease on a trail a goat would shun, and forage and keep in good condition on almost any herbage. Along with the burro, these sturdy animals have the longest history of any animal in transportation in North America, being introduced by the Spaniards around 1500. At one time they were used to pack from Sonora, Mexico to San Francisco, a distance in excess of 2,000 miles.

During Cataline's early days he packed from Yale to Barkerville. It was during this time that he took a wife, a Thompson Indian woman from the Spuzzum Band. When the railroad was completed in 1885, goods for Barkerville and the north country were packed from Ashcroft, which then became his headquarters. His wife and family remained in Spuzzum and lived with another family whose name they eventually took. Thus the name Caux was not perpetuated, but Cataline continued to contribute to his family's support — a

contribution always made in $20 gold pieces.

Over the years many stories concerning Cataline have been related — some legends, other fascinating lies. Disregarding the legendary tales and obvious fabrications, and stripping the rest of the usual accruement of embellishment of the years, we can picture him as a very good businessman, frankly fair and scrupulously honest in all his dealings.

As already mentioned, Cataline knew very little French, Spanish or English, and if Castillou was not around to act as interpreter, Cataline had great difficulty making himself understood. Eventually Cataline developed a distinctive language of his own. It was a combination of all the Indian languages he had heard, together with the words he learned from Spanish packers, all mixed in with words of English, Scotch, French and Irish. Unfortunately, no one could really understand this new vocabulary either!

His *corregidor* was named Ah Gun, while Dave Wiggins, a mulatto — half-Indian half-Negro — was his *secundo*. Cataline wore the same type of clothing year round, white boiled shirt: (a new one was donned for every trip and worn throughout the journey), heavy woollen pants and riding boots and no socks — winter or summer. He always wore a big, bucking belt, about 10 inches wide with little buckles all the way down. The Indians used to refer to it as his corset.

When Cataline had business to conduct he attached a collar, yellow with age, to his shirt and a little tie, not too clean, and wore a French hat. He also wore a long frock coat which was green with age. Around the coat he had a red French-Canadian wool sash. Cataline would then seat himself on a chair made of birch and rawhide, while everyone else usually sat on the ground.

Cataline had a luxurious head of curly, jet-black hair, worn shoulder length. When he took a drink he always poured a little in his hand and rubbed it in his hair saying, "A little on the inaside, a little on the outaside. Bon she maka de hair grow."

In 1898 Cataline conducted a party of soldiers from Telegraph Creek to the Yukon. The officer in charge was

Cataline's mule train loading supplies at W.B. Bailey's warehouse in Ashcroft, B.C.

very officious and aloof and always insisted that everything be done strictly according to military rules, which necessitated almost continuous bugle blowing to give the soldiers various orders. This irked Cataline no end and he complained; "Alla time blowa de buga, no gooda, scara de mule." But the bugle blowing continued, much to his annoyance. One day, however, when the colonel and his men were in the rear of the party, one of the animals fell and rolled off the corduroy road and became completely mired in the mud. Much as they worked to free the animal, they only succeeded in making a bad situation worse. Cataline rode back and watched the performance in silence. Finally the colonel looked up in exasperation and asked, "What shall we do now, Mr. Cataline?" After a brief pause, Cataline replied: "Blowa de buga, blowa de buga!"

One year a disease struck his trains and many animals died, although Cataline managed to get the cargo through to their destinations. This necessitated hiring an Indian backpacker to fulfil the contract, but at a severe loss to himself. The following spring he was forced to apply to the bank for a loan to replace the lost animals. The bank manager asked him how many cattle he had. "None," said Cataline. He was then asked how many horses. "About 75," he was informed. "All right" said the manager, "we'll loan you the money."

The next fall, when Cataline returned from packing,

(Above) This postcard view of Cataline was taken in Ashcroft.
(Below) Another postcard, this one showing Cataline's pack train loading at Bailey's for Babine Lake in 1897.

he went directly to the bank, opened his valise and counted out the exact amount owing. As he rose to leave, the banker suggested Cataline should leave the remainder of his money in the bank where it would be safe. The packer pondered this advice for a moment, then asked, "How many horses you have?"

"None," replied the puzzled banker.

Cataline then shook his head dubiously and said, "I tink I keepa de mon."

Although Cataline could not read or write he had a remarkable, retentive memory. His mule trains consisted of 63 to 66 animals, and Cataline knew exactly what was on every one of them, where they were to be delivered, and what price to charge. He kept all his records in his head without any notes whatsoever. A good example of this is told by Tom Manin, his friend and sometimes agent. Once Cataline had hired two men who quit the pack train after one trip. One of the men was like Cataline, unable to read or write. Cataline took them into Manin's store to settle up. There he called the items from memory for the storekeeper. The verbal account ran something like this:

"Six dollars cash to Soda Creek; two dollars 100 Mile House; three dollars Clinton; Lac La Hache five dollars; two dollars at Bonapart Reserve; twenty dollars at Ashcroft; 150 Mile House, 50¢ for tobacco; two dollars for whisky at Hazelton; pay fine at Hazelton, five dollars. He have coming $151 and two bits." He

Jean Caux's Pack Train loading at Harvey Baileys for Babine Lake 1897

then laboriously signed his name to the cheque which the storekeeper had filled in for him.

The second man, however, said that he could read and write and that his account differed from Cataline's. On his list there was a $3 difference in the total. Manin checked the list and found that the man had made an error in addition. Cataline was right.

To be in a better position to serve the north country where packing was more in demand, Cataline moved north to Quesnel and operated from there for a number of years. Later he went to Hazelton and continued to work from there into the Omineca and other mining districts until he sold his business to George Beirnes in 1912. Beirnes built him a two-room cabin on the flat overlooking the Bulkley River. The cabin was still standing in 1970.

It was Cataline's claim that he never lost an article, but on one occasion a small parcel disappeared. The consignee, however, was not the loser for on his return to Hazelton Cataline sent a man back with a replacement: one small package containing two pounds of Limburger cheese. It happened that one of the packers thought that something had gone rotten and had thrown the original package away.

By 1920 Cataline was beginning to feel his age and decided that the Hazelton winters were too hard and, henceforth, he would spend them in Victoria. But after spending the winter of 1920 in the Dominion Hotel in that city, he spent the remainder of his days in Hazelton. He found that he preferred the rigors of Hazelton winters to Victoria city life.

Jean Caux died in October, 1922, at the age of 90. He is buried in the old Hazelton cemetery, which overlooks the confluence of the Bulkley and Skeena rivers, the scene of his packing activities in his later years. Beside him are four other pioneers, his friends of 50 years: Jack Graham, the packer; Joe Lyons, the miner; Jim May, miner and prospector, and Ezra Evans, miner and one-time Deputy Mining Recorder of Omineca. Their wooden headboards have long since disappeared, but a small stone cairn marks Cataline's last resting place. A brass plate on the cairn bears the simple inscription: "Jean Caux — Cataline, the packer."

(Right) Jean Caux in his later years. (Below) Cataline's pack train preparing to leave Hazelton in 1911.

CAMELS IN THE CARIBOO

The only known surviving photo of a camel pack animal in British Columbia. Those used on the Cariboo Road wore special boots of rawhide and canvas to protect their tender feet from rocky terrain. Archie McPhail holds halter rope while Bill Smith poses for a pioneer photographer.

One moment the 60-mule pack train was moving serenely along the trail, the next all was pandemonium. Mules brayed, kicked and broke for the brush, packs flying every which way. They had just met up with a Cariboo camel train.

CAMELS in the Cariboo? You bet! And thereby hangs a most unique and intriguing tale, little known and long forgotten these past 130 years.

In 1862, John Calbraith, who had been connected with the construction of the Cariboo Wagon Road, appears to have suggested the use of camels for packing in the mines between Yale and Cariboo.

Calbraith had evidently read about the use of camels in the United States by the U.S. Army and their subsequent use in Nevada, Arizona, California and Washington, and that they were now available for purchase. Had Calbraith known *why* the animals were for sale, he probably would never have suggested their use. He did not, however, thus we find camels in Canada.

A bit of background history is necessary for one to better understand how these slow, mild-mannered creatures found themselves so far from their homelands.

Early in 1856, the U.S. Army Camel Corps was established in the American desert. By November 14, 1856, the ship *Supply* had delivered the second cargo of camels to Texas from Arabia. According to army records, the herd then numbered 70 head.

A pack train of camels was soon assembled and driven across the country to Albuquerque, New Mexico, under the charge of Lt. Edward F. Beale, who later thoroughly tested the animals out in the Mojave Desert. In his report of May 10, 1858, Lieutenant Beale wrote that he had tested the animals and had travelled 4,000 miles without accident. The results from the experimental introduction were so generally successful and satisfactory from a military standpoint that U.S. Secretary of War Floyd recommended in 1858 that funds be appropriated to purchase 1,000 more camels. This recommendation was repeated in reports of the Secretary of War for the years 1859 and 1860, but Congress, probably concerned with the coming Civil War, failed to grant the request.

From their headquarters at Camp Verde, a military post near San Antonio, Texas, the camels were used constantly by the Quartermaster's department in Texas, and in explorations in New Mexico, Arizona and California up to 1861. The western terminal of the U.S.

Army Camel Corps was at Fort Tejon, located a few miles south of present-day Bakersfield, California.

Lieutenant Beale had nothing but praise for his imported charges, claiming that one good camel was worth four good army mules. Other officers connected with the project had much the same attitude. It was concluded that the camel was much superior to the mule for army transportation purposes on the pack trails of the Southwest. In one test, Lieutenant Beale reported a camel rising and walking off with a load of 1,256 pounds, or more than five times the normal mule load.

The government's introduction to camels was, at the time, enthusiastically heralded and acclaimed by both the California and Nevada press which predicted a "lightning-fast dromedary express" carrying fast mail from Missouri River points to California in 15 days. Soon private interest was directed to the camel industry.

The American Camel Company was incorporated in San Francisco in 1859. A trial importation of 22 head of Bactrian, or double-humped camels, was brought to San Francisco by Otto Esche from the highlands of the Amur River, Manchuria, China. These camels were then sent over the rugged Sierra Nevada Mountains to western Nevada, arriving in 1860. There they were employed in carrying salt from Teal's Marsh, in the Walker River district, to the silver mines at Virginia City, a distance of 200 miles. Other shipments of camels were engaged from Manchuria and the San Francisco papers of 1860 contain several notices of pending camel sales.

The outbreak of the American Civil War doomed the U.S. Army Camel Corps. Those animals and facilities in Texas fell into Confederate hands when that state left the Union. Reports indicate that some were used by the Confederate Post Office Department, but most just wandered away into the surrounding desert where they fended for themselves. Some were utilized in packing to the mines in Arizona in the 1860s. But for the Civil War, and the contemporary completion of the Pacific railroads, the camel might well have become the accepted pack animal in the West.

The Bactrian camels owned by the American Camel Company and used in Nevada soon displayed a trait that was to prove their undoing wherever they were used. They were totally incompatible with horses and mules, who had an unconquerable fear of the strange, cud-splitting beasts and would stampede at the first sight or smell of them. Had this trait been more closely monitored, much trouble would have been avoided in the future.

The first unwise step in the handling of the camels appears to have been taken when the three Arabian camel drivers were permitted to return to their homeland. The second was the transfer to other duties of the officers that had experience with them.

The camels in Nevada soon showed their incompatibility with horses and mules. Complaints about damaged goods and the disruption of pack trains brought many lawsuits against the owners of camel caravans. Things finally got so bad that a law was passed by the Territorial Legislature making it a crime "to cause a camel to be on a public road during daylight hours." The foreign critters had to go.

Enter John Calbraith and his scheme to use camels in British Columbia. On March 1, 1862, a small ad appeared in the *Colonist* newspaper in Victoria. It read: "TO PACKERS. Twenty-five camels for sale. Apply to Henry Walton, general agency office, Commercial Street, near Yates Street."

Two weeks later the same paper reported that Cal-

This drawing of Lillooet appeared in The Illustrated London News *on December 24, 1864. After arriving in Victoria, the camels were taken to Port Douglas, from where they were used in transporting freight to Lillooet.*

braith had purchased the 25 camels in San Francisco for $300 each. The camels had been purchased from willing sellers in Nevada and driven back over the Sierra Nevada Mountains to San Francisco. There they were loaded on steamers and shipped to Victoria. On April 15, the camels, which were to be used as beasts of burden from Lillooet to the Cariboo goldfields, arrived in Esquimalt, the *Colonist* reporting: "Mr. Calbraith's twenty-three Bactrian camels arrived on the *Hermann* yesterday. They are singular-looking animals and when driven off the steamer frightened the horses at Esquimalt out of their proprietory and a week's appetite. The camels are just now engaged in shedding the winter coat of hair and present a very scalpy appearance. Each has two humps on the back and will pack from 500 to 600 pounds."

On April 22 the paper announced the birth of the first baby camel, which created some excitement. On May 2, the entire herd was driven to downtown Victoria and kept in a corral at the corner of Douglas and Johnson streets. Here they remained for the next two days as they waited transshipment to the B.C. mainland.

In purchasing the camels, it would appear that Calbraith had only acted for a syndicate consisting mainly of Frank Laumeister, Adam Heffley and Henry Ingram. George Schultz and Gustav Hoffmeister were also involved in the enterprise, although it is Frank Laumeister who has come to be chiefly associated with the ill-fated scheme.

Laumeister arrived in Victoria in 1859 and had soon established a saloon on the northeast corner of Johnson and Store streets. The following year he purchased a half interest in the Victoria Brewery. Laumeister envisioned making a fortune with animals that could easily carry twice the load or normal horses or mules, but he did not anticipate the problems that the animals would cause.

On May 4, the camels were placed aboard the steamer *Enterprise* and taken to New Westminster. All the camels did not made the trip, however. Somehow, the newborn baby and its mother escaped into the bush around Victoria. James B. Anderson, a former Minister of Agriculture, wrote in his journal that the young camel roamed the streets of the James Bay district for months, becoming "as friendly as a stray puppy and quite adroit at begging handouts from the interested population." The mother was also seen from time to time over the next six months, sometimes frightening those who came upon it unexpectedly. Apparently, these were not the only ones to go astray.

The *Colonist* had reported in its April 15 edition that 23 animals had arrived in Esquimalt. On April 23 the paper announced the birth of one baby and added, "Two or three more" are "expected daily." If the paper was accurate, this means there were at least 24 camels in Victoria and two or three more expected. Yet, when the Enterprise reached New Westminster, the *British Columbian* stated: "Camels, 21 in number," have arrived. What happened to the others is anybody's guess.

In any event, the remaining 21 camels were transported by barge to the town of Douglas, at the head of Harrison Lake, where they were soon put to work. On May 17 the *British Columbian* reported that the camels were "found to answer admirably" in packing over the Pemberton Portage. A week later the paper added: "The camels are still employed in packing over the Pemberton Portage. Although we believe these animals do not quite come up with the expectations of their owners, yet they answer very well, and we understand an advance of $600 has been tendered for them. While they carry from 500 to 600 pounds a load, being double that of a mule, they keep their costs less than nothing as they pick up all they require by the wayside — no small consideration when feed is from six to seven cents per pound."

Had Laumeister known the trouble that was in store for him, he would have unquestionably taken the profit

A mule train heading for the Cariboo goldfields. Although camels could carry far greater loads than mules or horses, they had one serious drawback: they terrified the other pack train animals and sent them scurrying in all directions. This was undoubtedly one of the main causes for their downfall as freight animals.

by selling his camels. But, except for some minor problems, the camels had adopted well to date, and he was soon busy putting his main goal into operation. On May 28 the *Colonist* announced that Laumeister's camels had crossed Seton Lake en route to their main objective of freighting to the goldfields. A week later, nine of the animals were packing from Seton Lake to Lillooet. The remaining dozen had been taken to the mouth of Bridge River, just above Lillooet, where the discovery of coarse gold and the construction of a toll bridge had led to the development of a small community. Then, near the end of June, 1862, the first of the camel pack trains pushed out from Lillooet for the long and dangerous trek to the Cariboo goldfields. One camel was killed when it plunged over a precipice near Pavilion Creek, apparently pushed over by a younger animal that became frightened by something on the trail.

Unfortunately, little historical record pertaining to the trip has survived. However, we do know that the camels were in Lightning Creek near Barkerville during the month of August, for on August 20, a young Englishman named Harry Guillod wrote in his diary: "Was bothered today by camels of which there are about a dozen here who have a neat idea of walking over your tent and eating your shirts."

Despite the initial high hopes that were held for camel pack trains, the enterprise soon proved to be a dismal failure. It had become apparent early in the venture that the tender feet of the camels, accustomed to soft desert sands, were ill suited for the rough rocky trails. To combat this problem, boots fashioned of rawhide and canvas were used to protect them while on the trail. But for their greatest drawback, there appeared to be no solution. The camels frightened and stampeded horses and mules of other pack trains wherever they met, and many accidents were caused. Commenting on the situation on October 15, 1862, the *Colonist* reported that there were only about a dozen camels left. "They are turned out to graze at the Forks of Quesnelle River, and are considered the greatest failure of the season." What happened to the other nine is not recorded.

Despite the setbacks, the camel owners apparently decided to give their venture another try, for in mid-May of 1863 the *Colonist* reported that a heavily-laden camel train had left from Lillooet for the Cariboo goldfields. But it was to be their last hurrah, at least as far as the historical record is concerned. Plagued by the same problems as before, numerous damage claims forced the owners to abandon the profitable Cariboo route. The beasts of burden were then placed on trails to Fort Hope, east into the Wild Horse and upper Columbia mines. Some were taken back to the coast and shipped south to the U.S.

Finally, many of the animals were turned loose on the range east of North Thompson River. For years some of these abandoned creatures were kept about by Henry Ingram at his ranch at Grand Prairie (Westwold), about 40 miles east of Kamloops. At least one attempt was made to use a camel as a draft animal, but as one man swore in disgust, "Camels make damned poor plow animals."

Some of the camels eventually ended up in the meat pot. John V. Campbell, described in the *Washington State Historical Quarterly* as "an intelligent quarter-breed," spotted a camel on Perry Creek not far from Fort Steele. After obtaining permission from the owner, John Galbraith, one of the first settlers in the region, (not to be confused with John Calbraith), he killed it for his winter meat. Galbraith, who received 40 pounds of the meat, pronounced it "delicious when fried."

Evidently most white men were prejudiced against the use of camel meat as food, however. When William Barry and Sam Adler, two prominent Cariboo pioneers, killed and dressed a camel for meat at their 150 Mile Roadhouse, they found no sale for it. Indians, on the other hand, never passed up an opportunity to kill and eat the strange creatures. In early Montana Territory, where a few animals were used in packing as late as 1866, owners had to be on constant guard lest the Indians kill their costly pack animals.

At least one American hunter achieved dubious fame as a "Camel hunter." James McNair, late of Kentucky and something of a drinking man, decided one day to go hunting for camp meat near Deer Lodge, Montana Territory. The intoxicated McNair soon spotted what he took to be several large moose grazing in a nearby field. Taking careful aim, he blazed away and dropped his prey with the first shot. He was about to shoot the second "moose" when the irate camel owner arrived on the scene, screaming to high heaven about "damn fools shooting his camels." McNair finally told him if the camel was his he was welcome to the meat. This, of course, did not pacify the angry owner, who confiscated McNair's money, watch, rifle and a deed for a claim in Alder Gulch. Then McNair found out just how big a camel really was when forced at the point of his own gun to dig the animal a decent grave. McNair acquired the nickname "Camel" from this incident, and thenceforth, is said to have been more careful in selecting his target when out hunting.

A similar incident had occurred in the Cariboo in 1862 when "Grizzly" Morris bagged one of the Laumeister's camels that had been put out to graze near Quesnel Forks, mistaking it for a large grizzly.

The last surviving camel on the open range in B.C. died near Grand Prairie in 1905. Prior to its death, children of the area enjoyed going for rides on its back. This camel was the only one to ever have its photograph taken for posterity.

It is interesting to note that the date of death of this camel corresponds to the date of death by natural causes of abandoned camels everywhere in North America. The last one in Washington State, for example, died in an apple orchard near the town of Brewster in 1905. Those that roamed the area of Gila Bend, Arizona, also passed away in 1905-06. This would indicate that all of the animals were of about the same age when imported, lived out their normal lives and died at about the same time.

With their passing, a unique, and somewhat unusual aspect of early B.C. gold rush history also elapsed. Although the impact of these animals was generally negative, they nonetheless contributed to the cultural mosaic of the province. They are long since gone, but certainly not forgotten.

The CPR steamship Amur *on the beach after striking rocks in Wrangell Narrows, June 3, 1911.*

Amur, Danube & Tees

The *Amur*, *Danube* and *Tees* were three pioneer west coast steamers that carried gold seekers to the Klondike in 1897-98. They survived shipwrecks, collisions and litigation for a combined lifetime of 149 years.

DESIGNED primarily as freighters, but with some passenger accommodation, the *Amur*, *Danube* and *Tees* were rather small ships: *Amur* had a displacement of 907 tons; *Danube* 887 tons, and *Tees* 679 tons. They were sturdy seaworthy vessels built along the lines of the North Sea coaster John Masefield describes in his poem "Cargoes." The *Danube*, an iron ship, was the oldest of the three, having been built at Govan, on the Clyde, in 1869. The *Amur* and *Tees* were both steel ships; the former built at Sunderland, England, in 1890 and the latter at Stockton-on-Tees in 1893.

All three had ample cargo space, and during their west coast service it was well utilized. Heavy cargoes of ore, lumber, coal, and canned salmon were carried as well as equipment and general supplies for a string of coastal settlements. Also, over the years, many passengers travelled on these steamers — sometimes many more than the accommodation officially allowed. This was especially true in 1897 and 1898 when eager fortune hunters sought transportation to the goldfields of the Klondike.

Like Masefield's British coaster, the *Amur*, *Danube* and *Tees* on this west coast experienced plenty of stormy weather and rough seas, despite the fact that much of their voyaging was through the more sheltered waters of the Inside Passage. There the dangers were from hidden rocks and shoals, made more hazardous by a treacherous current and periods of poor visibility. All three vessels had accidents — they ran aground, struck rocks, even sank — but amazingly, they all survived and after repairs were made they were ready to serve again. The *Amur's* career lasted for 38 years, the *Tees* operated for 44 years, and the *Danube* had a remarkable 67 years of service.

The *Danube* was purchased by Capt. John Irving's Canadian Pacific Navigation Company (CPN) in 1890 for

Two views of the Ss Danube. *The location of the above photograph was not recorded, but the photo below was taken at Port Essington.*

$38,400. She had already been plying west coast waters for the previous two years, operated by the Scottish-Oriental Steamship Company of Glasgow. Its Oriental Line steamers crossed the Pacific from Vancouver in conjunction with the recently completed Canadian Pacific Railway (CPR). The *Danube* had been used to transport passengers, mainly Chinese, between the deep-sea ports of Vancouver, Portland and San Francisco.

After being acquired by the CPN, the *Danube* was commanded for some years by Capt. William Meyers, who was later involved with the ill-fated *Cariboo and Fly*. The ship was put on the northern run serving the salmon canneries and settlements scattered along B.C.'s lengthy coastline. One cannery employee left the following record of a voyage aboard the *Danube*, southbound from the Nass River to Victoria, in December, 1890:

"The *Danube* left Cascade Cannery, Nass River, on December 24 and several hours later called at Port Simpson (originally the Hudson's Bay Company's Fort Simpson). On Dec. 25 the ship passed the mission village of Metlakatla and entered the estuary of the Skeena River, en route to Port Essington. In the river the state of the tide is always a consideration and the *Danube,* probably not for the first time, ran aground on a sand-bar. After five hours she finally floated free and began loading 7500 cases of salmon. About noon on December 26 the ship left Port Essington and arrived at Standard Cannery, near the river-mouth, at 3 P.M. where another 3000 cases were taken aboard.

"From there the *Danube* continued to steam south reaching Lowe Inlet Cannery about 2 P.M., December 28 and took on 6000 more cases of canned salmon. She left Lowe Inlet about 1:30 the next day but about 5 P.M. was obliged to anchor in Holmes Bay. The *Danube* left there early on December 30 but by 10 A.M. fog rolled in and she had to anchor again. The fog cleared about noon and the ship proceeded but anchored in an unidentified bay that night.

"On New Year's Day, January 1, 1891, the captain found his bearings and continued south. They encountered a gale in Fitzhugh Sound, passed Bella Bella in the afternoon, and later anchored in Safety Cove. Next day they crossed the rough waters of Queen Charlotte Sound and arrived at Alert Bay about 4 A.M. Jan. 3. There another 4000 cases of salmon were added to the cargo. The *Danube* continued her southern journey and arrived at Victoria on Sunday morning, January 4, 1891 — more than ten days after leaving Nass River."

There was a tragic sequel to the unloading of the *Danube's* cargo of canned salmon. On January 12 the deck of the wharf gave way under the extra weight and five longshoremen died in the accident.

The return journey to the Nass River for the 1891 canning season was accomplished in half the time of the southward one. The same diarist recorded a briefer account of the northward trip. He wrote:

"Left Victoria at 11 P.M. March 14 — arrived at Nanaimo on Sunday morning, March 15 — Alert Bay at 3 A.M. — crossed Queen Charlotte Sound — arrived Rivers Inlet at 3 P.M. Discharged freight at two canneries. Passed China Hat and Bella Bella during Monday night. Arrived at Lowe Inlet on Tuesday and on to Standard Cannery at 10 P.M. the same day. Reached Port Essington on Wednesday morning and left the Skeena via Inverness Slough. Departed Inverness Cannery at 10 A.M. Thursday — passed Metlakatla and Port Simpson — reaching Cascade Cannery, Nass River, March 20 at 5 A.M. — five days from Victoria."

In addition to serving B.C. coastal communities,

including the Queen Charlotte Islands, on a regular basis, the *Danube* performed some special assignments. In 1891 and 1892 the ship was chartered by the Canadian government to convey officials to the Pribiloff Islands with regard to arbitrating the international dispute about seal hunting in the Bering Sea area.

In 1893 the *Danube* became involved in another international affair. She carried an overload of more than 600 Chinese passengers to Portland, Oregon. The United States authorities said they were illegal immigrants and the papers they had testifying that they were merely returning to the U.S. after a visit to China were false. A warrant was issued to hold the *Danube* in port until the legal tangle was resolved. Captain Irving posted a $40,000 bond. However, when, after a week, fewer than one-third of the passengers had been cleared, Irving ordered Captain Meyers to slip away with 400 passengers and two U.S. immigration officers still on board. The *Danube* steamed boldly past Astoria, at the mouth of the Columbia River, without being stopped. The U.S. officials were put ashore near Fort Stevens and the *Danube* then returned to Victoria where the Chinese immigrants were disembarked.

All coastal steamers available played a part in transporting gold seekers to Alaska and the Yukon during the hectic years of 1897 and 1898. On August 1, 1897, the *Danube* sailed for Dyea, Alaska, with 150 passengers crowded aboard. A few days earlier, on July 29, the *Tees* had left Victoria with a similar overload. In 1898 the *Danube* made a longer voyage to St. Michael's at the mouth of the Yukon River and returned with $850,000 in gold.

Later, as the rush for gold diminished, coastal steamers returned to their more regular sailings. However, other changes were imminent. In May, 1903, the CPR bought out the CPN, thus acquiring ownership of the *Amur, Danube* and *Tees*. The new owners kept the ships in general coastal service for a few more years.

The *Danube*, being the oldest of the three, was the first to be sold. In 1905 she was purchased by the B.C. Salvage Company. Over the years the *Danube* had undergone so many repairs that her original iron hull had been almost entirely replaced with steel plates. Her new owners also installed more powerful engines and, because of her changed function, renamed her the *Salvor*. She operated in this capacity until 1918 when she was sold to a Montreal firm which used her briefly as a tramp steamer. She was finally acquired by a Spanish company who put her in service as an iron-ore carrier in and out of the port of Balboa. Renamed the *Nervion*, the sturdy old ship's career continued until 1936, when she was broken up for scrap. She had been in service for 67 years.

The steamer *Tees* came to the west coast in April, 1896. Although smaller than the *Danube* — 165 feet long compared to the latter's 215 — she was a more modern ship with a steel hull, a double bottom, triple-expansion engine, and electric lights. Her top speed of 10½ knots was not very fast, but she was an excellent sea boat with comfortable accommodation for 75 cabin passengers. The *Tees* was also equipped with a siren whistle which announced her coming in no uncertain terms. Capt. Joe

Gosse reported the siren's wail gave the natives of Port Simpson a startling jolt when the ship first called at this north coast settlement in 1896.

After participating in the Klondike gold rush during 1897 and 1898, the *Tees* continued serving the north coast and the open waters of the west coast of Vancouver Island where her seaworthiness was fully proven. However the *Tees*, like most coastal steamers, did suffer some mishaps. In 1899 both the *Tees* and the *Danube* ran aground — the *Danube* ran ashore at Oyster River on Vancouver Island's east coast on May 25 and again on June 19 at Denman Island. The *Tees* had a similar misadventure later in the year. Both accidents necessitated some costly repairs.

Steamer Tees *entering Metlakatla Harbour, on the northern coast of B.C.*

After being acquired by the CPR in 1903, the seaworthy *Tees* was kept on the west coast of Vancouver Island run for the next 10 years. The *Tees* stood up to plenty of battering from rough seas along that rock-bound coast. In November, 1911, the *Tees* experienced a rather unusual adventure by getting lost in the vicinity of Kyuquot Sound, near the north end of Vancouver Island. A weak wireless call for help from the *Tees* was received, but it faded before her position was given. Naturally this caused much concern and four ships were sent to Kyuquot Sound to look for her. Their search was made difficult by extremely stormy weather. However, after three days, the *Tees* was located in a protected inlet safely tied to some convenient trees. After leaving the settlement of Kyuquot she had struck a rock which had put her rudder and propeller out of action. The high surrounding hills had muted her distress calls. After the necessary repairs were made the *Tees* returned to the west coast service for another two years, but in 1913 she was replaced by the newly-built *Princess Maquinna*.

In 1918 the *Tees* was chartered by the Pacific Salvage Company (PSC) to replace the *Salvor* (formerly *Danube*). In this capacity the *Tees* was sent to Alaskan waters to assess the possibility of salvaging the stricken *Princess Sophia*, which had sunk with the tragic loss of 353 lives, after grounding on Vanderbilt Reef in Lynn Canal on October 24, 1918. Divers from the *Tees* inspected the wreck, which was badly damaged, and salvage was deemed not to be feasible. However the ship's safe containing $62,000 in bullion was recovered.

In 1925 the PSC bought the *Tees* and renamed her *Salvage Queen*. She worked as a salvage vessel until 1933. That year she was sold to the Island Barge and Towing Company who changed her name again to *Island Queen*. The former *Tees* had now become a tugboat towing scows loaded with hog fuel from the Chemainus Sawmills to Port Angelas in Washington state.

The old steamer performed this duty competently, but in 1937 she suffered a fatal accident. The barge she was towing into Victoria harbour one stormy day crashed into her with such force that it reduced the former *Tees* to a floating wreck. Her owners decided she was beyond repair and the once sturdy old vessel became scrap metal.

The *Amur*, the latecomer of these pioneer steamers, did not arrive on the west coast until 1898. A typical British coaster, she had been built at Sunderland on the Wear River in 1890. She was 216 feet long, 28 feet wide, and could travel at a speed of 12 knots. Although primarily a freighter, she had accommodation for 60 passengers. She was originally launched as the *Famous*, and operated for several years under that name.

In 1898, the Klondike Mining and Transportation Corporation, eager to cash in on the gold rush bonanza, purchased the *Famous*, brought her to B.C. and renamed her *Amur*. However their venture failed, and a year later the *Amur* was bought by Captain Irving's CPN for $39,350 — a bargain price. The *Amur* operated successfully in west coast waters, but she did experience some misadventures. In September, 1901, she ran ashore on Chilkat Island in Lynn Canal and was out of service for a month undergoing repairs. Soon after being acquired by the CPR in 1903, the *Amur* struck a reef off Port Simpson, breaking her shaft and propeller. In 1905 she grounded on a rocky shoal in Wrangell Narrows. These accidents were not necessarily the result of navigational incompetence but because some mishaps were almost bound to occur, especially during bad weather, in the poorly marked channels of this rugged coastline.

A newlywed couple, travelling north to the Skeena River in November, 1905, kept a record of their journey aboard the *Amur* and noted the precautions the captain took when landing them at Port Essington:

"We are now (10 P.M., November 20, 1905) on board the Ss *Amur*, northward bound. This boat is tiny compared with an Atlantic liner but very nicely fitted up. We have about the best cabin on the boat, with a settee, making it quite comfortable. There are about 20 passengers. We are going through an inland sea between islands and mainland. The water is very calm and it is raining.

"About 7 P.M. (November 21) we reached Alert Bay — where one passenger landed. There are houses all around the bay with totem poles in front of them. Many Indians were at the wharf.

"During the night we crossed Queen Charlotte Sound and this stretch of water was very rough. We were tossed from side to side, our trunks slid across the cabin, everything in chaos. However when we reached the sheltered channels again the water was calm. Passed two steamers southward bound. Heard from the Purser that our furniture is not on board — left behind for the *Tees* to bring up, which means we won't get it for another two weeks.

"About 11 P.M. (November 23) we anchored off Port Essington, about 15 miles up the Skeena River. Captain McLeod is very cautious and said because the *Amur* draws 10 feet of water he could not go to the wharf to land so we had to go ashore in a small boat. The baggage was taken ashore first and it was 2 A.M. before we landed. We had to climb down a ladder into the little boat, which had several inches of water in it. It was quite a distance to shore and pretty rough. We were carried in from the boat on to rocks and then taken by a wooden walkway to the Hotel Essington."

The *Amur's* accidents were trivial compared to the San Francisco earthquake and fire in April, 1906. However the *Amur* helped to ease the distress by carrying from Vancouver a cargo of relief supplies to aid the victims of the shattered city.

The *Amur* continued on the run to ports of call in northern B.C. and Alaska until June, 1911, when she again struck a rock in Wrangell Narrows, suffering severe damage. As she was due to be replaced by the nearly completed — and later ill-fated — *Princess Sophia*, the *Amur* was laid up and not repaired. In April, 1912, she was sold for $11,000 to the Coastwise Steamship and Barge Co. of Vancouver.

Her new owners had the ship refitted as an ore carrier and she functioned in this utilitarian way for the next 12 years. The *Amur* transported ore from Britannia Beach on Howe Sound, and later from Anyox on the north coast's Observatory Inlet, to the copper smelter in Tacoma, Washington.

In 1924 the *Amur* was sold again, this time to Captain Berquist who operated the old ship as a coastal freighter under her original name of *Famous*. In 1926 she was wrecked in the Skeena River but was salvaged to sail again for another two years. In 1928 her active career ended and for the next four years the *Famous* lay in the graveyard of old ships at Dedwell Bay in Burrard Inlet. In 1932 she was stripped and her hull sank in the deepest waters of Burrard Inlet's North Arm.

Such, in brief, was the story of three pioneer steamers. Each played an important role in the maritime history of B.C. Their namesake rivers continue to flow as they have done for many centuries, although much more polluted than in former times. As for the steamers *Amur*, *Danube* and *Tees*, they exist today only in written records, relics and photographs, and in a few personal memories.

THE MIDWAY RAILWAY WAR

With the domination of British Columbia's southern rail traffic as the prize, two major railways fought it out, toe to toe.

IT might seem surprising that the sleepy little border town of Midway, British Columbia, was the site of a war between two railway giants. But trouble between James J. Hill's Great Northern Railway (GNR) and the Canadian Pacific Railway (CPR) had been brewing for years. Finally, in the fall of 1905, the interests of both railways came into direct conflict. The result was a violent confrontation between two hastily recruited armies. That no one was killed was more a matter of good luck than good sense.

Hill's interest in the southeastern corner of British Columbia stemmed from dramatically improving world metal prices following the 1873-1896 depression. The Kootenay district represented the northern extension of the so-called "inland empire," and many of the new Canadian mines were financed by American capital. Hill's GNR already serviced the mines of the northwestern United States, so he had only to build relatively short spur lines to feed the production of B.C. mines into the American rail network.

In 1905, however, Hill's ambition went beyond the wealth of the Kootenay district. His goal was the rich ore deposits of the Similkameen Valley, and he intended to push a line, using the charter of the Vancou-

(Two-page spread) The Great Northern Railway station at Midway.

JAMES J. HILL

WILLIAM CORNELIUS VAN HORNE

ver, Victoria and Eastern Railway (VV&E), from Washington State into B.C. at Midway. The problem that Hill faced was that his proposed route brushed CPR company land, and his rival did not welcome increased competition.

Ironically, Hill, along with George Stephen and Donald Smith, had been the driving force behind the construction of the CPR. Even after Hill left the CPR to pursue his American railroad interests, he had maintained cordial relations with the CPR syndicate, and particularly Stephen. However, the relationship between Hill and the CPR deteriorated markedly when, in 1888, William Cornelius Van Horne succeeded Stephen as company president. Although Hill had earlier been responsible for recruiting Van Horne into the CPR organization, relations between the two men tended to be distant and formal. The basis of the difficulty between Hill and the CPR was the American railroad magnet's creation of the GNR out of the St. Paul, Minneapolis and Manitoba Railway and a number of smaller lines in 1889. The purchase of the

American Soo Line by the CPR the following year, put the Canadian railway in Hill's backyard. But Hill was not about to be outdone. As he pushed his own railroad across the United States, Hill positioned his line as close to the border as possible so as to allow short feeder lines to readily penetrate the Canadian market. Now, as southern B.C. experienced a major mining boom, Hill was ready to go after the developing ore traffic.

The CPR, however, was not prepared to give Hill an inch. While pushing its own Crowsnest Pass line into the rich mining district around Phoenix, B.C., the CPR succeeded for a considerable time in preventing Hill·from building his own line into the rugged, mountainous area. But eventually Hill overcame the obstacles of both man and nature and once his tortuous line was completed, he was able to secure two thirds of the Phoenix traffic.

A second, more serious concern facing the CPR was the extent of Hill's ultimate ambitions. The CPR rightly feared that the extension of Hill's branch lines into Cana-

da was meant as more than just snipes at the CPR's heels. The GNR branch lines could be easily combined into a major southern mainline reaching west as far as Vancouver. In fact Hill had openly stated in 1905 that he would push a mainline from Manitoba to the west coast. As the CPR knew, this would mean much more serious competition. The CPR had lobbied unsuccessfully against the awarding of the VV&E charter to Hill. Now, in the late fall of 1905, as Hill pushed his railway across the British Columbia-Washington border, the stage was set for a direct confrontation between the CPR and the GNR.

Trouble started when the GNR construction crew began cutting a tunnel through a rocky hill by Myers Creek, about seven miles from Midway. Although the GNR had purchased the land on the eastern end of the tunnel, the western approach was on CPR property. In essence, this narrow strip of CPR land — lot 2703 — was valuable only insofar as it was necessary for the GNR's tunnel construction. Even before the GNR had actually begun serious excavation at the western mouth of the tunnel, Hill's men found it convenient to dump rocks taken from the eastern approach onto CPR property. When it was discovered that the GNR was using a piece of CPR land as a dumping site, the CPR men angrily erected barricades and posted guards to keep GNR men off.

On the surface it seems hard to explain CPR truculence. A little strip of land in a remote region of the province could hardly be considered valuable. Further, the GNR had offered to purchase the land from the CPR. The CPR, also, was doubtlessly aware that neither the B.C. government nor the courts would permit its title to lot 2703 to stand in the way of the GNR line. However, bearing in mind how vigorously the CPR opposed Hill's expansion into B.C., the railway's likely intent was to make the GNR's advancement as difficult as possible.

Initially, CPR tactics were quite successful. The GNR faced an impasse — construction could not proceed beyond the CPR barricade. However, as the GNR construction crew was undoubtedly aware, the CPR property was defended by no more than a dozen men. On Tuesday, November 7, 1905, the GNR gang poured down the hill from the tunnel site and onto the CPR guards. With picks and shovels the GNR men pushed into the enemy camp, knocking down tents and routing the hapless CPR defenders. Outnumbered 10 to one, the only course for the CPR men was retreat.

The first battle had gone to the GNR. Now the CPR set about squaring the odds. Under the direction of Fred W. McLaine, the railway land agent, the CPR began recruiting all available men in the Midway area. The following morning, with more men and supplies, the CPR returned to lot 2703. McLaine and his men were in for a surprise, however. The previous night, the GNR had brought in 150 more men. The CPR force was still outnumbered, now two to one.

In the face of superior numbers, McLaine's men resorted to harassing their opponents. The CPR men ripped up and carried off GNR track or twisted the rails into giant corkscrew shapes. Increasingly, the GNR crew was on the defensive. The railway put guards along their right of way and began chaining their tracks to anchors drilled into solid rock. To give additional protection, the GNR brought in a carload of barbed wire from Spokane which was then strung across the grade. Dump cars were also strung along the track, turned upside down, and then loaded with rocks as additional anchors for the rails.

Despite this added protection, the CPR raiders continued to make off with or destroy GNR rails. As frustration among Hill's men mounted, some of the railroad workers pulled guns during the face-to-face fighting. By good fortune, no one was actually shot. In one of the skirmishes, however, McLaine himself was captured and locked in a GNR powder shed. Although McLaine was eventually freed by cooler heads, the GNR "charged" him with threatening to do physical violence to his kidnappers. McLaine was eventually charged by the Midway police with having committed breaches of the peace.

At this time the opposing armies were encamped on the disputed strip of land, a mere 25 feet from one another. When the men were not actually engaged in fighting over rails, they sat in camp and jibed at one another across the narrow no man's land. The men's existence in the railroad camps was extremely unpleasant. The weather was cold, and fog hung low over the tents. Most of the day the men did nothing but eat, and because GNR food was better and it was easy to slip across the frontier dividing the gangs, Hill's cooks often fed both camps. To the consternation of the provincial police, both arms and liquor were plentiful. When faced with two camps of armed, intoxicated, and often ill-tempered railway workers, it would seem unlikely that the small provincial police force enthusiastically enforced provincial alcohol or firearm laws.

On the afternoon of Friday, November 10, with cases of liquor being smuggled into the camps, it seemed certain that once night fell a full-scale battle would break out. The situation was so serious that the GNR brought in a doctor to care for the expected injuries. Surprisingly, however, no great

battle took place.

By now the press was roundly criticizing the actions of both railways. "There is," wrote one Toronto newspaper, "no right of private warfare in Canada." Similarly, as the situation dragged on, the B.C. government and its provincial police came increasingly under pressure concerning their inability to gain control of the situaion. As one Vancouver reporter wrote, "the Midway provincial police would be more at home playing. . .'Button, button who has the button?' rather than searching for weapons."

From the CPR's perspective, the fact that the American commercial rival was "dead in the water" was a sort of victory. The GNR was making no progress on its spur line, and was actually fighting to hold onto the rails it had already laid. On the afternoon of Sunday, November 12, the GNR finally pulled its men off the little strip of land claimed by the CPR. As the GNR men pulled back, they took out weapons and fired round after round into the air. These were the last shots of the Midway railway war.

Early the following week, the CPR obtained an injunction ordering the GNR men off lot 2703. Also, the charges against Fred McLaine, the CPR land agent, were dropped. But while the CPR was able to achieve early court victories, the most important legal victory went to J.J. Hill. The GNR commenced expropriation proceedings in order to obtain lot 2703, and on December 8, 1905, the British Columbia Supreme Court awarded ownership of the disputed land to the Great Northern Railway.

However, the CPR may have also won a victory. Despite what he said in 1905, Hill never constructed a southern mainline in competition with the CPR. The fight over lot 2703 may have been enough to warn HIll that when really threatened, the CPR could be a vicious foe. The bitterness between the two railways ended with Hill's death in 1916. Today, few if any British Columbians will remember when two great railway giants actually came to blows.

This 198-foot-high Great Northern Railway trestle was located near Phoenix.

PIONEER SMELTERS OF BRITISH COLUMBIA

The story of the rise and fall of the early smelters in British Columbia and their place in the history of mining and in the development of the province.

The Hall Mining & Smelting Co., Nelson, B.C. in 1899. Blown in in 1896, it was dismantled in 1907 and demolished in 1932. (Right) The Hall mines smelter crew, probably before 1900.

ALL the pioneer smelters of British Columbia, save one, were predestined to failure. Despite this ultimate doom a few did survive long enough to win their place in history by opening up one-half of the province and establishing an industry that was to become a giant.

The era of smelter building began in 1868 and lasted until 1915. During this period money was spent to start 24 smelters. All of these except the outstanding COMINCO smelter at Trail were to fail. Eighteen of them, a mortality rate of 75 percent, did not return even one penny on their investment; a financial fiasco, to say the least. Pioneering a new industry was difficult as well as costly. Two of the enterprises died on the drawing boards after sites had been obtained, and others were never completed. A few that were built operated only for very short times — as briefly as a day or two. The principal reasons for this dismal record appears to have been managerial incompetence and technological ignorance.

Five smelters, however, did savour temporary success that lasted from five to 19 years. Along with the flourishing operation at Trail, they were to bequeath a lasting legacy. They were responsible for the building of railroads that opened up the entire southern part of B.C. to settlement and development. Because the smelters needed coke, coal mining in the Crow's Nest Pass prospered. Most significantly, these smelters made hardrock mining of many metals possible by making it profitable. This gave mining the great impetus that enabled it to become the second largest industry in the province, a position it has held ever since.

Of the plants that did achieve profitability, five were located in the southern interior near established lodes of gold, silver, copper, lead and zinc. The sixth was a copper smelter situated on the northern coast at Anyox.

All the pioneer smelters were built in the wilderness and in those pristine areas they were spectacular. Out of the green valleys grew giant metallurgical complexes with huge buildings and roaring blast furnaces. Tall smokestacks billowed clouds of sulphurous fumes that proved to be lethal to trees in the nearby hills. The yards teemed with workers, while ore cars from endless arriving trains were constantly being shunted and noisily dumped. Small locomotives were forever whistling as they moved the hot slag to ever-growing piles. Who, at the time of so much activity, would have thought that such centres of heavy industry, so substantially built, could ever actually vanish? Yet, in a few years, most did.

Today the buildings, the tall stacks, the bricks and the railroads are gone. Virtually nothing is left. Even the monstrous accumulations of slag, which had been considered to be permanent relics, are disappearing as new technology has found uses for them. The crumbled concrete has been covered by vegetation and trees are growing again on the hills. Yet the pioneer smelters, now just a memory, played an essential part in the province's mining history.

The story of mining in B.C. probably began eons ago when some native wandering by a glacial stream found an attractive yellow pebble, then searched for more. If this was indeed "mining," it remained unchanged until 1849, when a man called Sutter found gold in a stream in California. His momentous discovery was the real beginning of mining in western North America. It made the nation gold conscious and attracted prospectors by the thousands to California and Nevada.

In a relatively short time all the major gold and silver lodes had been claimed. The less fortunate who found nothing continued their search. This horde of prospectors began to move northwards through the mountain trenches and eventually reached B.C. Here, major ore strikes were made at Rock Creek, Wildhorse Creek and in the Omineca and Cariboo regions before the tide moved still farther north, into the Klondike. It was not too long before much of the Canadian "pick and shovel" loose gravel had been claimed and worked out. The character of mining began to change as the first era of the province's mining history ended and the second began.

With the "easy picking" placer gold no longer to be found, prospectors turned their attention to hardrock, quartz. Such gold and other minerals were found, but mining them would be different. The day of the freelance prospec-

tor-miner was over. Mining now became a corporate venture because capital was required to blast the rocks, to build concentrators and to ship the ore which had to be processed. At first shipping ore was a very expensive and difficult problem. In the lode areas of the southern sections of the province there were no railroads nor roads as such. Only crude wagon trails and waterways were available. Then, too, there were no smelters in Canada and the ore had to be transported to railheads in the United States for transhipment to the American smelters at Everett, Tacoma and Butte. This also involved the payment of duties. Faced with expenses such as these, the mining of metals other than gold was uneconomic. As gold lodes were few, but many rich deposits of other metals had been found, it became obvious that there was a great need for smelters in Canada and for railways to transport the ore.

Fortunately the federal and provincial governments did recognize the needs and reacted favourably. They offered inducements by way of subsidies and land grants to the builders of smelters and of the railways to feed them. It was because of the smelters then being erected in the southern interior that railways were built. These eventually connected Alberta with the Pacific Coast, and were ultimately united to become the Kettle Valley Railroad under control of the Canadian Pacific Railroad (CPR), and it opened up the region for settlement, agriculture and resource development. Also, because of the smelting, numerous other short railways, even from the U.S., were built to bring in the ore.

Long before the railways, however, attempts had been made to process ore at the mine-sites. The earliest of these was probably that made in 1842 by the fur traders of the Hudson's Bay Company who, it is reported, had heated the ore from the silver-lead outcroppings of a mine on Kootenay Lake, later to be known as the Bluebell. After heating, they apparently had hammered the ore into little balls for their muskets.

This same mine, the Bluebell, was the first location in the province where ore would be smelted. In 1868 an American prospector named Henry Doane, by doing some high-grading, induced George Hearst, later to become a senator from California, to take over the mine. Hearst actually reduced some ore. But the ore was not

(Opposite page) Because of the success of the B.C. Copper Company's smelter, Greenwood grew to a population of 3,000. This smelter, shown in inset photo, operated for 17 years. Today its imposing smokestack, some slag and ruins are all that remain.
(Below) An aerial view of the Bluebell mine site and Riondel.

the same that had been given him for pretesting, and as his equipment was too primitive the results were very poor. Since a mine without smelting facilities was then worthless, Hearst abandoned it, but the remains of his attempts were still visible in the late 1880s.

The province's second smelter was also built at a mine-site and needed no transportation facilities for the ore. This was raised in 1883, 42 miles south of Golden City, on the south side of the Spillamacheen River where it joins the Columbia. It was well built of iron and stone by a John McRae. There is no record of any production. The stone from the structure, however, was used in 1906 to build piers for a railroad bridge.

In 1887, soon after the transcontinental CPR was built across the centre of the province, a smelter was built at Illecillewaet station. It was operated under the name of the Selkirk Mining and Smelting Company by the then well-known mining pioneers, Gustavus Blin Wright, Charles E. Poolet and Edgar Marvin. About 250 tons of ore from the Lanark mine was processed between July 25 and November 7, 1887. However, the smelter was inefficient and nothing more was heard of it.

Chronologically, the next smelter was erected in what is now the heart of Vancouver, near the old Hastings Mill site on what is now Powell Street. This was in 1888 when a Claude Vautin from London, using English capital, formed the B.C. Smelting Company Ltd. The smelter was apparently well built for a capacity in excess of 50 tons per day. In building, Vautin tried hard to meet all the requirements for subsidies and grants, which totalled $25,000 in cash and 31 acres of land from the City of Vancouver.

The buildings and equipment were excellent and included a 60-foot-high smokestack. The ore to be smelted was from the Monarch mine at Field, which Vautin controlled. However, ignorance of the nature of the sulphur and zinc content of this ore was eventually to wreck his endeavour. On February 14, 1889, when the furnace was blown in, an overheated flue caused a fire and an immediate shutdown. A few minutes later the furnaces were restarted and, using some limestone and scrap iron as a flux, some of the ore was actually smelted and poured into moulds. But it soon became clear that the ore was too sulphurous and would require processing by a roaster that had not been provided for. Also, other fluxing ores would be needed. Further financing was not forthcoming and, because of the mismanagement, the property was mortgaged in May. Vautin had been awarded the land but did not collect the cash bonus. In December that year a contractor bought the plant at auction and later dismantled it.

In 1889, a smelter was erected at Revelstoke by the Kootenay (B.C.) Smelting and Trading Company. The works were located on the south side of a sharp bend in the left bank of the Columbia River, about three-quarters of a mile west of the CPR station at Revelstoke. In 1891 some ore from the Monarch mine was smelted. This was the same ore that had proved troublesome in Vancouver and it did so again. Another type of ore might have saved the operation, but there were no other mines nearby to supply it. This lack of foresight caused the abandonment of the enterprise in 1892. Also, the site had been poorly chosen. The bank upon which the buildings had been erected became eroded and, by 1899, the buildings, machinery and the site had all vanished.

In 1890 a man named Best decided to establish a smelter at the mouth of Woodbury Creek, two miles north of Ainsworth on Kootenay Lake. S.S. Fowler, the mining historian, describes this plant as "almost mythical." According to *West Kootenay: The Pioneer Years;* "The smelter, with a 20-ton capacity, was scheduled for a trial run on October 17 after a test made earlier that week had proved satisfactory. But the trial run had to be delayed when the owners of the pack train refused to transport the ore from the mines for the price offered. Alas, it was to be a short reprieve for the smelter, for, during the first days of its trial run the heat generated proved to be too great." The smelter split in two and was abandoned. The mythical part for which there is no explanation was the fact, learned later, that the plant and pots had been a Mexican design similar to those used by the padres in Mexico in the 17th century.

The next smelter was built on the railroad at Golden by the same group that had failed at Revelstoke. The site was about one-half mile east of Golden station, close to the mouth of the Kicking Horse River canyon. Incredible, the same mismanagement team again counted on the troublesome ore from the Monarch mine. One car of ore was received and smelted. But that was the end as refinancing fell through. Fowler tells us that, after the First World War, the buildings were torn down, mostly by hoboes who tore off boards to make fires under the smelter roof. The white bricks from the tall smokestack were used to build many of Golden's chimneys and fireplaces.

Up to this time almost every smelter had been closed almost immediately after

(Opposite page) Beset by financial problems from the start, the Dominion Copper Company's smelter at Boundary Falls ultimately succumbed to its competitor at Greenwood. It is seen here in 1902.

(Below) The Kootenay Mining & Smelting Company's smelter operation at Pilot Bay in 1896. At its peak it employed 200 men: today, its surviving smokestack intrigues travellers on the Balfour-Proctor ferry.

opening. Closures due to technical ignorance, poor financing and lack of management acuity had made investment in smelters all but suicidal. After this unbroken record of failures it is remarkable that funds could be found for further projects, but they were. Fortunately, from this time on, the risks were considerably diminished and the building of the pioneer smelters continued.

The first of the new breed of ore processors was again built near the Bluebell mine on Kootenay Lake by the Kootenay Lake Reduction Company and blown in during March, 1895. Because of its location, this was to be known as the Pilot Bay Smelter. At its peak it employed 200 men and smelted lead and zinc. Partial success was achieved because the ores not only came from the Blue-

(Above) The Trail smelter c1896. Capacity was 250 tons daily. The main furnace was 310 feet long and 60 feet wide.
(Opposite page, top) Nelson, B.C., showing the Hall Mining & Smelting Company's smelter.
(Opposite page, bottom) Mountains of slag from the Granby smelter just north of Grand Forks, in 1977.
(Below) The Vanada smelter, Texada Island, 1903 It operated fitfully for a year or two, then failed. In 1911 an attempt to reactivate it by using oil for fuel was quickly abandoned.

bell but also from across the lake from the mines near Ainsworth. But, despite the use of barges for transporting the ores, the costs were too high and, as the equipment was not the best, the operation closed after two years. Later in 1909 a French firm called the Canadian Metal Company, Eduard Riondel, president, and the capable S.S. Fowler, manager, reopened the works. There was intermittent operation for a few years but it never was a complete success. Although all else has disappeared and the site is overgrown, modern-day tourists who ride the free government ferry from Balfour to Kootenay Bay can see a derelict smokestack yet standing.

The next pioneer smelter to be set up, the only one to survive until the present, was at Trail. Today it is the world's largest in zinc production and second or third in lead smelting. It succeeded because of sound management, adaptability, use of its own research, by diversification or ores smelted, by ensuring its ore supply, by owning its own mines, and by ensuring its own energy supply by owning a hydro-electric operation, and its own coal mines. It was a pioneer also in controlling air pollution and is known worldwide for its chemical fertilizers.

It was given its start in 1895 when a 26-year-old "boy wonder" copper baron from Montana, Augustus F. Heinze, was prompted by the ore finds at Rossland to start a smelter at Trail. He also built a railway to Rossland and Robson and obtained rights-of-way for the Columbia and Western Railway (C&W) to Midway. The CPR, entering the area from Alberta at this time, apparently resented the young man's ambition and bought him out. To do so, however, they also had to purchase his smelter. This was in 1898.

It was the purchase by the CPR, guided by the managerial genius of Walter Aldridge, that ensured continued success at Trail. In 1906, when the company acquired the St. Eugene mine at Moyie, and those at Rossland, the entire operation became the Consolidated Mining and Smelting Company (COMINCO). Later, the purchase of the Sullivan mine proved to be fortunate as it became a very rich producer of lead and zinc ores. Being innovative, the company, in 1914, began to produce zinc by electrolysis. Thus Trail produced a gross portion of the zinc needed to make the brass for the shells of the First World War. Again, in 1920, its own research department developed a differential flotation method to separate zinc from lead ore.

In 1930, using 400-foot-high smokestacks, sulphur that had previously polluted the air was collected and used to make chemical fertilizers. A further contribution to ecology was made in 1975 when hardware was installed for the elimination of smoke.

Not far from Trail, at the foot of Kootenay Lake at Nelson, and at about the same time in 1896, the Hall Mining and Smelting Company smelter was blown in. While this complex was to last only about 10 years, it was one of the more successful pioneers. Initially the ore came from the Hall Brothers' Silver King Mine. This mine produced for some years before the building of the reduction plant. From the mine located high upon a hillside the ore was originally "rawhided." This meant that the ore was packaged in raw skins and skidded down the moun-

tain. At the time it was shipped by water to Idaho and then transhipped to Butte, Montana, by rail.

Having a profitable mine and the prospect of being served by a railroad (the Nelson and Fort Sheppard Railroad of D.C. Corbin), the Hall Brothers built their own smelter. They brought the ore down from their Silver King mine by an aerial rope tramway that was four-and-one-half miles long, with a drop of 4,000 feet. Operated by manpower, each bucket could carry 150 pounds of ore at the rate of 10 tons per hour.

Another reason for their success was that they did custom smelting of copper and lead from the mines in the entire lake region. Later, reverberatory furnaces were added to refine the matte to blister copper. Eventually the ores being received needed fluxing.

The railroad that arrived in 1900 could bring fluxing ores from the Emma mine at Grand Forks, but this made smelting more expensive and, unable to compete with the smelter at Trail, the operation closed in 1907. No vestige of the plant is left, as a residential area and a highway now cover the site.

A smelter at Northport, Washington, is not included as one of the province's pioneer smelters, although it could, with considerable justification, be so called. It was built in 1898, right at the international border by the flamboyant Heinze to serve the Le Roi and other mines at Rossland. It operated intermittently until 1909, when the efficiency of the CPR plant at Trail put it out of business.

As a footnote to the mention of an American smelter, one had been built a few miles farther south from Northport, at Colville, in 1887. This one also had designs on Canadian ore but apparently failed to survive for long.

After the purchase of the Heinz smelter at Trail, the CPR planned to expand smelting operations and purchased a site farther west, near Christina Lake, at Cascade. About the same time still another pioneer smelter was planned, and a site purchased three miles south of Grand Forks, at Carson. However, these smelters died in the planning stage because of the rapid progress being made in the building of the Granby smelter at Grand Forks.

The C&W, under the operation of the CPR, rather than Heinze, laid tracks in 1899 as far as Midway. This made it possible to transport the ores of the copper rich mines at Phoenix to a smelter. Quick to take advantage of the approaching railway, Jay P. Graves, of Spokane, Washington, and S.H. Miner, of Granby, Quebec, formed the Granby Consolidated Mining & Smelting Company and, with efficiency and haste, built a smelter at Grand Forks which was blown in on August 18, 1900. After the COMINCO smelter at Trail, this was to be the province's most profitable pioneer smelter.

The main source of ores for the Granby smelter were the mines at Phoenix, namely: The City of Paris group, Old Ironsides, Knob Hill, Phoenix and Victoria. Because these were self-fluxing ores with proper portions of sulphur, silica and iron, and were used with coke, the smelting rates were cheap. The Great Northern Railroad arrived in 1902 to bring in American ores as well. In order not to have to ship matte, the first converter was installed in 1902. By 1910 the Granby smelter was the largest copper smelter in the British Empire. At that time it employed 300 men and processed 3,000 tons of ore per day. It was a pioneer also in starting the eight-hour day in Canada, in 1905.

In 1919 world prices of copper began to drop and profits fell. Weakened by its dependency upon a single metal, a prolonged strike at the coal mines in the Crow's Nest dealt it a finishing blow, and the smelter closed. The two mountains of slag that stood until recently are fast receding as the granules are being converted into insulation.

Near Grand Forks, but on the other side of Phoenix Mountain, two other temporary, successful smelters were established and opened at about the same time in 1901. One was located at Boundary Falls and the other, three miles eastward, at Greenwood.

Built by the Standard Pyritic Company, the smelter at Boundary Falls had financial problems from the onset. It was sold to the Montreal and Boston Company who, in turn, sold it to the Dominion Copper Company. They operated it fairly profitably for about three years, using ores from the Brooklyn, Lone Star and Stemwinder mines. It was idle for most of 1905 and when the competition of the Greenwood plant became too much they sold out to their competitor, who operated it inconsistently until they closed it in 1918.

The victor in this short-lived contest was the B.C. Copper Company, whose smelting operation helped Greenwood eventually grow to a population of 3,000. Blown in in 1901, it was one of the better operations and ran for 17 years, when problems besetting the Granby Company at Grand Forks caused it to close in 1918. Its biggest year was 1904 when 210,000 tons were processed.

In 1902, at the north end of Kootenay Lake, at Five Mile, between Ferguson and Trout Lake, a small smelter was assembled. It had a 30-ton capacity Vulcan furnace and two Howell roasters. The ore was to come from the Sunshine, Silvercup and Triune mines, but there is no record of these mines ever having produced a ton of ore.

That same year, a smelter development appeared on Vancouver Island. Here, again, two smelters were built close to each other. The first was that of the Northwest Smelting Company at Osborne Bay, Crofton. Although completed the first year it was not blown in until four years later, in 1906. It operated only for a short time, until its reason for being, the copper mining operations at nearby Mount Sicker, shut down.

Its neighbour, the smelter of the Tyee Copper Company at Ladysmith, was blown in one week before Christmas in 1902. It processed ore until 1904 and once treated 500 tons in a day. Here again, more technical problems with the ore made processing expensive because outdoor roasting was required. These costs and a falling supply of ore caused operations to cease.

About the same time, in 1903, the Vanada Copper and Gold Mining Company started a smelter on Texada Island. It operated fitfully for a year or two, then failed. In 1911 an attempt was made to reactivate it by using oil for fuel was quickly abandoned.

During this period, 1903 to 1905, there was further activity near Golden. The new smelter builder was the Laborer's Cooperative Gold, Silver and Copper Mining Company. Apparently the location chosen on Hospital Creek was quite good, for power was received from a dam two miles up the same stream, and limestone for fluxing was only half a mile away. The plant was designed to handle 65 tons of ore, brought down from Canyon and McLean creeks, per day. One hundred tons from the Lucky Jim mine was shipped for a test run, but the smelter only operated for a single evening. Fowler suggested that the entire operation may have been a stock promotion scheme.

On Slocan Lake, at Roseberry, three miles north of New Denver, a small smelter was built to serve the Sandon and Three Forks mines. Apparently it was built by the Carnes Creek Consolidated Company Ltd., and was scheduled to open in May, 1905. No further information has been uncovered.

The financiers of the Roseberry project, under the name of the Kootenay Ore Company, also built a small smelter at Kaslo, on the site now occupied by the marina. In 1905 the Lucky Jim mine, which had also tried a shipment to Golden, shipped 100 tons here for testing.

Later in 1905 the Sullivan Mining Company at Kimberley built a smelter near the mine at a site called Marysville. Although technical and financial problems caused several changes of management, it did process some ore. However, the smelter was considered a failure and it closed in 1908. A year later, when it became the property of COMINCO, the smelter was scrapped and the ore shipped to Trail.

The last of the pioneer smelters was blown in on March 14, 1914. It was located on the coast, at Anyox, north of Prince Rupert, at the end of a long inlet. It was a project of the Granby Company which had been doing so well with its operation at Grand Forks. The ore came exclusively from the nearby Hidden Creek mines, and its coal came from Nanaimo. Earlier, in 1911, it had been planned to ship this ore to Tacoma. Analysis of the costs determined that it would be better to ship to a local smelter. This was later proven to be correct. During the 20-year lifespan of a reasonable profitable operation, 2,700 people lived in the company town. After Grand Forks closed in 1919, Anyox inherited the title of the largest copper smelter in the British Empire.

During the early years the Anyox plant had many problems with ore that was very inconsistent in its silica, iron and alumina content. By 1935 the ore reserves had become exhausted. With copper prices too low to warrant development of new prospects, the smelter was closed and the town abandoned. Today there is little evidence of its existence. Of the smelter, little more than some vegetation-covered concrete ruins remain.

With the death of Anyox, the era of the pioneer smelters was over. After 1914 no new heavy metal smelters were built until the Afton mines did so at Kamloops in 1978. The pioneer smelters had risen, then disappeared, but, in the interval, they had made a permanent and very beneficial mark in the history of B.C. They opened up the southern interior of the province and gave the momentum to the mining industry that has made it the giant that it is today.

The Upper Kootenay River Canal

Grohman was not the first to try to divert water from the Kootenay River to Columbia Lake by means of a canal. During the Wild Horse Creek gold rush 19 years earlier, the feat had been attempted by 25 men so that they could pan the river-bed.

This two-page spread shows the remains of W.A. Baillie-Grohman's canal in May, 1986.
(Below) The canal under construction at Canal Flat in 1888.
(Opposite page) A point of interest plaque at Canal Flat.

CANAL FLAT

In 1808 David Thompson named this flat "McGillivray's Portage" as he crossed from Columbia Lake to the Kootenay River. In 1889 W.A. Baillie-Grohman joined the two waterways by a canal with a single lock. Regulations aimed at preventing Columbia River flooding so restricted the operation of the canal that only two steamboats passed through—the Gwendoline in 1894 and the North Star in 1902.

PROVINCE OF
BRITISH COLUMBIA

19 66

THE first man to conceive the idea of reclaiming Kootenay Flats, in the Creston Valley, was William Adolphe Baillie-Grohman, a British sportsman and author, who was on a hunting expedition in West Kootenay in 1882. He theorized that the level of Kootenay Lake could be lowered by widening its very constricted outlet, enabling the spring freshet to flow freely, and thus prevent the rise of the lake.

When Grohman returned the following year, he added another idea to his proposed scheme; to lessen the amount of water in the Kootenay River by diverting it, or part of it, into the Columbia River at the place which David Thompson had called McGillivray's Portage. Here the two waterways were only about a mile and a half apart, and Grohman saw no difficulty in attempting to cut a canal to connect the two. In fact, by his own admission, he was not the first to attempt such a diversion. During the gold rush at Wild Horse Creek, some 19 years earlier, 25 men had attempted the same thing, but for a different reason. They hoped to divert the entire Kootenay River so they could wash for gold in the river-bed. They expected to complete the project in one season, but a shortage of provisions and funds prevented them from carrying it out.

With the modern mechanical means available today, such projects as digging the canal and widening the outlet of the lake would be considered small and could be easily and quickly accomplished. But in 1883 the Kootenay District was a sparsely inhabited wilderness without benefit of railway or steamboat transportation, and with only a minimum of trails. Baillie-Grohman's one-man reclamation and colonization scheme, therefore, made history.

In negotiations with the B.C. government, Grohman was seeking a concession to the Kootenay bottomlands, situated between the south end of Kootenay Lake and the International Boundary. However, another group, headed by Capt. J. Ainsworth, had also been negotiating for a land concession in Kootenay which would include the 48,000 acres Grohman was hoping for. Ainsworth offered to build a railway from the Kootenay River outlet to its confluence with the Columbia, a distance of some 26 miles in exchange for 750,000 acres free of taxes, as well as other valuable rights.

A public meeting of protest held in Victoria objected to the passage of this private bill, which was to convey such a large tract of land to a group of Americans, and the act was later disallowed by the federal government. But Ainsworth was persistent and eventually succeeded in getting the act of incorporation passed, although the Columbia and Kootenay Railway Company was given a much smaller land grant than had originally been sought.

Grohman's concession, dated December 10, 1883, took the form of a 10-year lease. It covered 47,500 acres of the bottom and marsh lands known as Kootenay Flats. Although there was no mention of any land or works in the Upper Kootenay-Columbia Valley, subsequent events would show that at the time the document was drawn up Grohman had a canal in that district in mind: "Provided also and it is hereby agreed and declared that the Lessee shall from time to time and at all times during the currency of this lease have a right of way over and full egress upon any Crown lands and the right to construct a ditch or works thereon for the purpose of carrying into effect the reclamation scheme attempted by the Lessee. . . ."

This "ditch" would later evolve into the canal at Canal Flats, although the document gave no indication as to where the ditch might be constructed, nor did it refer to, or give permission for, the diversion of the Kootenay River.

For the first five years of the lease an annual rental of $100 was to be paid, and an additional 5¢ an acre thereafter "on land reclaimed and brought into the state of actual cultivation," both payable in gold coin. The sum of $15,000 was to be expended in B.C. by the lessee within the first three years to further the reclamation, and during the following seven years an annual sum of not less than $10,000 was to be spent. No part of the premises could be assigned or sublet without written consent of the government.

The lands and all buildings and improvements were to be free from provincial taxation during the term of the lease, unless Grohman should apply for the purchase, which he had the privilege of doing after the survey was made.

Grohman's next step was to interest some of his friends in England in his Canadian enterprise, and the Kootenay Lake Syndicate was formed as a temporary means of raising the initial funds required. With this assurance of financial aid, Grohman returned to Victoria to make a formal proposal to the government on behalf of the syndicate, a proposal which now asked for partially free grants of land in the Upper Kootenay Valley of approximately 22,500 acres. Grohman outlined 18 primary conditions under which he thought that the land concession should be provided. One condition was that the syndicate should place a steamboat on the navigable part of the Lower Kootenay River and Lake during 1884; another, that within six months of the commencement of the Kootenay canal a similar steamer or steam-tug should be placed on the Upper Columbia River to ply from Golden to the Columbia Lake. This appears to be the first written suggestion by Grohman to the government as to where the canal was to be, for he calls it "The Upper Kootenay River Canal."

The steamer on the Kootenay River and Lake had been arranged for by Grohman even before his proposal was approved, and in so doing he became the first man to operate a steam-craft on the Kootenay waters. The boat was the *Midge*, which had been consigned to Grohman by English investor Venables Kykre. When the *Midge* arrived at Montreal, on the deck of the *Polynesian,* customs officers demanded a considerable amount of duty on the little old steam-launch. Learning that "settler's goods," including certain agricultural implements, were admitted free of duty, Grohman declared the *Midge* to be an agricultural implement: the boat, he explained, was required to pull a steam-plough on the flooded lands he intended

to reclaim. Ottawa accepted this idea and, much to the consternation of the Montreal officials, the *Midge* was cleared free of duty. The boat was then shipped on two flatcars to Sandpoint, Idaho, the nearest railway point to the Kootenay. From there she was carried by a dozen white men and a number of Indians over the Pack River Trail to Bonner's Ferry, rollers and pulleys being used where necessary. It took three weeks to transport the boat the 40 miles.

The *Midge*, needless to say, was never used as an agricultural implement, but for cruising and exploring the lake and river. The Indians all along the way were intrigued and delighted by the sight of her puffing about, and willingly cut wood for the boiler in return for being allowed to blow the whistle or to have their canoes towed by the little steamer. Later, she was abandoned by Grohman and taken over by T. Davis, one of the prospective settlers, who renamed her the *Mud Hen*. When he returned to Wales, the *Mud Hen* was abandoned forever.

It was in his formal proposal of 1884 that Grohman first recorded officially that a canal was to be used for diversion of the Kootenay River. The pertinent clause now read: "That in order to carry out the reclamation works we shall have a right of way over and full ingress and egress upon any Crown lands, and the right to construct a ditch or canal, or such other work, between the Upper Kootenay River and the Upper Columbia Lake, that will enable us to turn the Upper Kootenay River into the Upper Columbia Lake. . . ." Thus the purpose of the canal was now made known.

The proposal was approved and the articles of agreement were signed on September 7, 1885. The new agreement, which contained 26 clauses, was substantially the same as Grohman had proposed, except that the canal and the river diversion now assumed more importance. Grohman later admitted that this was the vital point on which his whole undertaking was based. The relevant clause, now No. 15, read thus: "In order to carry out the reclamation works, the said William Adolph Baillie-Grohman, his heirs or assigns, shall have full ingress and egress upon and over any Crown land at or near the works, and the right to construct such a ditch or canal, with a dam between the Upper Kootenay River and the Columbia Lake, as will enable him or them to turn the whole or a portion of the Upper Kootenay River at point A on the said plan No. 1 into the Upper Columbia Lake. . . ." The increasing importance of the canal in the reclamation scheme is shown by the fact that several clauses hinged upon its being completed: no Crown grants were to be issued until the canal was completed, or, if it was not completed by July 31, 1889, until Grohman could establish that no less than $50,000 had been expended in B.C. in furtherance of the reclamation works. Such expenditure could include steamboats, machinery, material, equipment, etc., brought into B.C. Clause 2 stipulated that before December 1, 1886, a steamer or steam-tug of not less than 90 tons gross was to be placed on the Upper Columbia River to navigate the stream from the Canadian Pacific Railway (CPR) (east crossing of the Columbia) to the Upper Columbia Lake, providing, as had been stated in the original proposal, that there was no other steamer then navigating that river. No mention was made of any steamer to be placed on the Kootenay River and Lake, since the *Midge* was already in operation on those waters. Before September 1, 1886, Grohman or his company was to deposit $7,054 with the B.C. government, this being 10¢ on the dollar per acre.

It should be made clear that the B.C. government did not, as is often supposed, assume the authority for the Kootenay River diversion. True, it entered into this agreement of September 7, 1885, with Grohman, an agreement which included the diversion clause quoted above, but the document also included the all-important clause 21, which is here quoted in full:

"This agreement, not withstanding anything herein contained, shall have no force or effect unless and until the Government of the Dominion of Canada shall have lawfully authorized the turning of the water of the Upper Kootenay river at the point of diversion marked A on the plan hereto attached, marked No. 1, into the Upper Columbia Lake, and also the like authority to the lowering of the water of the Kootenay Lake by the deepening and widening of the outlet of the Kootenay Lake at the places designated on the plan hereto attached, marked No. 2. In the event of such authority not being given, and if the said William Adolph Baillie-Grohman shall have deposited the aforesaid sum of seven thousand and fifty-four ($7,054) dollars, the same shall be returned to him."

From this clause it is clear that the B.C. government had made the entire reclamation works subject to assent being given by the federal government. If assent was not given, Grohman would have his deposit refunded and could assume that the deal was off unless some other scheme satisfactory to the federal government could be worked out. It is true that the original concession of December 10, 1883, made no reference to any assent being required from the federal government, but neither did it give Grohman the authority to divert the Kootenay River or to build a canal. It only gave permission to construct a "ditch or works." Grohman later said that the attorneys for the B.C. government, as well as his own attorneys, had overlooked the fact that the province had no jurisdiction over canal works, yet clause 21 makes it plainly evident that the point had not been overlooked.

Whether or not Grohman and his associates were aware of this complication, they continued with their plans. The Kootenay Syndicate Limited had been incorporated in England on May 18, 1885 and, after obtaining the agreement, proceeded with the financing. The required deposit of $7,054, was made in May, 1886, and acknowledged by a letter to the directors from William Smithe dated May 7, 1886.

But between the time of the incorporation and the payment of $7,054, events occurred which appear to have upset the proverbial apple-cart. A public official notice, dated November 3, 1885, stating the intention to divert the Kootenay River, or a portion thereof, into the valley of the Columbia, was posted at Golden City. The residents of this settlement, otherwise known as the Fifth Siding of the CPR, then under construction, did not let the suggestion go unnoticed. Along with other settlers in the Upper Columbia Valley, they held a public meeting at

Golden on March 5, 1886, for the purpose of sending a petition to Ottawa protesting the diversion of the river. The petitioners considered that the canal scheme would cause great damage to lands within the railway belt if the additional volume of water from the Kootenay should be emptied into the Columbia; that the gently flowing Columbia would be unable to carry off the water from the swifter-flowing Kootenay and thereby much of the low land in the Upper Columbia Valley would be flooded; that farming and ranching were dependent upon the hay grown on these lands; that much valuable timber would be destroyed; that future settlers would be deterred; that the scheme would preclude the possibility of building a road in the valley which was necessary to mining and timber interests; that the diversion might lead to foreign complications; that, in short, the reclaiming of the Kootenay Flats, which was the object of the diversion, would be greatly overbalanced by the amount of damage which would be caused by overflow into the Columbia Valley. The petitioners concluded by asking for suspension of the work until a careful investigation of the possible consequences could be made.

The petition was well prepared and signed by 30 individuals, one of whom, Robert Lang, a merchant of Golden, forwarded it on March 6 to the Hon. Thomas White, Minister of Interior, Ottawa. Apparently it had effect, for an Order in Council, dated May 26, was transmitted to the B.C. government calling attention to the representations and submitting a copy of the petition for comment. The reply, dated July 5, quite properly, simply pointed out that the assent of the Dominion government was necessary before Grohman could proceed with his reclamation work.

The responsibility for securing this consent naturally was Grohman's, and he made application to the Federal Minister of Public Works. An engineer employed by the Department of Railways and Canals made an examination of the locality which would be affected. In his report he recommended that a lock be built into the canal to make it a navigable waterway. On that basis, it was recommended "that permission be given to Mr. Grohman to carry out his modified scheme, subject to the conditions mentioned by the Chief Engineer." The modification secured from Grohman was a "guarantee, under pain of forfeiture of permissions given, that his Company shall so construct its works, viz, the canal & the widening of the Kootenay's outlet, that the level of the Kootenay shall not at any season of the year, or at any point of its course, be lowered below the ordinary low water level at present in existence, and that with reference to the canal he is prepared to undertake, under a suitable penalty, to keep the gates or lock of the canal permanently closed after the last day of August except at such intervals when steamers and other craft may pass through the Canal." In addition, the Crown retained the whole of its rights in so far as the navigation of the two rivers was concerned, not permitting "Mr. Grohman or his Company to assume any control or the right to interfere with the navigation of the river by other persons or Companies" except for the payment of tolls for passing through the canal, which tolls would be subject to approval by the Dominion government.

(Above) A Chinese gang of workers excavating the Grohman canal. Note the odd-looking, side-dumping wheelbarrows.
(Opposite page) All that remained of the Grohman canal "locks" in 1986.
(Opposite page, inset) Grohman's canal at Canal Flats, showing the locks under construction.
(Below) Two views of the same section of the Grohman canal in 1986. The left photo shows a dry canal in May. Three months later, however, the canal was full of water.

These modifications were to have far-reaching consequences for Grohman, who was facing heavy financial losses to himself and his company if the work did not proceed. In applying for the consent of the Dominion government, Grohman had represented his scheme as primarily concerned with the improvement of navigation of the rivers, and while the modifications met that situation, they threatened to defeat the original and true purpose of the canal — the reclamation of land. Short of complete abandonment of the project, however, the terms had to be accepted.

Negotiations with the B.C. government were reopened and a new agreement, cancelling that of September 7, 1885, was made. Dated October 30, 1886, this final agreement embraced the modified plans as approved by both governments and, reluctantly, by Grohman. To compensate him and his company for the alterations, the B.C. government agreed to a free grant of 30,000 acres of land in the Upper Kootenay Valley, to be Crown-granted on completion of the canal. Of the 18 clauses in the new agreement, the first 11 dealt with the canal and the various conditions and specifications pertaining to it. There was now no reference to the diversion of the Kootenay River into Columbia Lake. The particularly relevant clauses, No.'s. 1 and 18(f), clearly defined the modification of Grohman's original scheme and are here quoted in part:

"1. The said Company will well, truly and faithfully make, build, construct, complete and equip, in an efficient and substantial manner, in accordance with certain plans and specifications hereinafter mentioned, a navigable canal between the Upper Kootenay River and the Upper Columbia Lake across a certain flat known as the "Canal Flat," and in such manner as to allow craft to pass from one water to the other, and so as not to affect the volume of water in the said river or lake or the Columbia River....

"18(f). That, in order to carry out the aforesaid works, the said Company, their servants and agents, shall have full ingress and egress upon and over any Crown land at or near the works, and the right to construct such a canal between the Upper Kootenay River and the Upper Columbia Lake. . . ." Permission was also granted to widen and deepen the outlet of Kootenay Lake at the points known as the "Rapids" and the "Narrows" on the west arm of the lake.

At no place was the canal to be narrower than 30 feet from bank to bank at water-level, and the depth of water not less than four feet. The lock, if either timber or stone, was to be 30 feet wide and 100 feet long. The company was given the right to exact tolls for boats, persons, and goods passing through the canal, not to exceed 25¢ for each passenger; goods on board, 10¢ per 100 pounds; the craft itself, 50¢ per ton; cattle and horses, 50¢ per head; sheep and pigs, 25¢ per head.

Finally, after four years of negotiation, Grohman was ready to start on his reclamation scheme, albeit on a considerably different plan from that which he had first formulated. Armed with the revised agreement, he went once again to England to form yet another company which would carry on the financing of his project. The

Kootenay Valleys Company Limited was incorporated in April, 1887, and capitalized at £100,000 in 20,000 shares of £5 each.

In his position of managing director, Grohman returned to B.C. to supervise the canal works. To facilitate the construction of the necessary buildings and of the timber lock, a small steam sawmill was ordered. It was shipped from Brantford, Ontario, to Golden, the nearest railway point, and there loaded on an improvised barge for the journey up the Columbia to Canal Flats. At its best, water transportation on the Columbia was slow, and it was particularly so in the late summer when the water-level was low. This caused the barge to run aground so many times that it became routine to unload, push it off, reload, and start again. Finally, 23 days after it left Golden, the machinery was unloaded, for the last time, at its destination.

There a small settlement soon grew up, which was named Grohman. A store and post office, a hotel of sorts, the sawmill, and various other buildings appeared. Gangs of men began digging the Kootenay Canal, using horses and scrapers. There was also a unique brigade of Chinamen which operated something like a human conveyer-belt, pushing odd-looking side-dumping wheelbarrows. The work of excavation was comparatively easy: the material to be moved was mostly gravel which contained no boulders of any formidable size. The actual dimensions of the canal were 6,700 feet long and 45 feet wide; of the lock, 100 feet long and 30 feet wide.

The construction of the lock was not, however, as simple as the excavation. Grohman had disapproved of the plans from the start. He had argued that if the lock were constructed as designed, it would not allow for easy navigation, but he had been unable to get the plans changed. According to the government specifications, the foundations had to be sunk to a considerable depth. When the excavation for the ground-sills got below the level of the Kootenay River, a large amount of seepage water hampered the work, and steam-pumps had to be brought in to alleviate this condition and allow the work to continue.

On July 29, 1889, just within the two years allowed, the canal works were completed. The 30,000 acres were Crown-granted accordingly, and the canal became public property, being accepted on August 20 of that year by the Hon. F.G. Vernon, Chief Commission of Lands and Works, on behalf of the province. The cost had been excessive — over $100,000, more than twice the amount estimated in the prospectus.

The canal being of no further consequence to the Kootenay Valleys Company, the next part of the project was begun — the actual reclamation of the land of Kootenay Flats. The work of lowering the level of the lake by widening the outlet was started by Messrs. Selous and Louis, of Nelson, and about $16,000 was expended in slashing timber and brush, excavating loose rock, erecting a boarding-house and a bunk-house, and so on. But things did not run smoothly for Grohman. Not only was there friction within his company, but funds were now exhausted and he was using his own money to carry on the project.

In 1890 another small controversy arose when J.C. Rykert Jr. published a notice in the *Kootenay Star* that he intended to apply to purchase 640 acres of land that was under reserve to Grohman. Grohman objected that Rykert was not a settler, as he claimed, having built his home and office at the same time as he was paid to reside on the spot as a customs officer. The dispute was settled in Grohman's favour; the Surveyor-General advising Rykert that he was merely a squatter on land that was not open for preemption or sale.

Throughout most of 1890 the work of widening the outlet of the lake continued. In August of that year the Kootenay Valleys Company had made an agreement with yet another London company, the Alberta and British Columbia Exploration Company Limited, to transfer all interest in the concession of Lands B, and Grohman now became manager of the new company as well as managing director of the former one. But when he returned to London seeking payment of the money he had expended from his own funds, he found the company unwilling to reimburse him. Then, as holder of the original concession of December 10, 1883, he claimed that the right to Lands B reverted to him because the Kootenay Valleys Company had not paid for the necessary surveys and works, and he cabled Victoria to defer the transfer. The Company thereupon notified the B.C. government that Grohman had ceased to be their managing director, and the Chief Commissioner of Lands and Works notified Grohman by cable that he could no longer be recognized in connection with the concession and the Kootenay Valleys Company.

Grohman then began action against the Kootenay Valleys Company in the Supreme Court of B.C. for an injuction to restrain the company from dealing in any way with Lands B. But the government made an agreement with the Alberta and British Columbia Exploration Company. Grohman then commenced a petition of right against the Crown, the affidavit to the petition being dated December 14, 1891. Other business now necessitated Grohman's absence from Victoria, and while he was away some of the legal documents pertaining to the case were forwarded to him contained insufficient postage. Thus it was sent to the Dead Letter Office and destroyed. When Grohman returned to Victoria he learned that his lawyer, to whom he had paid a retainer of $500, had absconded. This was the last straw. Grohman threw up his hands in disgust and decided that he had had enough. Thereafter, the Kootenays saw him no more. He had spent a fortune and nine years in the attempt, and he had not reclaimed a single acre of land.

The Alberta and British Columbia Exploration Company now abandoned the works at the outlet of the lake. Instead, selecting 7,700 acres north of the International Boundary, the company began the construction of dykes to reclaim that acreage. The greater part of this new program was completed in 1893, but the extremely high waters of 1894 broke through the dykes and flooded the land again. Further attempts were made to complete the dyking, and the company, along with other settlers, carried on farming to some extent. But the rebuilt dykes still did not prevent the flooding of the land, and the company terminated its farming operations.

Today thousands of acres of the Kootenay Flats are producing bountiful crops of grain. The work was accomplished chiefly through dyking and drainage by pumping. Of great assistance, however, was the excavation work done at the Grohman Narrows by the West Kootenay Power and Light Company when it removed 334,585 cubic yards of gravel and 17,927 cubic yards of solid rock.

WILLIAM BAILLIE-GROHMAN
A BRIEF BIOGRAPHY

WILLIAM Baillie-Grohman was born on April 1, 1851, in London. His mother, a cousin of the Duke of Wellington, was Irish; his father was English.

Young William's early years were divided between his father's inherited estate in Austria, "Schloss Wolfgang," and his mother's old home in Rosecrea, Tipperary. At "Wolfgang" he received lessons in natural history, rock-climbing, stalking and shooting, and he shot his first stag at the age of nine. Until he was 14 he studied under private tutors; then he entered Elizabeth College, Guernsey. At 18 he left school and tried working, first in a lawyer's office in London, then in a merchant's office. But his restless spirit could not be imprisoned in the city and he spent the next few years in Europe, travelling, shooting, and mountain-climbing.

In 1875, at the age of 24, he published his first book, *Tyrol and the Tyrolese*, which was an instant success. In 1878 he crossed the Atlantic, in order to visit the hunting-grounds of North America in the Rocky Mountains of Wyoming and Idaho. Within two years he had made four trips of exploration in the great mountain system of the new world. An interesting account of these adventures is found in his third book, *Camps in the Rockies,* published in 1882.

It was while searching for the haunts of the mountain-goat in 1882 that he discovered the Kootenay Flats and formulated his reclamation scheme. In 1887, while on one of his many trips to England in connection with his Kootenay works, he married Florence Nickalls, of Nutfield, Surrey, and brought her back to Canada with him. They lived at Grohman and at Victoria, where in 1888 their only son was born, while his father was in the midst of the construction of the canal. A daughter was born the following year. When in 1893 Grohman and his family returned permanently to Europe, he had crossed the Atlantic 30 times.

The outbreak of war found Grohman and his wife in Austria. Because of his intimate knowledge of the country they were at first forbidden to leave, but in 1915, after their son-in-law had been killed in action, they were given permission to go to England, where they remained until the war was over. The Germans commandeered "Schloss Matzen" as billet for officers, and when the Grohmans returned there in 1919 they found that all was well with their home, but that the people were starving in consequence of the British blockade. Grohman plunged into relief work and became executive secretary of the Tyrolese Relief Fund. This exhausting work, made more difficult because of the war-damaged railways and other hardships, weakened his heart, and on the morning of November 27, 1921, he fell forward on the breakfast table at "Schloss Matzen," dead. He was buried near by, beside his mother. His wife survived him by 24 years.

PORT ESSINGTON:
ONLY A DREAM

Port Essington was once a bustling seaport where Saturday night brawls were commonplace. Today, the town-site's crumbling buildings lie deserted, and muddy bear tracks on the decaying wooden walkway are the only remaining signs of life.

AN old fashioned egg beater rusting on a window ledge; newspapers strewn across the floor reporting "War In Europe"; piles of Sunday School papers, yellow with age, and the abandoned organ in the muted church, all reveal that families once lived and cared and hoped in Port Essington. Today, as you walk peacefully along the silent, decaying boardwalk, their presence is felt, their memories linger. But who were these people who built their lives and dreams on the muddy, misty banks of the Skeena River?

Robert Cunningham was the founder and main driving force behind the establishment of Port Essington. Arriving at Matlakalta, north of Prince Rupert, in the spring of 1863, Cunningham worked under Father William Duncan for two years before joining the Hudson's Bay Company (HBC). Five years later Cunningham resigned from the HBC and opened a trading post at the mouth of the Skeena River with Thomas Hankin.

The Skeena River was fast becoming a favourite route for miners intent on exploring the new goldfields in the northern interior, and the two partners were intent on capturing some of this trade. They selected a site on the north bank near the present site of Inverness Cannery, where a man named Woodcock had built an inn to accommodate travellers. The area thus became known as Woodcock's Landing, and in the spring of 1871, Cunningham and Hankin constructed a large store there and began an active trade.

Soon over a hundred eager miners had arrived, all waiting impatiently for the ice-congested river to clear. The Tsimshian Indians, sensing an opportunity for employment, offered their services for $1 a day, or rented their canoes for $1.50 a day. The only means of freighting from Woodcock's Landing to Hazelton, 180 miles upriver, was by canoes, and this became a prime source of income for the Indians. They used large Haida war canoes, 30 to 60 feet in length, which were constructed from cedar trees on the Queen Charlotte Islands. Manned by five men, each could carry about 4,000 pounds. Cunningham and Hankin, who had the bulk of the shipping contracts, also operated two freight canoes on the Skeena.

But the Skeena, or "K-Shian," river of mists, as it was known, was a treacherous waterway, and travel by canoe was slow, costly and dangerous. The 180-mile upriver journey to Hazelton could take up to three weeks, while the return trip with the current took just a few days. Once at Hazelton, the goods and supplies were loaded onto awaiting pack horses for the overland trip to the goldfields.

(Opposite page) The remains of Finntown, the Finnish settlement at Port Essington, in 1985.
(Above) Robert Cunningham, 1837-1905, was the founder of Port Essington.
(Left) Pilings that once supported a Port Essington cannery stretch into the Skeena River.

With all the miners passing through Woodcock's Landing, Cunningham and Hankin did a rousing business. Never one to miss an opportunity, they decided to set up a branch store at Hazelton, which was rapidly becoming a busy settlement, and Hankin started out with eight tons of supplies as soon as the ice melted. Although both businesses were prospering, Cunningham ran into difficulties with Woodcock over the land survey, and decided to look for another location. The site he selected, on the south bank of the Skeena just below the mouth of the Ecstall River, was known to the Tsimshian as "Spok-sut," which meant "fall camp ground." Here, in 1871, Cunningham preempted and built a large trading post which he named Port Essington, the name first given to the whole Skeena River estuary by Captain Vancouver in 1793.

Cunningham reserved some of his pre-emption for the Indians and encouraged them to stay and settle permanently. He parcelled the remainder into lots which he sold to settlers, and gradually a small settlement began to emerge. Cunningham later built a sawmill on a small stream south of town which began to supply the demand for lumber on the north coast.

With all this activity, Port Essington grew into a busy centre. The HBC bought three lots and set up their store, Skeena Post, in direct competition with Cunningham. Other businesses sprang up along the wooden main road, Dufferin Street, which extended upriver from the Ecstall. Cunningham's large store had been built at the main intersection of Dufferin and Front streets right off the main dock. As there was no banks, Cunningham issued his own currency, made from brass, for trading. The HBC meanwhile, had currency made from copper.

By the time the Cunningham and Hankin partnership was dissolved in 1877, prospectors heading for the northern goldfields had discovered alternate routes. But, as this means of commerce was diminishing, another was springing up to replace it.

Each year millions of salmon crowded the Skeena on their way upriver to spawn, and in 1876 the first salmon cannery was built at Woodcock's Landing. Other canneries quickly followed, and by the 1890s there were seven scattered over the Skeena River estuary. Two of these, Cunningham's, built in 1882, and the Boston Cannery, were located at Port Essington. As salmon fishing and canning quickly became the dominant industries, Port Essington remained the centre of the region.

During the winter month's Port Essington's population dwindled to 300-350; but with the coming of spring it increased dramatically. In May, steamer after steamer would unload crowds of men from the south, "and every tide brought canoe loads of dusky Indians." All were intent on capitalizing on the brief salmon fishing season. It only lasted two months, June and July, but during that brief period Port Essington was in a frenzy day and night. By the end of July it was all over, and transient fishermen returned to their homes, while Port Essington residents settled back to their peaceful existence, enjoying "the fruits of the great upheaval."

In 1884 Bishop William Ridley opened a mission in Port Essington under the care of Rev. A.H. Sheldon. During the next four years Sheldon worked fervently with his flock, laying the foundations of the historic church deep and wide. The church was a wooden building, painted white, and lined inside with beautiful dark red B.C. cedar. A rectory was connected to the church by a small hall, which was used "as a schoolroom for the white children, for Bible classes, choir practice, as a medicine room, Indian room, vestry, and on certain evenings of the week as a reading room by the white men."

Sheldon was well liked by all who knew him, and it was a tragic loss when he was drowned in a canoe accident off Point Lambert in 1888. His wife and Mrs. Robert Cunningham were drowned in the same mishap. It was several weeks before Sheldon's body was recovered, and it was then buried beside the Anglican Church he established and loved so much.

After the death of Reverend Sheldon, no one was sent to minister the Anglican Church until Rev. B. Appleyard was appointed in 1895. Appleyard remained at Port Essington until relieved by Rev. W.F. Ruskbrook in 1903. During his tenure, Appleyard submitted reports to the *Mission Field*. From an 1897 report, we can get an early glimpse of the town, whose setting Appleyard described as "truly beautiful and inspiring."

"The mountain sides run sheer down into the river, rocky precipitous walls of frowning crags; here and there are breaks or gaps, forming coves or small inlets, into which the water washes, sometimes making a few yards of muddy beach around the base of the rocks. These are used as fish cannery sites; but so limited is the space gained from the universal perpendicular, that half of the necessary buildings are often built upon huge posts or piles, which are driven firmly into the bed of the river. Port Essington is an exception to this rule; it stands upon a few low foothills, which extend over a space of about half a square mile. The streets are narrow, because level ground must be used with great economy. As I walk down the centre of the only street we can boast with buildings on both sides, I can hit every door as I pass with a walking stick; in fact, the street proper is composed of a few rough planks laid upon the ground, forming a walk about a yard wide — this is used for all purposes. Horses and waggons we have none; all heavy articles are moved upon trucks, such as are used around railway stations, or in the winter time upon small sleighs. A portion of the village stretches in a single row of houses, which follows the graceful curve of a small bay; streets, or the beginnings of streets, struggle up the foothills from this line as a base. I often think how beautiful this village will be when it has pushed these streets backwards, and up the gradually rising elevations at its rear, until they reach a small but beautiful level plain, which extends backwards about an eight of a mile, where again the mountain rears up its side in majestic grandeur."

Although natives formed the nucleus of the town, Port Essington's population also included Indians, whites, Japanese, Chinese, and new immigrants from Europe. The Japanese built their homes at the end of Dufferin Street past the business section, while Finntown, the Finnish settlement, was built further along on the banks of the Ecstall River. Unlike other B.C. communities where the Chinese and Japanese were avoided or shunned, here "they enter into the totality of our lives," wrote Appleyard, "and wield their influence and play their part it it."

In May, 1891, the HBC steamer *Caledonia*, under Captain Odin, made her first successful trip up the Skeena River to Hazelton. Although the journey took nine days, it ushered in a new era of transporting freight. In 1900, Cunningham bought the *Monte Cristo*, although many doubted that a private trader could compete successfully with the well established HBC. When Cunningham hired Captain Bonser from the HBC, everyone anticipated a strong rivalry to develop. But, with their new vessel *Strathcona*, the HBC felt they could easily compete, so they ignored their former employee.

Cunningham, however, was not through yet. That same winter he sent Captain Bonser to Victoria to design a stern-wheeler especially for the Skeena, and by the spring of 1901, the *Hazelton* was ready. During her first season she made 13 trips to Hazelton, steaming upriver

(Above) A view of "downtown" Port Essington, with a general store and the Hotel Essington on left. The large building on the right is the town hall.
(Below) This postcard of Port Essington was published by Harrison Campbell & Mills Co., druggists at Port Essington.

(Above) A view of the harbour at Prince Rupert c1908. At first, the arrival of the Grand Trunk Railway hinted at prosperous times for Port Essington. However, when the railway bypassed Port Essington on the opposite side of the river, the town rapidly declined.
(Opposite page) Only a few dilapidated buildings remained standing at Post Essington when this photo was taken in 1985.
(Below) The remains of the general store on Dufferin Street in 1985.

in 40 hours and returning in 10. The HBC were no longer competitive, and to meet this challenge, they built the *Mount Royal.* The intense rivalry everyone had expected was now on.

To outrace their competition, Captain Bonser of the *Hazelton* and Captain Johnson of the *Mount Royal* took unprecedented actions. They stole from each others woodpiles, often ordering passengers off to help load; and they sometimes steamed off with part of their cargo still on the dock. In 1904, this competitive zeal almost led to tragic consequences.

The *Hazelton* and *Mount Royal* were at Port Essington loading up for their first trip of the season to Hazelton. Loaded first, the *Hazelton* churned away from the wharf. At Hardscrabble Rapids, about 105 miles upriver, the *Hazelton* put ashore at a wood stop to take on fuel. Captain Bonser, who was not aware that the *Mount Royal* had departed Port Essington only a short time after the *Hazelton,* suddenly spotted a column of smoke downriver. Realizing its significance, and with only half of the wood loaded, he immediately signalled to let go the lines. But before the *Hazelton* could attain top acceleration, the speeding *Mount Royal* pulled abreast of her.

Art Downs, in *Paddlewheels On The Frontier* describes the encounter: "Coming up in fairly slack water, the *Mount Royal* quickly gained and soon the vessels were bow to bow — smoke, steam, and cinders belching skywards; paddlewheels frothing rapids white, passengers urging their vessels forward. Gradually *Mount Royal* thrust ahead, then suddenly was jolted as *Hazelton's* bow crushed into her starboard quarter. Fortunately her overhanging main deck absorbed the blow or *Hazelton* could have slashed into her engine room, with deadly results."

After being butted a second time, *Mount Royal* was forced broadside to the current, swung around and carried downstream. The *Hazelton,* meanwhile, sped upriver, her whistle tooting triumphantly.

Following this incident, Cunningham and the HBC realized that their rivalry was futile and dangerous. It was said that the HBC paid Cunningham $2,500 to tie up his vessel, and agreed to haul his freight for free. The HBC further agreed to purchase the *Hazelton* from Cunningham if future traffic warranted, and this was in fact done. As for the *Mount Royal,* she was wrecked in Kiteselas Canyon in 1906 with the loss of six men.

Meanwhile, since 1903, surveyors for the Grand Trunk Pacific Railway (GTP) had been in the region seeking a suitable route for their transcontinental railway. Prince Rupert, a port just north of the Skeena River estuary, was to be the western terminus. This news excited Cunningham, who owned a great deal of property in Hazelton and Port Essington. In 1904, he renovated the Essington Hotel and built the Cunningham Hall, which was opened with a grand ball.

Everyone began gearing up for the anticipated boom times. Frizzell's Hotsprings, a short distance up the Skeena River, was made into a recreational facility with a new bath house. A new school and jail was erected and the wooden boardwalk replaced. Other businesses were also improved. The cannery, Skeena River Commercial Co., had many repairs as did Herman's Hotel. (Peter Herman, who started working for Cunningham in 1885, later went into business for himself, operating a store and a cannery on Dufferin Street. He also took over the operation of the post office from Cunningham in 1901. Herman drowned in the Ecstall River at the age of 44, leaving a wife and six children.)

To take advantage of the railroad construction, the HBC sold the *Caledonia* and ordered a replacement, and on January 30, 1908, the Victoria *Colonist* reported that there "will be five, possibly six steamers in service on the Skeena River this summer." The *Inlander,* last of the Skeena River stern-wheelers, arrived in 1910. Built in Victoria for a group of Skeena River businessmen, she was soon earning a profit.

In *Skeena: River of Destiny,* Dr. Richard Large gives us an excellent description of Port Essington during the heyday years of the early 1900s. As with earlier years, most of the residents drifted south for the winter after the salmon fishing season. Those that remained behind, however, lived the good life. "It was then that the community social life blossomed, with Saturday night dances, community concerts and church activities; and for those whose tastes were of a more Rabelaisian type, the friendly atmosphere of the brightly lighted bars of the Essington, Caledonia and Queen's Hotels, with their black jack and poker games in the back rooms, or the sociable gatherings at the houses of Blanche Hart and others of her ilk, were waiting to supply their needs."

Later, Dr. Large went on to describe the town in detail. Port Essington was "laid out on two arms of a right angle, centered on a rocky point at the confluence of the Skeena and Ecstall rivers. Cunningham's establishments occupied the central location around this rocky point and the settlement extending downriver was the portion laid aside for the Indian village. The upriver half of town lined both sides of Dufferin Street, the one roadway, which consisted of a 12-foot sidewalk built on posts over the tidal flats. The buildings on the water side of the road were all on piles and the tide flowing under the buildings every 12 hours adequately cared for garbage and offal disposal. On the other side the buildings clung to the rocky hillside or again were built on piles over the sloughs projecting in from the river.

"On Saturday night Dufferin Street was a seething mass of humanity, with representatives of every race, and the vast degree of them in some degree of intoxication. The married women of the town wisely stayed home on Saturday night, for the two Provincial constables were totally inadequate to maintain order; and brawling frequently halted the stream of people as they eddied around in a struggling group. In fact, the constables were often as bad as their charges, and one time were directly interested in the operation of the numerous gambling dens which were muleting the careless fishermen, so that, during the days of railroad construction, the district Chief of Police had to come in to clean up the mess.

"Stores and restaurants stood open all evening and threw their shafts of light onto the darkened streets. As one walked east on Dufferin, the side wall of Cunningham's store stood flush with the sidewalk on the right,

Store and hotel at Port Essington.

while the homes of the staff were grouped around the rear of the Cannery on the water side. Beyond them stood the 'Chinahouse,' where the Chinese laborers in the cannery silently shuffled in and out of the darkened door, or sat in groups on the steps stolidly watching the passing crowds and smoking their long tubular pipes.

"Across the street was Charlie Katsayama's restaurant. Charlie was a thin wiry Japanese, invariably dressed in work pants and heavy woollen underwear, with a woollen scarf around his waist, while he performed the innumerable tasks of serving meals, and, in between, dishing out ice cream cones to the children clustered about the door. Kind-hearted as he was energetic, he brought up a healthy, happy family.

"Next were Louis Hepenstall's poolroom and Lee Wing's restaurant, Mrs. Frizzell's dress shop and Morrow and Frizzell's Meat Market, while on the water side was the No. 2 dock — Frizzell's wharf — the only one not connected with a cannery, and the point of call for most of the upriver sternwheelers. The Anglican Church and the Dominion Fishery office faced each other at the half-way mark, and then came the old Herman buildings — later occupied by Kameda's store and restaurant."

The Kamedas were a hard-working Japanese family whose restaurant became the scene of Port Essington's bloodiest murder when three intoxicated fishermen burst in and in their drunken stupor, began tearing the place apart. The Japanese, retreating before a hail of crockery, returned armed with knives and soon got the upper hand. One fisherman, "clutching his throat, slit ear to ear, rushed out the door and staggered down the road, his blood spraying both sides of the street until he fell in a pool a hundred yards further on. Another spent some time in hospital paralysed from a stab wound in the back of the neck. The community's sympathies were with the Japanese and only jail terms were exacted by a lenient court.

"Waldham's Cannery was next on the left — where Peter Herman's original cannery stood — and across the street the Queen's and Caledonia Hotels, with the proprietor George Kirby, sitting on a chair outside the door; and Kishimoto's store — a wonderful collection of Japanese art and merchandise. A.B.C. Packing Company's Boston Cannery and store marked the end of the road, where a trail led along between shacks occupied by cannery workers and others whose profession is the oldest known to man."

During construction of the GTP, Port Essington was thriving as loggers, fishermen and railway workers kept the town lively. Many came to Port Essington for the poker games, saloons and the working ladies. Often these men ended up in jail for fighting or being drunk. For long jail sentences, prisoners had to be sent to Vancouver as there was no long term accommodation in Port Essington. Here as elsewhere, it was against the law to sell liquor to the natives, and a six month jail term was enforced for this offence. Keyhole Johnny was a constable in Port Essington and Jimmy Adams was Justice of the Peace. Their methods were practical and efficient, but probably not totally legal.

But the GTP was bypassing Port Essington on the north side of the Skeena, and its completion in 1914 sounded the death knell for the town and the sternwheelers, as the train became the main form of transportation. Most of the population moved to the new seaport of Prince Rupert. In 1912, the *Inlander*, under Captain Bonser, was the last stern-wheeler to make a trip on the Skeena. The *Inlander* was then beached at Port Essington and left to rot. A sad end to a colourful era.

For many years, approximately 400 to 500 people remained at Port Essington. These were mainly men that fished for salmon during the summer months while the Chinese and native women were proficient at working in the canneries. For a time the Provincial Fisheries Department kept a flat bottomed stern-wheeler at Port Essington on weekends during the fishing season. The *Snag Scow* was used to locate and remove logs from the river bottom that caused problems for the gillnet fishermen. These logs were removed to an area called "the boneyard," where no one was allowed to fish.

Like all frontier communities, constructed of wooden frame buildings, Port Essington lived under the constant threat of fire. Over its history, several fires devastated large portions of the town; but, during its heyday, it was quickly rebuilt. The Anglican Church was completely destroyed in the fire of 1909. Rebuilt that same fall, it was destroyed in another fire a year later. This time, fortunately, it was insured, and that, plus generous donations from the Japanese Association, was sufficient to rebuild it once again.

However, in later years it was a different story. With modernization in the fishing industry, canneries along the Skeena River were no longer required. So businesses and canneries destroyed by later fires were not rebuilt.

In 1961, Port Essington was devastated by a fire that levelled most of the remaining buildings and homes. For the few that survived, another fire in 1965 turned Port Essington into a ghost town.

Today, all that survives are the memories, and the remains of a few crumbling buildings. Yet, to walk down the broken and overgrown boardwalk is to step back into the past; a past that envisioned roots for future generations. The ambitious people who proudly built Port Essington are long gone, but, hopefully, they will not be forgotten.

SOINTULA
Malcolm Island Utopia

Proud and often well educated, the Finns had emigrated to Canada to escape the oppression of the Russian Czar. Many settled in Nanaimo and laboured in the coal mines under grim working conditions. Isolated and ridiculed, they decided to form their own island community.

(Opposite page, left) This photo of Matti Kurikka was taken in Finland in 1899.
(Opposite page, right) An early view of the Sointula waterfront.
(Below) Boat sheds at Sointula in 1990.

A tall man with dark, flashing eyes arrived in Nanaimo, British Columbia in August, 1900. Matti Kurikka, dedicated to the emancipation of the oppressed and the working class, brought along with his battered suitcase nearly 20 years of experience in promoting socialism. His dream was to form a utopian society where Finns could live together in harmony, away from the tyranny of Russia and the dictates of the Church.

Kurikka was just what the Finnish coal miners in Nanaimo were looking for. Working conditions were grim and men lived with the constant threat of fire, cave-ins, and death from "after damp," the lethal gas created when coal dust explodes. Above ground the miners received inadequate wages and lived in rough wooden shacks. The mining company suppressed any attempts to improve living or working conditions, and mine owner James Dunsmuir often ordered the men to relocate from one site to another, moving themselves and their homes at their own expense. A frequent source of solace was the tavern located near each mining settlement. Dunsmuir further encouraged drinking by allowing two breweries to make wagon deliveries to the camps each day. The miners even had the convenient option of charging their purchases against their monthly pay cheque.

The majority of the Finns who emigrated to Canada at this time did so to escape the oppression of the Russian Czar. They were proud and often well educated, but due to the language barrier they were isolated, ridiculed, and treated like ignorant foreigners. Frustration led to further drinking and fighting.

"To know the toil and burdonsomeness of descending into the bottomless jaws, never knowing whether one will surface alive, dead, or badly injured to live the rest of one's life a cripple at the mercy of others," was Finnish miner Matti Halminen's description of life in Nanaimo.

Halminen and many of the other Finns wanted to quit the mines, but the prospects of outside employment were minimal, and their financial resources were meagre. Then, in early 1900, Aatami Korhonen, Viljo Jokinen, and Heikke Kilpelainen arrived in Nanaimo from Queensland, Australia. They brought several pamphlets written by Matti Kurikka, a Finnish visionary and idealist. Kurikka had emigrated to Australia in 1899 to escape the tyranny of the Russian Czar. In two public meetings that attracted over 800 people, he had outlined a plan for a utopian society called the Kalevan Kansa (The People of Kaleva). Work, food production, learning, and entertainment would be experienced communally.

That summer 180 Finns left for Queensland with approximately half that number being firmly committed to Kurikka and the Kalevan Kansa. The Australian government subsidized their passage and offered to pay Kurikka 3,000 marks if he would write a book in Finnish about the colony.

Kurikka arrived in Australia in October and his first letter home, dated October 7, Brisbane, sounded ominous. Land was available for the Finns to begin farming, but the Australian government also hoped to employ them to clear land for sugar plantations. No funds were forthcoming for the establish-

FRONTIER DAYS IN BRITISH COLUMBIA

ment of a utopian commune. Hoping to raise money for his project, Kurikka organized a contract to construct railway sleepers near Chillagoe. Not long into the contract, the Finns felt that they were cheated on their payments, and Kurikka as leader was held responsible. The men drifted away taking jobs for 12 shillings a week, and Kurikka's utopia, "El Dorado," never got further than 10 tents pitched near the railway line in Chillagoe. Kurikka found himself alone, ill, and in financial straits. Then Matti Halminen's letter arrived from Nanaimo asking him to come to Canada and lead the Finns to a new life.

Kurikka replied immediately: "I am ready to leave Australia and to come to you, but I am as poor as a church rat. . . . If you were able to procure for me the travelling expenses, I would give myself solely to the services of founding that community. I am prepared to do work of any kind. . . . I have hands as calloused as anyone. I want to be with you to plant the seed of betterment from which bountiful crops shall rise for the joy of humanity and for the glory of Finland."

The Finns scraped together the $125 fare and Kurikka arrived in Nanaimo in late August, 1900. To raise money for the commune a joint-stock company was formed with membership shares of $200 per adult. These fees were to be the company's primary financial resource. Kurikka and Halminen visited government offices obtaining maps and descriptions of available land.

Early in 1901 Malcolm Island (Malkosaari), approximately 180 miles northwest of Vancouver, was chosen as the site of the new utopian community. It seemed an ideal location. It was designated as prime agricultural land, was heavily forested, and was near major shipping lanes between Vancouver Island and the mainland.

One Sunday, shortly after the site for the commune was chosen, Halminen, along with some others, met at the Oberg residence in Nanaimo where Kurikka lived. The men were shocked to find that Kurikka had his bags packed. He had agreed to work on the Finnish newspaper *The Lannetor*, in Astoria, Oregon, and planned to leave the next morning. The Finns felt that without Kurikka's moving speeches and sharp pen, the Kalevan Kansa Colonization Company (KKCC) was doomed to failure. After a long silence Halminen offered a solution to the problem, "Let's establish a newspaper here in Nanaimo."

Kurikka responded, "If you can organize such a thing I would be willing to run it only for the price of my food."

Halminen quickly found 10 friends and convinced them to donate $10 each for a share in the newspaper. The *Aika (Time)*, the first Finnish newspaper in Canada, began weekly publication on May 17, 1901.

Kurikka, recalling the censorship he had experienced when he was editor of the *Tyomies*, revelled in his new freedom. "The Harmony Idea," espousing his religious and philosophical beliefs appeared in an early edition of *The Aika*. He wrote: ". . .the only road to a better life lies in cooperation, love and generosity. But this cannot be obtained immediately. It will be necessary to prove that mutual help and organization is possible and then endeavor to get the surrounding disorder to organize."

As well as writing, Kurikka travelled as far away as New York speaking of his socialist ideas and plans. Many

of the Finnish communities were strong Lutherans and saw Kurikka as the Anti-Christ. When he received letters threatening his life if he did not stop attacking the church, even Kurikka realized that he had gone too far. He requested the KKCC Board of Directors to send to Finland for Austin Makela, "his best and most trusted friend." The board of directors took a collection for travelling expenses and soon Makela and his wife were enroute to British Columbia.

On November 27, 1901, the KKCC, with Immigration Minister Gosnel acting on behalf of the Crown, signed the formal papers for Malcolm Island. Among other things, the agreement stipulated that ownership of the island be passed to the Finns in seven years, provided that 350 men (one for each 80 acres) had built homes on the island and made improvements to the amount of $2.50 per acre.

What the colony needed now was capital. Kurikka was confident that at least 2,000 settlers from Finland and the United States would eventually emigrate to Malcolm Island, but he was afraid that lack of financial resources would doom this utopia just at it had his "El Dorado" in Australia. Desperate to procure prosperous members, Kurikka made a deal with coal mine owner James Dunsmuir. Dunsmuir agreed to hire up to 200 Finns on Kurikka's recommendation, at a daily wage of $2.50. Kurikka would only recommend men who agreed to join the KKCC, and to pay at least $5 each month towards their membership fees. This plan could put up to $1,000 per month into the company account and would provide enough money for work to begin on the island.

The standard daily wage at that time was $3, and the thought of providing cheap labour to an already hated employer was too much for the miners. The KKCC board of directors and Kurikka had their first serious argument.

Kurikka pounded his fist on the table and roared: "We have no responsibility towards those others, we have the Kalevan Kansa to whom we have a responsibility."

The board replied that the KKCC "will not be founded by trampling the wages of other workers, injuring them, and irritating them to be against us."

At this time a group of miners were attempting to organize a union and, at a large meeting at the Nanaimo Opera House, men began to ask questions about this plan to enlist low paid Finn workers. Dunsmuir heard about the meeting and travelled to Nanaimo from Victoria. When he found few workers present at the South Wellington mine, he ripped a paper from his pocket and wrote: "At this mine work shall be discontinued indefinitely." With one sentence Dunsmuir exerted his authority, and with the mine closed, Kurikka's plan came to an end.

On December 6, 1901, Johan Mikkelson, Teodor Tanner, Kalle Hendrikson, Otto Ross and Malakias Kytomma left Nanaimo in a sailboat for the 175-mile journey to Malcolm Island. Mikkelson was injured in a shotgun accident and was taken to Alert Bay, but the other four men arrived on Malcolm Island on December 15. In mid-January they were joined by Viktor Saarikasi and Heikki Kilpelainen, one of those who had emigrated to Australia with Kurikka. Work quickly began on a large log cabin.

In June, many members of the company and their families travelled to Malcolm Island for the "Juhannus" (celebrations). Speeches and readings were given by Kurikka and others, and it was decided to call the settlement Sointula (Harmony). Kurikka was unanimously elected president and work crews were formed in the areas of logging, fishing, cultivating, blacksmithing and machining. One hundred members were present for the reading of the first annual report. Already the company had an outstanding debt of $1,300. Money had been borrowed for the tools and equipment necessary to begin building and many members had been unable to pay their membership fees. Those lacking in cash were allowed to work for their shares.

The *Aika,* meanwhile, continued to churn out articles about Sointula, hoping to recruit new members with capital. More people did come to the island but few had any money, and most were unpleasantly surprised by the conditions they found. The *Aika* had described a thriving, communal colony, but the reality was a heavily forested island being laboriously cleared by hand. Enthusiasm and a willingness to work was evident, but many of the men were shoemakers, tailors, and other professionals who were unsuited for, and largely ignorant about, the tasks they were to perform. The two buildings, the cabin and a hall, were already crowded and many of the newcomers slept in tents.

Kurikka encouraged the colonists to place spiritual matters above materialistic concerns and to sacrifice their own means and personal desires, but by the end of August there were over 200 persons living on the island. The housing situation, already cramped, became unbearable when the fall rains came. Work began on a large building to be used as a kitchen, cafeteria and storage room. Construction was also started on a sawmill, but work was painfully slow. The fall of 1902 was miserable and uncomfortable but by November a large building had been constructed, with the two lower floors designated as living quarters and the top floor to be used as a meeting area. On the bottom floor, near the back of the building, was a large baking oven made of mortar. Pipes passed from this oven through the walls to form a type of heating system.

The apartment, as it was called, came too late for some. Several families had left the commune and a few wrote maligning letters to outside newspapers. One of the letter writers, Martin Henrickson, was a well-known working class agitator and lecturer. He had been one of Kurikka's best friends, but soon the two were arguing so much that Henrickson left the island. This was to be a recurring theme for Kurikka, those that admired him the most, eventually became his worst enemies.

The entire colony was living on credit and, as president, it was Kurikka's job to obtain it. This was not always easy and Kurikka admitted to stretching the truth at times. Whenever the colony was desperate, he would travel to Vancouver and soon supplies would arrive. Near the end of January, 1903, Kurikka was again in Vancouver soliciting funds, but now the colony's creditors demanded to know exactly what was on the island. Kurik-

ka returned to Sointula accompanied by J.W. Bell, a trustee assigned to assess the island's forest and other assets.

As usual, when Kurikka returned, the colonists met on the third floor of the communal living quarters to discuss the company's current situation. It was just after 8 P.M. on a Thursday evening, Kurikka was in the chair and approximately 50 men and women were present in the room, when someone yelled "Fire!" In a matter of minutes the narrow stairway was impassable with smoke and the only escape was by window. Parents searched the smoke filled lower rooms for sleeping children and people jumped from windows with clothing and hair on fire.

Morning dawned on a grim site. There had been 137 people in the building which was now a smoking ruin. In the ashes lay 11 bodies; three adults and eight children. Many colonists had been badly burned or injured while escaping. All supplies stored in the building were destroyed and everyone living in the apartment was now homeless as well as destitute.

An inquiry held to look into the tragedy determined that the fire began at the end of the building where the baking oven was. The heating pipes passing through the wooden walls had nearly started a fire once before, but grief lay heavy on the hearts of the Finns, and rumours began to circulate. It was said that Bell had been sent by the government to examine the KKCC books. There was talk of embezzlement, and even accusations that Kurikka and others had burned the building to destroy the company ledger.

A meeting was called to deal with the issue and Kurikka requested that the two primary slanderers be expelled from the island. The directors suggested that Kurikka and August Oberg, whom the majority of the slander was directed at, take legal action against their accusers. At the annual meeting on February 21, 1903, Kurikka moved that P.J. Vinahan and another man who had talked of arson have their memberships cancelled. These two men had already left the island and the majority of the assembly was against revoking their memberships. A debate took place and in the heat of the moment Kurikka threatened to resign as president and leave the island. In the interest of harmony the board agreed to Kurikka's motion. Makela strongly opposed this decision and the two men faced the first serious conflict in their friendship.

On December 19 a special company meeting was called to discuss finances. It was decided to consolidate the debts of the colony by using various buildings and equipment valued at over $20,000 as collateral. That spring Kurikka went to Vancouver. While there he noticed an advertisement seeking tenders to construct a bridge over the Capilano and North Seymour rivers. Kurikka had a man named Jacobson draw up an estimate and then placed a $3,000 bid with a non-refundable deposit of $150.

When Kurikka returned to Sointula a new estimate was done. Based on these figures, the majority of the colony voted to forfeit the $150 deposit rather than risk losing money in the long run. Kurikka argued that the cost would be less since all the lumber would come from

(Above) A Finnish farm house at Sointula in 1990.
(Below) The breakwater at Sointula.

Malcolm Island, and even if they did lose money, the project might lead to more profitable contracts in the future. As his last argument Kurikka said that the financial affairs of the colony were so bad that all supplies, even food, would end if the contract was not taken.

Once the bridge construction began, however, it soon became apparent that the estimates had totally overlooked the major expense of foundations, and had been minimal for miscellaneous items such as bolts and nails. In addition, the building materials had to be transported three-quarters of a mile from the ocean to the building site and a team of horses and a sleigh had to be purchased. Belatedly, Kurikka realized his mistake, and encouraged the men to strike, but no one would listen. The men worked for four months with no wages, and thousands of feet of Malcolm Island's best timber went into the project.

The *Aika* commenced fortnightly publication on Malcolm Island in November, 1903, and Kurikka's editorials never failed to promote emotional discussions and debates. The

Matti and Anna Kurikka with daughter Aili and Anna's mother, Albina Palmqvisttin, Finland, 1888. (Below) The Sointula Co-Op store on First Street, Sointula, in 1990. Established in 1909, it is B.C.'s oldest Co-Op

motto of the *Aika* was "Freedom with Responsibility" and Kurikka personally advocated responsible freedom in the area of sexual relations. In the May 1, 1904, edition of the *Aika* he wrote: "Let us aid woman into a position of unconditional freedom and responsibility. Let us build marriage on a foundation of ideal love. . .let us dissolve those unnatural marriages. . .let us refuse to acknowledge a marriage in which the relationship is not centered on love, goodness and tenderness." Kurikka felt that a man and woman could live together without the sanction of marriage if they loved each other and produced children, but he did not advocate dissolving marriage lightly.

These articles on free love drew a lot of attention, both on and off the island, and a formal complaint had reached the government. As usual, Kurikka was dealing with theory and not fact as to how things were in Sointula. On the whole the members of the colony were in opposition to free love. They worried that if men started to come to the island because of this, soon the clergy and government would become involved and the KKCC could be in jeopardy, since granting title of the island to the Finns required that they "honour and obey the laws of the land."

When Kurikka and the

bridge crew returned to Sointula at the end of September, the tension erupted. On the one side was Kurikka, who had practised his theories, and the single men of the island, and on the other side was Makela and the rest of the colonists. There was no middle ground and neither side would compromise. The discord between Kurikka and Makela grew so strong that it was suggested that they both leave until the island cooled down. Neither would leave, however, and it was eventually decided to hold a general meeting and decide on the issue once and for all. Kurikka felt that his position was threatened, and at a directors meeting on October 10, 1902, he resigned as president and left the island.

From Vancouver he wrote to his daughter. "My dear Aili, much has happened here. My separation from the Kalevan Kansa is the result of personal persecution. The best members follow me. The island with the buildings and machinery remain with Makela and his supporters, to them are also left the debts. I regret the split but feel that it was inevitable. Materialism in Sointula began to be so brazen that it was impossible for a civilized person to stay. Greetings to your mother."

Approximately half the colonists left Sointula with Kurikka. They stayed in a hotel on Heatly Avenue in Vancouver while Kurikka moved into the KKCC's former office building. In the basement he raised chickens and upstairs he attempted to raise money by writing for various Finnish-American newspapers. Late in the year he obtained a shingle bolt contract in the Fraser Valley near Websters Corner (Maple Ridge). A new association, Sammon Takojat (Forgers of the Place of Sampo), was

formed. Sammon Takojat differed from the KKCC in that it was an all male commune. Kurikka felt that women were a disrupting influence. He wrote to Aili, "The best men — almost all bachelors — have joined me."

The first group of Finns arrived in Sammon Takojat on January 1, 1905. The colony was completely cooperative with no person owning anything individually, the 24 men worked together and slept in one large room. The settlement operated as an utopian socialist society with theosophy as its religion. Sointula was still in Kurikka's thoughts though, and in a letter to Aili he wrote: "Think what it means, when it is necessary to leave machines

and cultivated fields, the visible assets of four years work, simply because your best friend betrayed you."

Kurikka left Sammon Takojat in February to lecture and raise funds, but he confided to his daughter that he had left certain problems behind also. "I have again had great difficulties to overcome because enthusiastic materialists, my own students, are now agitating against me. But that has always been the reward of idealistic thinkers." The men living at Sammon Takojat were frustrated with a communal life of poverty, and by July Kurikka received word that women were now living at the commune and that he need not bother to return.

The idealistic dreamer was not without a cause for long, however. In Finland the Pan-Slavic Party was pushing for Russification, even though Alexander I of Russia had granted the Finns freedom of language, parliament and religion. Kurikka returned to his homeland and spent many hours writing and giving speeches. He became editor of *The Elana (Life)*, and through it he continued to attack the church and capitalism. Later he published a book entitled *School of Life II — The Idea of Sointula*, in which he advanced economic theories. To Kurikka, Sointula was a dream that embodied the ideal of living together, as well as the name of a place. He talked of starting a communal farm in Finland, but was unable to obtain funding.

Having observed a "marriage of conscience" for some time, Kurikka officially remarried on May 23, 1906. He was proud of Hanna Raiha. She was fair, beautiful, and 20 years his junior. In December Hanna gave birth to a daughter, Auli Annikki. Two years later, just in time to celebrate Christmas, Kurikka, Hanna and Auli travelled to North America and settled in Penker, Connecticut, where Kurikka earned a living writing for Finnish-American newspapers and by raising chickens.

Always in his thoughts though, were dreams for new utopian settlements. He planned to purchase 300 acres near Vancouver to form a cooperative, and when that failed, he attempted to interest a friend in founding an all woman's colony. Kurikka still considered himself a director of the KKCC, and as late as 1913, entertained plans for a New Sointula in India, or Penker, Connecticut. In 1914 the Kurikka's travelled to Finland to visit family and Kurikka returned to Penker alone.

Matti Kurikka's realization of forming a utopian community ended on a damp October evening in 1915 when neighbours found his body on his farm in Penker. He lay face down in the brush and in his hand was the machete that he had been using. Kurikka died as he had lived, attempting to clear a path. But with El Dorado, Sointula, and Sammon Takojat, he established himself as one of the great utopian founders of his time. Few men could generate such enormous energy and expectations, and few men pursued their dreams with such tenacity.

(Opposite page, top) Finnish settlers pose in front of the newly built log house at Sointula.

(Opposite page, bottom) An early view of Sointula, B.C.

(Right) This photograph of Matti Kurikka was taken in his Penker, Connecticut home c1914.

WHEN WHALES WERE FAIR GAME

Whales once migrated along the coast of British Columbia in vast numbers. Between 1910 and 1943, Rose Harbour, in the Queen Charlotte Islands, and other whaling stations, sent small whaling steamers out into the Pacific to hunt prey sometimes as large as the ships themselves.

THREE blasts of a steamer whistle brought Capt. George Heater to the deck of the sealing schooner *Jessie* as she rode at anchor in Rose Harbour one evening in late May, 1911. He fixed his gaze on Houston Stewart Channel, waiting for his brother's new ship, the steam whaler *W. Grant,* to round Ellen Island with a tow of whales for the whaling station. Already, he had learned from the station manager that William Heater had shot 47 whales in only a few weeks. That matched the record catch he had made the previous year in the station's first three weeks of operation. It was a remarkable record for the sealer-turned-whaler who had just learned the art of shooting whales and was already exceeding the catches of his Norwegian mentors.

William Heater was one of several sealing skippers who had joined the Pacific Whaling Company when the prospects for sealing in the North Pacific began to dim. Most of them were signed on as "pilots" of the whale catchers because of their knowledge of the British Columbia coast. The Norwegian gunners, who had delivered the boats from Norway, stayed with them in B.C. as skippers, their experience indispensable to the new venture. Whaling activity in the North Atlantic had declined from over-exploitation, but Norwegian whalers were in demand in every ocean where their countrymen's modern whaling methods were coming into use. After a few years, most who had commanded the B.C. whale catchers moved on to Norwegian-owned operations in Alaska, Mexico and the Antarctic.

The Norwegian gunners were none too eager to teach Canadians how to shoot whales. They came from a tradition where "whale shooter" was a job with high status as well as high pay. Nevertheless, William Heater was coached by one of them and became the first B.C. whaler to get his own command: a whaling vessel ordered from Norway in 1910 for the new whaling station in the Queen Charlotte Islands.

The *W. Grant,* towing three whales and listing slightly to port from the drag of an extra whale lashed to that side, appeared momentarily in the harbour entrance and eased toward the haul-out slip. A shout from the bridge assured the sealer that his younger brother had seen him. George Heater studied the little ship as her crew fussed about the float, tying up this trip's catch. He had seen her docked at Point Ellice in Victoria's upper harbour the previous winter, but this was the first time he had seen her at work. The vessel looked much like the company's four older whalers and as good or better than the five new ones that had sailed around the Horn from Norway, arriving in weather-beaten condition just before he had departed on his sealing voyage. Hard to believe the *W. Grant* had been sent from Norway the previous year in sections aboard a Blue Funnel liner!

(Opposite page, left) This 1883 line and stipple engraving by M. Bouquet shows a whaling ship preparing a whale while still out at sea.

(Opposite page, right) When whales were caught early in the hunt, they were flagged and left to drift at sea while the hunt continued. Upon completion of the hunt, the whalers would return and tow the whales to the station.

(Below) This 1883 line and stipple engraving, coloured by hand, was made by the artist Morel. It depicts a whale hunt during the age of sail.

FRONTIER DAYS IN BRITISH COLUMBIA

Her whales secured, the 91-foot steamer moved across the tiny harbour and tied up next to the coal pile on the wharf to refuel. As this was being done, Capt. George Heater rowed over for a "gam" with his brother, whom he had not seen since the *Jessie* had left Victoria for the sea otter grounds in early March. The *Jessie* had come into Rose Harbour to leave 524 salted sealskins for transhipment to Victoria by way of the Canadian Pacific Railway's steamships *Amur*. Soon she would be heading for the Bering Sea, and the two brothers would not meet again until late October in Victoria.

As the *W. Grant*, refuelled and provisioned, steamed back out to the Pacific a short time later, the two skippers' farewell waves were weighted with the recognition that the Heater brothers were no longer a pair as they had been in their 19 years of sealing in the north Pacific Ocean and Bering Sea, each with a schooner and Indian seal hunters. They had come west together, bringing their families from Harbour Grace, Newfoundland in the early 1890s, forced out of the maritime industry there by hard times. Both had done well, but now hard times in the Pacific sealing industry demanded another change of course.

Most of the sealers, like William Heater, had already abandoned the sealing industry. With the fur seals almost gone, only four schooners left Victoria to participate in the hunt in 1911, compared to between 60 and 70 in the early 1890s. The controversy over conservation of the seal herds was being settled even as the two brothers talked on the wharf in Rose Harbour: representatives of Japan, Russia, Great Britain and the United States had gathered in Washington, DC to sign a treaty that would end off-shore sealing (i.e. from boats), except for natives in canoes using traditional spears. This was to be George Heater's last voyage after fur seals, and despite his optimism and dogged determination, the catch turned out to be meagre. The following year he fitted the *Jessie* with a gasoline engine and tried his hand at halibut fishing. From that he turned to the herring and pilchard fishery. George Heater died literally with his sea boots on at age 65, having caught pneumonia when his vessel was disabled in a winter storm.

William took a different tack. He was 45 years old when he turned to whaling and, at age 78, was still in command of the *W. Grant* when the company closed down in 1943. He was so crippled with arthritis in the later years that his crew had to push him up the ladder to the bridge. Let anyone else shoot the whales? Never! He would struggle down again and forward to the gun every time a whale was sighted from the lookout barrel on the mast. And that could be several times a day!

The whaling company itself had been organized in 1904 by former fur sealers. Like the Heater brothers, Capt. G.W. Sprott Balcom and his brother Reuben, master mariners from Nova Scotia, had been fur sealing in the Pacific since 1892. When it appeared that the industry was in trouble, they returned to Halifax and organized fur sealing expeditions to the South Atlantic and Antarctic. By 1903 the Balcoms had a fleet of six schooners making the nine-month voyages out of Halifax. They initially made handsome returns, but profitabil-

ity waned when the Falkland Island Dependency levied a tax on every fur shipped through Port Stanley to London. Using the corporate structure and financial backing of their South Seas Sealing Company, they returned to Victoria, and, changing the company name to Pacific Whaling Company (PWC), began catching and processing whales. Capt. William Grant, managing director of the Victoria Sealing Company, who had invested with the Balcoms in South Atlantic sealing, was now a partner in whaling and became president of the company.

The PWC opened its first station at Sechart in Barkley Sound, on Vancouver Island's west coast, late in 1905 with a modern steam whaling ship, the *Orion*, ordered from Norway and delivered by way of Cape Horn. Two other Vancouver Island stations were operating by 1907; one at Kyuquot, and the other near Nanaimo at Page's Lagoon. The latter was closed down after one season because of a disappointing catch of whales in the Straits of Georgia.

Corporate expansion had reached a dizzying pace by 1910 when two more station sites were acquired in the Queen Charlotte Islands: Rose Harbour, at the south end of the archipelago, and Naden Harbour at the north end. Five new chaser boats were ordered from Norway, expanding the whaling fleet to 10 vessels. A freighter was also purchased.

The business weathered bankruptcy, corporate convolutions, the Great War, depressions and marketing crises until in 1943 the last surviving station, Rose Harbour, was closed. The whales, like the fur seals, had become much less plentiful and the ships and guns were worn out: but the *coup de grace* for the industry was the loss of its Japanese labourers to wartime internment. At the end of the Second World War the Consolidated Whaling Company, as it was now called, was liquidated and what was left of the ageing fleet was sold for scrap. A final flurry of whaling, developed out of Coal Harbour on Vancouver Island in the late 1940s. With its demise, in 1967, Canada's west-coast whaling was finished.

Situated on Houston Stewart Channel between the Pacific Ocean and Hecate Strait, on the north shore of Kunghit Island, the Rose Harbour site was chosen for its sheltered location, depth sufficient for deep-draught vessels, and a plentiful fresh-water supply. For the whalers, it was an easy tow with whales from either direction, and when the Pacific was too stormy, whaling could be carried on in the lee of the islands. The plant began converting whales into oil, whalebone and fertilizer in 1910, with only the *W. Grant* hunting for the better part of the first season.

By 1911, each of the company's four stations had two or three whalers hunting within a radius of 30 to 50 miles, bringing in sometimes three to five whales at a time. Cruising at about 10 knots, the 91-foot ships were designed to turn quickly and could handle extremely heavy seas. All 10 catcher boats used in the B.C. whaling industry were built in Norway following the design Svend Foyn had perfected in the latter part of the nineteenth century. Steam power, exploding harpoon heads fired from a large cannon, and powerful steam winches to pull whales in, allowed these boats to hunt species of whales

Capt. William Heater and his crew hand lancing a whale from the Ss W. Grant c1919.

that had not been accessible to hunters in the days of sail whaling. The whalers had bunker capacity for coal to last six or seven days. They inflated and flagged the whale carcasses, leaving them for collection later. The whale's tail was notched to identify which boat it belonged to. Drifting at night, they stayed out until they had enough whales to justify a tow to the station. Daily catches of three or more whales were rare after the first few bonanza years.

Whalers were meant to be whaling, and when the weather turned bad, the ships took refuge in sheltered bays along the coast. They were not welcome back at the station, although in some years whaling was hampered by weeks of storms or fog.

Three whalers had been bought second-hand: one from a Norwegian company whaling in Chile, and two from Newfoundland. The others were ordered direct from Norway. With the exception of the *W. Grant*, these were sailed from Oslo (then Christiania) to Victoria by way of Cape Horn, a journey that took four months. Dr. J.N. Tonnessen with A.O. Johnsen, in their definitive history of modern whaling, said of the *Orion's* maiden voyage: "It was a brilliant achievement sailing this small boat of 108 gross tons in mid-winter, through raging storms, across the North Sea and Atlantic, through the Roaring Forties and all the way up to Victoria. Whaling is often considered more the province of industry than of shipping, and for this reason, in the history of seafaring generally, little mention is made of the fact that some of the finest seamanship has been displayed by crews on board tiny whale catchers operating in the stormiest seas of the world."

Among the 11 men who shared the damp, crowded, continually rolling confines of a steam whaler, there was a willingness to chase down the most elusive prey. Each got a bonus for every whale caught according to it's value in oil. In the early years, sperm whales paid the highest bonus because of their valuable case oil. Next in value were the much bigger sulphur-bottoms or blue whales, sometimes reaching 90 feet in length, and the fin whales. Least valuable, though most plentiful and easiest to chase, were the humpbacks. Sei whales were too small and low in oil to be prized. Gray whales, if even seen, were not hunted. Almost eliminated by sail whalers in the nineteenth century, they have only reappeared as a result of years of protection.

The whaling season lasted from April until October. During the off-season, Ships wintered at Captain Grant's wharf in Victoria's upper harbour. Each spring the captains, who were kept on retainer over the winter, supervised their outfitting and signed on their crew: a mate, a cook, four seaman, two engineers and two firemen. Once they stepped off Grant's wharf, they would rarely be ashore until the end of the season. Kora Larsen, seaman on the whalers in the 1920s, thought the most exciting moment of the whole voyage was when the ship's whistle sounded for Victoria's Johnson Street bridge to raise, allowing the whaler to return to her berth at Grant's

wharf for the winter and the crew to go home. Occasionally a Chinese cook susceptible to seasickness would sign on quite unprepared for the physical duress of working in a rolling and pitching galley. It was said that the only reason he stayed aboard for the season was that there was no place to get off.

The most successful gunners were those with an intimate knowledge of whale habits. Spotted from the swaying barrel atop the mast, the whales' characteristic spout and movements indicated what kind of whale it was, whether it was feeding or travelling, and its direction and speed. Whales differed according to species in the length of time they would stay below, a critical factor in positioning the boat for a shot. Rising and dipping with the ocean swells as he

(Left) a whale's jawbone lies in the shallows where it fell off the haul-out slip at Rose Harbour. All other jawbones were cooked, dried and ground up as fertilizer. (Below) A coloured postcard depicting the Pacific Whaling Company's steamer Orion *harpooning a whale.*

manned the harpoon gun at the bow, the captain steadied himself with feet planted well apart. Sighting down the cannon, the captain waved signals to the mate on the bridge as he waited for his prey to surface. Not only must he be close enough when he fired the 90-pound harpoon, he must strike from the best angle to be successful. Once the whale was hit and wounded, it had to be played in. Frequently a second explosive harpoon had to be shot to end its struggle, or a long hand lance plunged deep. The process sometimes took hours. A whale might take off at such speed that even with the ship's engines in reverse the vessel would be towed by the whale at six knots until it tired. Humpbacks had a habit of sounding and surfacing in unpredictable ways, often astern. The chase required cunning and patience.

Captain Heater's whale-hunting technique was more than science. It was charged with a mixture of faith and determination that fixed his image in the memories of his crew for the rest of their lives. Heater, wearing his "sperm hat" with the little feathers for luck, sang "Jesus, Lover of My Soul" when his prey had sounded (dived), and swore mightily when it surfaced behind him. Heater was also the last skipper to call it quits when the weather got too rough to hunt. He also had a theory, adopted by others, that sperm whales could be counted on to appear at the change of the moon.

In 1913, the Victoria *Times* reported that Captain Heater had steered his disabled ship back to Rose Harbour using the whale which had damaged the ship for a rudder. The harpooned whale, desperate to escape, had sounded so close to the stern of the boat that its tail had broken the rudder and two blades of the propeller. After eventually killing the whale, Heater had lines attached to its tail flukes and run forward "port and starboard." With the whale's nose tightly lashed under the stern, the "steering" lines were brought alongside the *W. Grant* to the huge winch drums on the forward deck. Heater, steering by pulls on the whale's tail, brought the *W. Grant* slowly back to Rose Harbour. He even whale-steered her up to the wharf, according to the news story.

Whale-inflicted damage to the vessels was not uncommon, though in the history of B.C. whaling no ship was actually sunk by an enraged whale as happened to the *Lizzie Sorensen* in Alaska. Most damage was the result of whale carcasses hitting the side of the boat under tow. A report was made to the company headquarters in June, 1916, that the *Orion*, whaling out of Rose Harbour, began leaking when an unexploded bomb in the whale they were towing pierced the side of the vessel. A temporary repair was made, and on arrival at the station, the vessel was listed to port while loading coal so the blacksmith could make a permanent repair.

On the crescent-shaped stretch of shore west of the factory site at Rose Harbour, one can see at very low tide that a wide swath of the sea bottom has been cleared of boulders. This is where the whalers were careened for repairs. It was used in August, 1934, to repair the *Green* which, like the *W. Grant* in 1913, had

The old whaling station at Sechart. The first of the Pacific Whaling Company stations, it opened in 1905.

been struck by a harpooned whale. The whale was cut loose in order to save the ship. Canvas was stretched over the hole in the hull and the crew bailed frantically for six hours. With the engine room flooded, she was helpless. Fortunately, another whaler, the *White*, appeared on the scene and towed the *Green* back to Rose Harbour where she was beached, repaired, and sent whaling the following day.

One Norwegian who stayed with the B.C. company years longer than the others was Capt. Knut Halvorsen. A quiet bachelor, Halvorsen was always welcome at the Rose Harbour station manager's house in 1916 to play a game of cards. It was a violation of company policy, for whalers were expected to be off hunting more whales the minute they had dropped their catch. But the manager, William Rolls, and his wife, liked Halvorsen. It was a year of stress for Rolls. He was having difficulty with "something stronger than tea" somehow getting to the whaling crews. Little did he know that Captain Halvorsen and the crew of the *Brown* kept a still in Sperm Bay!

Standing today on the rust-encrusted rocks of Rose Harbour at low tide, with the fresh salty smell of seaweed in the morning air, a bald eagle's musical cry piercing the silence, one can barely imagine the stench and clangour of industry that identified the place in the whaling days. Today, four modest homes, built partly with reclaimed material from the whaling operations, mark this as the only community within the Queen Charlotte Islands' South Moresby Park Reserve. Other than a few relics of rusting machinery, little remains at Rose Harbour to indicate that it was once the site of a profitable whale rendering plant and base for a fleet of steam whalers. Shells of barnacles knocked off humpback whales and a few seaweed-covered bones in the shallows are the indicators that close to 4,000 whales were once landed here. Nothing save the beaching area, tells of the ships.

(Opposite page, top) The steam whaler Orion. *This photo was taken by Asahel Curtis when the* Orion *went to assist the doomed* Valencia.

(Right) The lookout sights a whale.

(Opposite page, bottom) The Coal Harbour whaling station. Winches hauled the whales up a concrete ramp formerly used by seaplanes. Skilled workers using flensing knives strip off the blubber, the fatty outer layer of the whale. The man on the right is using a giant caliper to make sure that the whale comes within the requirements of the International Whaling Commission.

ROSE HARBOUR

Established as a whaling station in the Queen Charlotte Islands during the first half of the twentieth century, Rose Harbour growled and hissed with the industry of 100 men converting whales into profits. Today there is no sign of the grease, blood, guts, guano dust and stench that once identified Rose Harbour.

WHEN, late in July, 1910, Capt. William Heater finally headed his new whaling steamer *W. Grant* northwest from Vancouver bound for the Queen Charlotte Islands, the whaling season was half over. His destination was Rose Harbour, on the north shore of Kunghit Island. The new whaling station had recently been completed after suffering some frustrating delays. While he waited, Heater had whaled out of the station at Sechart, Vancouver Island. Now the new Rose Harbour facility was finally ready to begin processing whales.

The coastline of British Columbia was as familiar to Heater as the back of his hand. However, although he had sailed fur-sealing schooners along the northwest coast since 1892, Heater had never had occasion to go into the anchorage on the south side of Houston Stewart Channel near the southern tip of the Queen Charlottes. At that time, there was nothing there. Now, as he turned in the channel to round Ellen Island, it was plain that statement was no longer true.

Framed by Kunghit Island's low spruce-clad hills, with islands, rocks and shoals on either side, a tiny harbour, possibly not more than one-half mile across, came into view. Facing the mountains of Moresby Island, directly across the channel, it appeared completely sheltered from storms. Along the crescent shore stretched a line of buildings with all the elements of the whaling stations the company had operated for the past few years on Vancouver Island.

Starting from a small creek, Heater's eye scanned the shore from right to left. There were three bunkhouses and a cottage, then the haul-out slip with loft behind where the whales' thick layer of insulating blubber would be rendered into oil. Leading from the slip at an angle, were the carcass platform and sheds where he knew the butchering and cooking would take place. A nearby smokestack indicated the location of the drier and guano sheds where cooked meat would be pressed, dried, then ground into fertilizer. There was the wharf, new and sturdy, loaded with oak barrels ready to receive whale oil, and a pile of coal. A tall smokestack behind the plant indicated the boiler house where a single man would shovel coal into four furnaces continually all day long to keep up steam power for the plant. A water tank stood on stilts nearby. Finally, the manager's house completed the scene.

The machinery was not new, having been used one season in the ill-conceived whaling station on the eastern shore of Vancouver Island at Page's Lagoon near Nanaimo. A disappointing lack of whales had forced that station's early demise; but the failure was not a total loss. The plant was dismantled and shipped north to a much more promising site at Rose Harbour: from the shortest-lived whaling station in the company's history to the longest. For Rose Harbour was to prove the most productive of all the stations operated by the company that, between 1904 and 1947, evolved through four corporate names: Pacific Whaling, Canadian North Pacific Fisheries, Victoria Whaling and finally, Consolidated Whaling Company, Ltd.

(Above) An aerial view of Rose Harbour today. A cluster of spruce trees outline the whaling plant.

(Opposite page, far right) A plan of the Rose Harbour whaling station drawn from a 1928 appraisal.

(Opposite page, right) A painting of an early whaling scene.

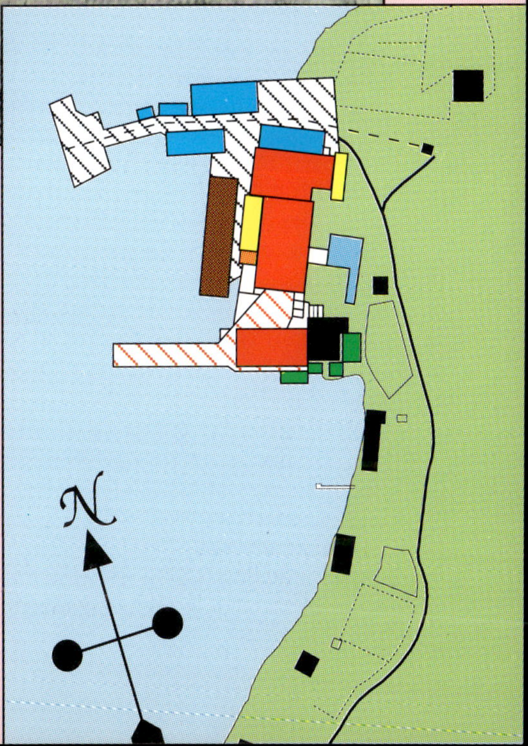

FRONTIER DAYS IN BRITISH COLUMBIA

Actually, it was the same people operating under the name of Queen Charlotte Whaling Company, Ltd., who had established the station at Rose Harbour. The purpose of the disguise may have been to acquire more licenses from Ottawa without appearing to have a monopoly. In less than a year, the Queen Charlotte Whaling Company, president William Grant, was sold to the Pacific Whaling Company, president William Grant. George Huff, who seems to have been the front man in the licensing process, managed the Rose Harbour facility for just one season. That may have been all he wanted after being confronted by some unforeseen managerial challenges.

Resolution of his biggest crisis had come just a couple of weeks before the whaling steamer arrived to begin work. At 9 o'clock on the evening of June 23, 22 of the Japanese workmen who had been building the station returned to their bunkhouse to find Jentoro Kawasaki in a drunken rage. It was a scene not unfamiliar to Japanese labourers of that time. Isolated from family, bored, and with nowhere to spend their earnings, they entertained themselves with gambling. Home brew for a man who had lost everything at poker was like an open powder keg waiting for a spark.

Kawasaki, who had been drinking for days, grabbed an axe and followed his countrymen upstairs, challenging them all to fight. Nobody, apparently, took him seriously except to complain that they could not sleep. When a senior member of the crew took the axe away from Kawasaki, he simply went downstairs to the kitchen and returned with a butcher knife and a stick. Kawasaki then pulled Watakabe, a much smaller man, from his bunk. In the ensuing melee, a bloody and bruised Watakabe ended up with the knife as they rolled on the floor. Kawasaki got up and staggered downstairs to the kitchen to rearm himself yet again. Before resuming the attack, however, he collapsed, the multiple slashes and two fatal stab wounds in his back finally taking their toll. The dying Kawasaki was then carried to his bunk where he laid for three days, wheezing air out of his wound. Medical care was out of reach.

On June 26, 1910, Kawasaki died. George Huff, who had anxiously attended him, had his body laid in a rocky crevasse on Ellen Island and covered with branches. Huff then sent Watakabe, escorted by three men, in a small boat some 25 miles to the provincial constable in Jedway. There, on July 16, the body, which had been retrieved from Ellen Island, was viewed by a coroner's jury and a doctor. They concluded that Watakabe had killed Kawasaki in self defence. Oral tradition has it, however, that more than one hand, coming to Watakabe's defense, had plunged a knife in Kawasaki's back. Only the Japanese knew the truth, and they never told.

Kawasaki's death inspired a "make work" program the following season to circumvent the drinking and gambling that inevitably accompanied idleness when there were no whales to cut up owing to bad weather. To keep his men busy when fog or storms prevented the whalers from bringing in whales, Moichi Kosaka, the Japanese foreman, devised a plan to build a "park." Trails were brushed out and pole benches, even a gazebo, were placed where there was a pleasant view of the channel.

Close to 100 men lived at Rose Harbour between April and October, most of them cutting up or processing whales. Japanese and Chinese made up the bulk of the work force, mainly because, as in the fishing industry, they could be employed cheaply. White labourers came on contract from the dying Newfoundland whaling industry. Each race was housed in a different bunkhouse, ate different food and spoke a different language. For most, homes, wives and children were an ocean or a continent away.

Kinoe Kosaka, wife of Japanese foreman, sitting on a "park" bench with her sons Gorge and Isamu, and Arthur, Nick and Douglas Raine, sons of the station engineer, 1916.

Moichi Kosaka was one of the fortunate few who had his family with him. Kosaka, who had arrived in Victoria in 1905 with his wife, was originally headed for Boston to study mining engineering. However, United States immigration rules, which were more stringent than Canadian at the time, stopped him at the border because of an infected eye. So Kosaka took up residence in Canada. After five years of working in restaurants, he ultimately found a job supervising his less-educated countrymen in the whaling station at Rose Harbour. His wife cooked for the 50-or more men, and raised two small sons in their room in the Japanese bunkhouse. Her motherly instincts extended to the many young men who arrived from Japan hoping to make a relative fortune for needy families back home. Years later, Kinoe Kosaka told her children how she had agonized over the pressures of loneliness and boredom that fuelled the drunken gaming and fights that she often heard upstairs. Perhaps it was she who dreamed up the idea of building a park.

Each bunkhouse had its own antidote for boredom. The Chinese, generally older men who had emigrated to Canada in an earlier era, were avid gamblers too. Solace for them was found in an opium pipe. Long after opium became illegal it was used in the Chinese bunkhouse in Rose Harbour. From the whitemen's bunkhouse one might have heard an accordion playing a Newfoundland jig. In the early years of B.C. whaling, 20 or more men were brought west on two-year contracts from Newfoundland, their skills no longer marketable in the colony. Whales had almost disappeared in the Atlantic and companies that had been hastily organized to reap a bonanza anticipated in 1900, were dying fast.

Managerial staff had also been imported from Newfoundland for the fledgling Pacific Coast whaling industry. Their expertise was essential for the enterprise's success. Whaling station managers Scaplen, LeMarquand, Garcin, Ruck, Gosney and Rolls all brought their families across the continent to live in isolated whaling communities on the rugged B.C. coast. With newspapers and mail brought once or twice a month, with no village in which to gossip and shop, with no church associations, with sometimes not so much as another woman to talk to, some of the women found the solitude hard to take. Visits from the passenger steamers bringing mail were big

events. Those passengers whose curiosity was strong enough to overcome their revulsion to the stench of the place were greeted with delight as they came ashore to look around.

Rose Harbour had more families than the other stations during the first eight to 10 years of operation. Children from three households, the station engineer's, the manager's, and the Japanese foreman's, played along the rocky beaches on pleasant days. On rainy days, they hung out in the warm boiler house with the amiable fireman, Mike Benson. On other days they shot the blisters in heat-swollen whale carcasses with a .22 calibre rifle. On one rare occasion, they even bounced on the tongue inside a huge whale's mouth.

Although racial animosity was high in the urban centres of B.C. at the time Rose Harbour was established, the Kosaka family were friends to the manager's and engineer's families. The children were included in Sunday picnics and their mother, when time permitted, visited with the two other wives on the station. Being a teacher from a literary Japanese family and fluent in English, she prevailed upon the LeMarquand children's tutor, a maid-

Rose Harbour whale flensers, 1918, pose inside a whale's mouth with station manager H. Diuckitt and station engineer J. Raine, Moichi Kosaka, foreman, squatting in bib overalls. Flensers cut the whale's blubber with scalpel-like knives.

(Above) Rose Harbour whaling station in a cloud of dust. Fallout fertilized lush vegetable gardens, but it reeked of ammonia. (Right) Flensers making the first cut into a humpback whale. The strips of blubber were peeled back like banana skins. (Below) A rusting winch is all that marks the haulout slip today. The beach across the harbour is where damaged whale boats were repaired.

en aunt, to include Isamu, her oldest boy, in their classes.

Newfoundland labourers gradually were replaced by Japanese and Chinese. These men worked 10 hours a day, six days a week for less than white men would have been paid. If there was a run of whales, they worked on into the night. After the whaling season was over, a crew of Japanese were retained at the station to do plant maintenance jobs.

Many of the whale processing jobs were extremely hazardous, and fatal accidents were not uncommon. Men occasionally slipped into the vats of boiling blubber. The station first aid man, doubling as bookkeeper, had only the most basic supplies for medical emergencies, and it sometimes took hours of waiting for

(Top) An abandoned steam winch, one of several that were used to move whale carcasses.
(Centre) Brick-housed furnaces are all that remain of the steam plant.
(Below) Meat digesters lay where they fell through the carcass plant.

(Above) An aerial view of the Rose Harbour whaling station in 1944.
(Below) A pile of whale bones waiting to be processed at Rose Harbour in 1918.

a whaler to come into port, and hours more for it to carry the injured man to the mainland hospital in Bella Bella. In the meantime, one first aid treatment was to smear the poor man's body with molasses and dust him with flour.

The late Alan Armour, son of the last Rose Harbour manager, and himself a former seaman for the company, erected a cairn in the summer of 1983 to the memory of those workers who had died in the service of the whaling company. Some of them, he believed, were still buried up in the woods behind the station.

In the first decade of whaling on the B.C. coast, newspaper reporters covered the activities of the company, its fleet of ships and its stations with keen interest. Magazine articles described the exciting exploits of whalers and tried to explain the whale reduction process. None were successful in describing the most remarkable feature of a whaling operation: its stench. A Victoria newspaper reported in 1910 that longshoremen demanded extra pay to unload sacks of whale fertilizer from the new Rose Harbour station. Their reason was that the smell would not come out of their clothes. In later years the Ss *Prince John* stopped coming up to the wharf at Rose Harbour because the skipper claimed the putrid air actually discoloured the ship's paint. "If you want your mail, you'll have to row out and get it!" he declared.

Whale oil and guano (whale fertilizer) production in the early part of the century was a thriving industry. Company profits in 1906 had provided dividends of 23 percent on preference shares and 18 percent on common shares. Though oil markets fluctuated frighteningly and weather curtailed good catches in some years, still the company pressed on, expanding at a reckless rate. The whale hunt intensified. Rose Harbour's second year of operation, 1911, was a banner year for the company. A total of 1,624 whales were captured and processed at the company's four stations.

Blacksmith Karl Larsen, remembering the shore whaling industry's demise, first in his native Norway and then in Newfoundland, muttered to his sons, "It can't go on like this." And he was right. It was all downhill from there. The four station's kill decreased to 1,109, 705, and 564 whales in the following three years as whales were became harder to find. By 1926 the fleet of whaling ships had been reduced from 10 to six, and two stations had been closed. In 1943 Rose

Nicholas and Arthur Raine pose with a crewman in a whaler's lookout barrel at the Rose Harbour wharf.

Harbour, the sole surviving whaling station of Consolidated Whaling Co. Ltd., processed only 91 whales, and the company folded. After World War II, some of Rose Harbour's machinery was moved to Coal Harbour on Vancouver Island where one last whaling flurry started hopefully. The new enterprise carried on until 1967 when it too succumbed. The whales were gone.

An aerial view of Rose Harbour today shows a green and pleasant shore with a few homes and gardens. Yet closer examination shows that nature has outlined the old whaling station plan with trees. Rows and clusters of spruce grow where once stood factory and living quarters: wood giving life to wood. A string of spruce trails up the incline from the rotting wharf piles, nurtured by coal spilled from the coal car that ran between the wharf and the engine house. At the top of a small meadow a miniature forest thrives in the ashes of the manager's house, and over the unused land a thick carpet of moss shrouds a dead industry's debris.

Mail comes even less readily today to a Rose Harbour address, dropped off by float planes if and when they have a charter hop that brings them to the south end of the Charlottes. Yet the residents love the beauty and solitude of Rose Harbour and seldom complain. They use the bone meal, left over from the whale processing days, to fertilize their gardens, while used brick and whale-oil-preserved lumber are utilized in their building projects. Here and there relics of the whaling plant stand like weird statuary. Rotting wharf piles lean at crazy angles; rusting meat digesters loll where they fell through the crumbling carcass platform; brick furnaces pose as fortifications at the back of a vegetable garden; a steam winch lies askew like an agonized cadaver clenching a power no longer needed.

In 1862 Francis Poole, an English mining engineer, sailed to the Queen Charlotte Islands. As his schooner approached what 50 years later was to become the Rose Harbour whale hunting grounds, he wrote: "Astern of us lies spread out the vast Pacific Ocean, completely alive with whales and porpoises. . . . Who dare foretell how soon these frequenters of this half-known ocean path will be driven from the field of their sports, and their inheritance be taken possession of by the fleets of civilization?"

Vancouver Coal Mining and Land Company's Shaft No. 1 at Nanaimo in 1884. Three years later it was the scene of a horrible mine disaster.

The Nanaimo Mine Disaster Of 1887

To drive the new wheels of industry, fuel was needed, and though wood was used when nothing else was available, the superiority of coal was plain from the beginning. Even on the west coast of North America it was in use whenever possible, despite the fact that almost all of it had to be brought around Cape Horn from Wales.

THE discovery of coal in the Nanaimo area is credited to an Indian who visited Victoria in the fall of 1849 to have his musket repaired. While watching the Hudson's Bay Company (HBC) blacksmith at work, he remarked that there were plenty of "black stones" where he lived. The Indian was told that if he would bring some to Victoria, he would not only have his gun fixed without charge, but would also receive a bottle of rum. In due course he returned with his canoe full of coal, which proved to be of excellent quality. In 1852 Governor Douglas sent a party headed by Joseph McKay to take possession of the deposits for the HBC. At this time the location was known as "Wentuhuysen Inlet."

Douglas, who foresaw a steady demand for Vancouver Island coal, decided that the new deposits should be developed without delay. Coal miners were transferred from Fort Rupert to the new location, and soon a small settlement developed around it. The famous bastion, still standing today, was begun in 1852 and finished the following year, the work being done by French-Canadian woodsmen. Almost 500 barrels of coal were shipped to Victoria in 1852, and a few months later the first shipment was made to San Francisco. By the summer of 1853, when Douglas visited the workings, the settlement contained 12 houses, a forge and a lumber store. It was a modest beginning, but a new industry had been put on firm foundations.

The new location, although officially known as Colville Town until about 1860, soon came to be known as Nanaimo. Despite rough beginnings, some of the amenities of 19th century civilization were gradually introduced. When Douglas visited the first settlers in 1853, they asked that a school be established. He transferred a teacher from Victoria, and each family henceforth paid one pound a year toward his support. When Vancouver Island's first legislature was elected in 1856, Nanaimo became represented by John F. Kennedy. Missionaries appeared in 1859, and the first church was opened in 1861. A literary institute, a temperance society and a cricket club were formed, and a bank was opened; while July 10, 1865 saw the appearance of the first Nanaimo newspaper, the *Gazette*. A fire brigade was formed the same year, and in 1866 a volunteer militia was established in case of trouble with the natives.

The population, about 125 in 1853, slowly grew. A census of Vancouver Island gave Nanaimo's population as 151 in 1854. By 1863 there were estimated to be 400 whites in the community, and in 1869 about 650. By 1874 the population was close to 1,000, of whom 400 were men employed in the mines.

The output of coal steadily increased, as the world moved from sail to steam. Between 1852 and 1859, 25,000 tons were shipped from Nanaimo, mostly to California. By 1862, when the HBC sold its coal interests to an English firm called the Vancouver Coal Mining and Land Company, 55,000 tons of coal had been produced. In 1863, output reached 100 tons a day, and, by 1866, nearly twice that.

(Above) Nanaimo, the coaling station on Vancouver Island in 1859.
(Below) This painting by Paul Grignon depicts a colliery engine and coal cars at Wellington during its prime.

By 1887 Nanaimo was enjoying a boom. Coal was still the basic fuel of industry and the demand for it seemed unlimited. The main market continued to be San Francisco. The output of the Nanaimo mines, which had been 80,000 tons in 1874, rose in the next 10 years to five times that figure.

In the Nanaimo area three collieries were in operation in 1887: the Wellington mines, a few miles from the city, owned by the Dunsmuirs; the Vancouver Coal Mining and Land Company's mine, much of it underneath Nanaimo and the adjacent inlet; and the East Wellington colliery, controlled by R.D. Chandler, a San Francisco man. Between them they produced more that 400,000 tons of coal annually.

However, accidents in the mines, some of them fatal, were frequent. Eleven men were killed by an explosion in 1879 and 23 in 1884. A constant danger was that of an explosion of coal dust; this produced a deadly gas, largely carbon monoxide, called "after-damp." The safety lamp, invented by Humphrey Davy in the early years of the century, had long been in use, its distinguishing feature being the avoidance of an open flame. Nevertheless, despite strict orders to the contrary, some men occasionally carried and lit matches, and some accidents were probably attributable to this fact.

In spite of these dangers, Tuesday, May 3, 1887, began like any other working day. The Vancouver Coal Mining Company was working two day shifts, and one shift went on duty at 2 o'clock in the afternoon. There were about 160 men, white and Chinese, deep beneath the city (some of the workings extended a mile out under the sea), when, at 5:55 P.M., disaster struck. A sharp tremor shook the whole Nanaimo area. A few moments later, black smoke began pouring from the Number One shaft of the Vancouver Coal Company. It was immediately realized that a calamity had occurred, and everyone in the city rushed to the pit-head.

As flames poured from the shaft and rose high into the sky, some suggested cutting a channel from the sea and flooding the mine. This drastic course was rejected as, not only would it extinguish the fire, but it probably would cost lives which might yet be saved, and destroy the livelihood of many families for as much as a year. Instead, men worked valiantly at pumps and formed a bucket brigade. But it was plain that the fire had spread throughout the workings and that no rescue work could yet be attempted.

It took 24 long, agonizing hours before the flames near the main shaft were extinguished, and it became possible to penetrate a short distance into the mine. An exploring party found that the giant fan which had circulated fresh air throughout the mine had been demolished. The Colonist reported that it had been the finest on the Pacific coast, having cost close to $30,000, and noted that "The heat of the fire must have been intense. The immense machinery is curled and twisted into all conceivable shapes, and practically useless."

The bodies of five white men and six Chinese were found near the main shaft, and Samuel Hudson later died from the effects of gas after participating in the first rescue operation.

About noon on May 5, another body was found 750 yards from the hoisting shaft. It was identified as that of Michael Lyons, and the Colonist printed some further details:

"He is a mule-driver, about 18 years old, and was found at his station near his dead mule. Lyons was taken to the schoolhouse, where he lies terribly burned about the face and breast. The former is as black as coal from the effects of the gas."

Altogether, about a dozen bodies, divided equally between whites and Chinese, were recovered that day, and preparations for the first of many funerals were begun. It was feared that close to 50 women had been widowed, many of them with sizable families. All the schools and most businesses in Nanaimo were closed, flags flew at half-mast, a special train carrying medical supplies and mining experts arrived from Victoria, and sailors from ships in the harbour gave what assistance they could.

All day an anxious and sometimes hysterical crowd surrounded the mine shaft. The Colonist portrayed the tragic scene:

"As each cage comes up, anxious hearts look for the glad tidings that never come. Women tear their hair in the agony of their sorrow, and with babes to their bosoms continue to walk up and down mourning their loss. Many are determined that they should go into the cage to find their loved ones. The entrance to the main shaft is being fenced, to prevent a rush when the bodies are being brought up. Most of the men are from Cornwall, Yorkshire and Wales, with a few from Nova Scotia."

A heavy rain in the evening of May 5 drove most people indoors, but, next morning, they resumed their vigil. Early on May 6 another penetration of the workings was made by a group which included men of some importance in the area. Among them were John Bryden, manager of the Wellington mine, Archibald Dick, provincial inspector of mines, and E.G. Prior, who had at one time held this post but was now a member of parliament for Victoria. Prior was to have a remarkable career as inspector of mines, MP, prominent hardware merchant, premier of the province, and, finally, its lieutenant-governor. The group, carrying safety lamps, descended the shaft about 6 a.m., and soon came upon grim evidence of the disaster.

"The first man found was Andrew Muir, foreman, and just behind him 22 white men and 12 Chinese, all lying between five and ten yards of each other. Muir had evidently been guiding the way out, the men following his lead. He evidently tried to get into the slope, but found it was caved in and had to retrace his steps to the air course. Just as they had come into the slope of the air course, the after-damp struck them and all succumbed. The Davey brothers were found kneeling down, their arms around each other, and had pulled their coats over their heads to shield themselves. There were no signs of burning. They had simply been killed by the after-damp.

"As soon as the bodies were found, word was sent for the relief party, who bore the bodies to the shaft, where they were wrapped in canvas and sent up in the cage. Two others, Woobank, father and son, were a few yards behind the others and could not be got at. They could see them, six or eight feet around the corner, but the wall of damp was between. The men rushed in, however, and secured them. The lights would not live in the damp."

Another party which entered the mine on Sunday, May 8, made equally tragic discoveries:

"Sunday morning opened gloomily, and no news came from the mine of the finding of the bodies until about 11 o'clock, when it was stated that 25 white men and 10 Chinese working in No. 1 level had been found. The exploring party found the gate barricaded, evidencing hard work on the part of the imprisoned men. They had evidently come out of the level, and reaching a cave-in through which they could not pass, had retraced their steps and made the barricade, hoping that assistance would soon arrive.

"One young fellow, a general favorite about the mine, had written in white chalk on his shovel, 'Thirteen hours after explosion, in deepest misery, John Stevens.' On one of the timbers was '1, 2, 3, o'clock'; and again, 'William Bone, 5 o'clock.'

"The Chinese had also inscribed their hieroglyphics on the timbers, but no Chinaman would venture down the shaft to decipher them."

A reporter who accompanied the party gave readers of the *Colonist* some idea of the conditions under which others had spent their entire working lives:

"The trip down into the mine was quite an experience. Darkness reigns supreme, and except for the safety lamps in hand there was not the faintest ray of light. The solid walls of coal through which runs the slope is all there to be seen, except for the far-away twinkle of the miners' lamps. After living in the bowels of the earth, one fully appreciates God's sunlight when he emerges."

Only seven men who were in the mine when the explosion occurred escaped with their lives. One of them was foreman Richard Gibson, who was also mayor of Nanaimo. He had managed to make his way through an air shaft to the stables where the mules were kept, where he and six companions were found by one of the first rescue parties.

"He was very much dazed from the effect of the afterdamp, and was not able to give a connected account of the explosion, no more than when the mine fired, he was knocked down by the force of the explosion and can hardly say how he managed to reach a place of safety.

"The first intimation he had of the explosion was when a tremendous blast knocked him down, rolling him over three or four times and bruising his body. He felt no gas or flames, and it took him three long hours to get to the shaft where, insensible, he was found by the exploring party and saved."

A coroner's inquest was opened on May 10 by Dr. Walkem, but adjourned for two weeks to enable experts to examine the mine and for survivors of the explosion to recall their experiences more clearly. Most

of the miners who eventually testified at the inquest said that the ventilation of the mine had been good. After a wide variety of witnesses had been heard, the jury brought in its verdict. The *Colonist* commented on it in its editorial of June 26:

"The verdict of the coroner's jury in the Nanaimo disaster is one which will be read with a great degree of interest. They find that the explosion was caused by the firing of an unprepared and badly planted shot in the face of the diagonal slope, causing the ignition of whatever gas had accumulated or was circulating in the air in its immediate vicinity, intensified by the addition of coal dust. The jury submit that in view of the fact that the mine is an acknowledged dry and dusty one, and that coal dust is a recognized factor in colliery explosions, proper precautions were not taken for minimizing the probabilities of a catastrophe. Criminal negligence is not, however, attributed to any one."

Gradually the community recovered. Money was collected by public subscription for the widows and children of the dead, while the living continued to descend deep into the earth each day to earn their daily bread.

More bodies were recovered from time to time: one in June, one in July, two in October, and two in December. In late July it was discovered that part of the mine was becoming hotter, and might break out into a fresh fire at any time. Accordingly, it was filled with water and not pumped out again for several months. Altogether 148 men (including Samuel Hudson) lost their lives, of whom the bodies of five whites and two Chinese were never recovered.

The survivors and their companions continued to labour in the shadow of instant death; less than a year later, on January 24, 1888, 77 men lost their lives in an explosion in the No. 5 pit in the Wellington colliery, and lesser disasters occurred from time to time. Non-fatal accidents were much more frequent, as the annual report of the Department of Mines makes clear.

The coalfields at Nanaimo reached their peak production in 1922, when more than 1,400,000 tons were produced. After that there was a steady decline, caused partly by the change by many industries from coal to oil. The last mine at Comox closed in 1966 and at Nanaimo in 1968. With them closed an era.

No. 1, most famous of all Nanaimo coal mines. Here, on May 3, 1887, 150 men died in an explosion, the worse Island disaster of an industry haunted by tragedy.

GRAPPLER'S
Fateful Voyage

For eight years the gunboat HMS *Grappler* provided protection to the pioneers of Vancouver Island. Decommissioned in 1868, the *Grappler's* career took a turn for the worst. Grounded and nearly shipwrecked several times, the *Grappler* miraculously escaped. But her fateful voyage in 1863 would have a far different ending.

E VEN to a coast which has known disaster at sea from the beginning, the *Grappler* tragedy ranks as one of the all-time worst.

Sudden storms, treacherous currents, uncharted reefs, marauding Indians; many were the dangers which stalked mariners a century ago. Yet a far greater threat accompanied every voyage in that perilous age of sail and steam — fire. Hand pumps and courage were pathetic defence against this killer.

There was no warning of the coming holocaust when the *Grappler* cleared Victoria for the last time, early in the evening of Saturday, April 28, 1883. To Capt. John F. Jagers, it was just another routine run. No stranger to B.C. waters, the 32-year-old German's career included a long stint as mate and master of the famous Hudson's Bay Company (HBC) steamer, *Beaver*.

The 104-foot *Grappler* was no newcomer either. All of 37 years, she was a maritime pioneer. Built during the Crimean War, the 232 ton vessel accompanied sister gunboat HMS *Forward* to Esquimalt in 1860. After eight hectic years as watchdogs — accomplishing every duty from that of coast guard to hunting whiskey peddlers to capturing Indian murderers — the aging twins were decommissioned and sold at public auction on March 14, 1868. The *Grappler* was not used by her new owners, however, and on June 30 she was resold to Capt. James Train for $2,400.

Thus began the *Grappler's* hectic and troubled career in B.C. coastal waters and rivers. In March, 1871, she entered the Skeena River trade. In August of the same year she rescued the tug *Cornelius* off the entrance to Howe Sound. But when Captain Boor of the *Cornelius* refused to pay the *Grappler's* $3,600 salvage fee, the vessel was seized and was not released until the claim was paid.

On December 16, 1874, the *Grappler* was sold to Broderick & Company of Victoria for $6,000. Broderick in turn resold her to the B.C. Towing & Transportation Co. less than a month later. On December 27, 1875, the old screw propeller was acquired by Capt. William Moore for $5,000. Born in Germany in 1822, Moore had sailed in schooners on the North Sea by the age of seven. He had reached New Orleans and was operating a towboat service on the lower Mississippi while still in his early 20s. After fighting in the Mexican War, Moore headed for the California goldfields, eventually following the golden lure to the Fraser River and Cariboo. He was destined to be one of the first into the Klondike, and would eventually establish the town of Skagway. For the present, however, he was active in the Stikine River trade, and for this he desperately needed another vessel. Three days after he purchased the *Grappler* she was loaded with freight and heading north.

Under Moore, however, the *Grappler* suffered nothing but bad luck. Moore struck Beacon Rock in Nanaimo Harbour the third week of March, 1876. Aground on the reef for 12 hours and taking on water, she was rescued by the

This original acrylic painting by B.C. artist Bill Maximick depicts "HMS Grappler Anchored at Komox Bay," on the Salish Reserve, October 2, 1862.

Emma and beached at Millstream for repairs. It was not long after these repairs had been made that the *Grappler* was aground once again, this time on Sidney Island Spit. This time, however, she was floated off by a high tide.

This latest incident had followed an accusation by a local shipbuilder that the *Grappler* was "rotten." Responding to this charge, steamship inspector Thomas Westgarth had examined the *Grappler* before she left Victoria. He later reported: ". . .she appears sound, staunch and seaworthy in every respect and carries a certificate for twelve months of which not more than four months have expired."

But *Grappler's* ill fortune persisted, and on July 15, with Capt. Henry Smith at the controls and the bark *Henry Buck* in tow, she left Victoria for the Stikine River. After running aground on Darcy Island, Captain Smith

was attempting to back her off when he saw the tethered *Henry Buck* charging down on him. Only a last minute manoeuvre prevented a disastrous collision, but the heavy strain on the hawser rolled *Grappler* on her starboard beam and she began taking on water. A short time later the tug *Goliath* was spotted and hailed, arriving just in time to prevent the *Henry Buck* from grounding also. But the *Grappler* would lay at the mercy of tides and weather for another three weeks.

On July 19 the tugs *Leviathan* and *Emma* salvaged the *Grappler's* 80 tons of cargo, which was later sold at auction. A week later, *Grappler* settled into deeper water where she lay until Capt. Edward Walker, arriving with salvage equipment, rescued her on August 6.

But *Grappler's* ill-fated career was still not over. In late November, 1880, while steaming from Victoria to

Nanaimo with a load of machinery, she encountered a severe storm. In an unpublished manuscript, Fred Rogers relates what happened.

"A storm that had blown up while she was bound from Victoria to Nanaimo with a load of machinery for Dunsmuir & Dingle Coal Company, gave *Grappler* a rough trip. To compound the difficulties, her former engineer had quit. The new man, who had already experienced problems with an engine breakdown while yet in Nanaimo, was still unfamiliar with her engines.

"Weather was boisterous when *Grappler* cleared Nanaimo November 30 with a load of supplies for Cunningham's Canneries on the Skeena River, and after travelling 20 miles, she sprang a leak. The pumps were started, but as often was the case, ashes and cold dust accumulated in the bilges to clog them up. When Captain Meyers beached the ship in Northwest Bay, she sank to her guards.

"Tug *Skidgate* was chartered to help *Grappler,* and with a Receiver of Wrecks by the name of Mr. Peck aboard, fought her way through another stormy sea. Peck returned to Nanaimo while Meyers' crew patched *Grappler's* punctures at low tide. Then tug *Pilot* arrived. When all was ready, *Pilot* pulled her off the beach and took her back to Nanaimo. Fate was kind to the old ship, for they no sooner reached harbour than another storm blew up."

Thus the battle-scarred *Grappler* lived to sail again. To date, she had been involved in enough near disasters to sink a merchant fleet, yet each time, miraculously, she had survived. Three years later, however, she would not be as lucky.

Bursting with cannery supplies, gunpowder and 100 passengers, mainly Chinese cannery workers, *Grappler* put in at Departure Bay for 40 tons of coal. Unloading 50 kegs of powder at Nanaimo Sunday afternoon (a fortunate schedule in light of later events), she continued northward on the last lap of her fateful voyage. About 4 P.M., Captain Jagers acquired the services of pilot Sidney Franklyn from the inbound steam schooner, *Grace.*

By 10 o'clock that night, Duncan Bay was astern, the weather mild, the seas calm. As passengers squirmed restlessly in their cramped quarters, Engineer William Steele was anxiously sniffing about his ancient boiler. Seconds later, he hissed in Jager's ear: "Captain, there's a fire in the for'ard hold!"

Jagers instantly summoned Mate John Smith from his berth and informed him of the danger. "For God's sake, say nothing about it to the passengers — keep it quiet!" replied the first officer, then streaked below.

He ordered two Indian firemen to clear the coal from 'tweendecks, but as the smoke increased with every shovelful, Smith realized the fire was well advanced. Shouting for the hatches to be sealed, he and a deckhand wrestled a hose into position. On the bridge, Captain Jagers gave four sharp blasts from his whistle in the hopes of alerting anyone ashore, and told Franklyn to put about for Duncan Bay.

Passenger David Brown was retiring when he "heard hurried trampling and thinking all was not right went forward and saw smoke and smouldering fire outside and back of the furnace.

"I immediately returned to where my uncle, H. McClusky, was asleep and said in a low voice: 'Get up at once, the ship is on fire,' telling him at the same time not to alarm the other passengers. The injunction was, however, unnecessary, for all in a moment, as it seemed, the vessel became a mass of flames and then ensued a scene which beggars description."

Another passenger, Capt. John McAllister, was shipping four skiffs to his up-coast cannery. Aroused by shouts as flames swept the engineroom, he hurried below to offer his services. Engineer Steele was desperately trying to couple a hose. Racing topside, McAllister shouted at the panic-stricken passengers pouring from their cabins to form a bucket brigade. It was no use. The terrified Chinese could think only of reaching the lifeboats — with a total capacity of 22 persons.

By now *Grappler's* feverish decks were grey with smoke. Seeing he had little hope of launching the mobbed lifeboats, McAllister ran aft to clear his fishing skiffs. Lungs heaving in the acrid fumes, as *Grappler's* abandoned engines thundered at full speed, the mariner could loose only one craft, which he tumbled over the stern, then leaped after it. By the time he pulled himself over the gunwale, a white man and a Chinese had already boarded.

Ears ringing with the shrieks of the dying, McAllister looked about for oars. There were none. Undismayed, he salvaged a broom and a bamboo cane from the floating debris and began sculling his unwieldy skiff toward Valdez Island. Within minutes his hands were raw, but the heroic canner struggled on. Suddenly, the alarmed expressions of his passengers made him wheel about.

Blazing from end to end, steering gone, *Grappler* had reversed course and was charging down on them at full speed! The galloping inferno lunged at the skiff, then arched away. They were safe, for the moment. As she flew by, like some hideous, flaming bird, singeing them with her fiery breath, several passengers saw their last chance and leaped over the side. Painfully ferrying his craft back and forth, McAllister rescued "five or six men. . . and two or three Chinamen."

One Oriental had been supporting himself on a plank, which McAllister split in two for paddles, handing them to his strongest passenger.

"In the meantime," said the *Colonist,* "the steamer kept going backwards and forwards in an erratic manner, the passengers shrieking and yelling for assistance and the flames spreading rapidly over the vessel."

Landing his survivors on Valdez Island, McAllister paddled to where *Grappler* had made her last turn, picking up a "Chinaman, a Siwash, Steele, the engineer, and several other white men, making about a boatload. . . Although. . .loathe to go ashore from the shrieks which were being incessantly given from those around discretion compelled him, his boat being full, to put to shore again."

By now, almost exhausted, hands blistered and bleeding, McAllister "had terrible hard work to land. Being exceedingly close to the (Seymour) Narrows and the tide increasing rapidly, he did not consider it safe to venture out again, but lit a fire to warm those who were half dead with the cold, some having been upwards of an hour in the water."

The most dramatic account of that horror-filled April night was that of passenger David Brown. Upon rousing his uncle, named McClusky, they hastened on deck. "Men, some of them half-dressed," Brown recounted, "running frantically to and fro half bereft of reason, calling on others to save them, the cries of the horrified Chinamen adding to the fearful confusion. . . !

"As fast as a boat was lowered men jumped down into it — whites, Chinese, Indians — the coolies actually attempting to save their property, throwing clothing and bags of rice into the boats which capsized almost as soon as they were lowered. I could see there was no chance of saving my life by these means and took a set of steps, made it fast to a line, and threw it overboard, allowing it to tow alongside. When I saw the vessel had become unmanageable and that there was no possibility or running her ashore I dropped overboard, cast off the line and supported by the steps was rapidly borne away with the current."

He had not been in the water long when he spotted one of McAllister's skiffs, drifting keel up, and managed to "scramble on top of it, but had great difficulty in keeping there owing to the boat turning and tumbling in the numerous eddies." Nearby Ripple Rock's lethal rips churned his precarious float "among some Chinamen who were supporting themselves with various articles. Two or three grabbed my legs and as I felt my hold slackening I exerted all my strength and managed to free myself."

He "had scarcely done so when I saw a white man clinging to a small plank and called to him, as he appeared nearly exhausted, to keep up a little longer and was shortly enabled to assist him on the boat.

"I had long before this lost sight of the ill-fated *Grappler* but my companion and I kept up our spirits till we heard the roar of rapids and felt the increased strength of the current. We were spun round and round in the whirlpools, sometimes under the water and sometimes above, but held on like grim death. At last, about an hour after sunrise (they had been adrift for more than eight torturous hours) we drifted ashore on an island and were found in the afternoon by a couple of Indians in a canoe, who took us to a camp of loggers."

Upon being awakened by his nephew, Henry McClusky dressed and sped topside, where he became separated from Brown in the chaos. Seeing a group of whites axing down one of the ship's yards, to serve as a float, he helped them muscle it to the rail. But the timber was too heavy; in the frantic twilight it slipped over the side and vanished astern. At this setback, McClusky decided to chance the water and jumped. By extreme good fortune, *Grappler's* wake swept him right alongside the runaway spar. Clinging to the pole, he watched *Grappler* "disappear round a point of land, a perfect sheet of flame and oh! how my heart bled for them, knowing there were none near to save."

Finally he was picked up by McAllister and taken ashore, where he saw the dying steamer return with the tide, "burnt nearly to the water's edge and sink almost in the same place where she had been when the fire started."

One elderly passenger, Robert K. Hall of Vallejo, California, had a close call. He had helped Captain McAllister launch his skiff, then leaped to the assistance of some deck-hands trying to lower a starboard lifeboat. But the after tackle fouled, allowing the boat to swing by its stern. Jumping into the almost vertical craft. Hall and company clutched the seats as a volunteer hacked at the tackle with a knife.

When the rope parted, the boat somersaulted into the sea, pitching its nine occupants in every direction. As Hall, desperate, decided to try swimming ashore, all about him "the spectacle presented was a most dreadful one, heightened by the shrieks of the drowning Chinamen."

He was almost exhausted and about to give up when Mate John Smith and three others found him. Their boat was half-submerged, but Hall gripped its stern until another passenger, Edward Lane, rescued him in one of the ship's boats, taking him ashore.

The escape of passenger Henry Halenkamp, meanwhile, was miraculous. When the lifeboat he had helped launch capsized under the weight of too many bodies, Halenkamp was dragged under. Although it was but seconds, it seemed an eternity that he remained under, unable to surface. He was "full of salt water and my senses were beginning to leave me" when "some object striking the boat caused her, though full of water, to right herself." He gratefully clambered aboard with four others, to be rescued by some of *Grappler's* crew.

Others told dramatic and heart-rending tales of escape. Passenger John Cardano broke an arm when his boat capsized upon launching. He had to use his remaining fist to punch his way into one of McAllister's skiffs, occupied by two panicky Chinese. Sailor Mike Conlin and five comrades were trapped in the forecastle by flames. One managed to beat down a hatch — with his head — and reach deck, Conlin at his heels. But the three others were burned alive.

Like Captain McAllister, Captain Jagers, First Officer Smith and Pilot Franklyn, who remained at his blazing post in a vain attempt to steer the ship, Conlin was a hero. When *Grappler* had passed within a half-mile of shore, someone had cried: "For God's sake, somebody get a line ashore!" Conlin volunteered.

Unfortunately, his lonely swim became a nightmare. Two hundred feet from the ship, he looked back. At that instant, some of "the poor wretches who were being burned" fastened themselves to his hawser. Lest he be pulled under, cursing and sobbing violently, the courageous seaman let go of the rope. Finally struggling ashore, he collapsed on the beach. It was four frigid hours before Captain McAllister found him and hustled him to a fire.

But even hell must know an end; by morning it was over, and valiant McAllister rowed to Nanaimo for help. When *Grappler,* charred to the water-line, sank she had claimed almost a hundred lives. The exact figure was not known, as ticket records were inaccurate.

Early History Of
HEDLEY CAMP

THE little gold-mining town of Hedley, in the Similkameen Valley of British Columbia, lies at an elevation of about 1,700 feet above sea level and is situated at a point where Twenty Mile Creek, after swinging around the western base of Nickel Plate Mountain, emerges from its canyon and has cut a boulder-strewn channel through the river-benches to flow into the Similkameen River a short distance below the town. Nickel Plate Mountain rises out of the Twenty Mile Creek in a series of bluffs with nearly vertical faces, but its southern slope is less rugged and is covered more or less with a scattered growth of Douglas fir. Prospectors and others travelling over the Dewdney Trail would notice the beds of limestone, quartzite, and other rocks outcropping on the slope above the river valley. Looking up the Twenty Mile Creek the iron-stained rocks of Red Mountain would attract attention, as would also the folding of the stratified rock of Stemwinder Mountain on the west side of the creek. All of these together would indicate an area where conditions might be favourable for ore deposition and would, at least, warrant careful prospecting.

The first record of mineral claims having been staked on what is now known as Nickel Plate Mountain was in 1894, when James Riordan and C. Allison located three claims for the Hon. Edgar Dewdney, and J.O. Coulthard, of Keremeos, had a claim on what later became the Kingston Mineral Claim. These four claims were recorded at Granite Creek, but were not considered worth doing the annual assessment work and were allowed to lapse. In 1897 Peter Scott located the Rollo and about the same time C. Johnson and Albert Jacobson, grubstaked by W.Y. Williams, then manager of the Granby mines at Phoenix, staked the Mound and Copper Cleft claims. In 1898 Peter Scott returned to do the assessment work on the Rollo and afterwards staked the Princeton, Warhorse, Kingston, and other claims. In August of that year C.H. Arundel and F. Wollaston staked the Horsefly, Sunnyside, Nickel Plate, Bulldog, and Copperfield, and still later located other claims on the mountain. It was the Nickel Plate, however, which was to prove to be the bonanza claim and become the first producing lode mine of the Similkameen, as well as one of the major gold mines of B.C.

It was about this time that Peter Scott and others agreed on "Camp Hedley" as a fitting name for the new camp, in honour of Robert R. Hedley, then manager of the Hall mines smelter at Nelson, B.C., who had grubstaked Peter Scott the summer before when the Rollo had been staked. As news of the strikes began to circulate around Fairview, quite a number of the prospectors came over to the new camp in the early fall of 1898. Amongst the new arrivals to Camp Hedley were Harry Yates, Fraser Campbell, and George Cahill. Duncan Woods, for whom George Cahill staked the Mascot Fraction, did not come in until the spring of 1899. Later in the camp's history it was the Mascot Fraction which was to become famous, for, although it contained only eight or nine acres at depth, it was to prove one of the camp's richest spots. Seldom in the history of lode mining in B.C. has so small an area produced so much

(Right) The Chuchuawa Indian church about one mile east of Hedley is still in use today. It stands on reserve land and permission is required to enter grounds. The gravel road in background zigzags up the mountainside and leads to the site of the Nickel Plate mine.

(Opposite page) M.K. Rodgers packing out the first load of ore from the Nickel Plate mine in 1898.

(Below) The remains of the Nickel Plate mine's stamp mill and cyanide plant in 1986. Compared to the photo on page 125, only the building on the top of the hill remains standing.

wealth in gold. During the spring of 1899 many more prospectors came into Camp Hedley, and by the end of the year the surface of Nickel Plate Mountain was almost entirely covered with mineral claims.

In the fall of 1898, Wollaston and Arundel exhibited samples of Nickel Plate ore at the New Westminster Fair, where M.K. Rodgers, who was more directly connected with the early history and development of the camp than any other person, first saw them. At that time Rodgers was travelling through the country in the interests of Marcus Daly, of Butte, Montana, and he was so impressed by the appearance of the samples that he immediately left for the Nickel Plate to make a close examination. The inspection proved so satisfactory that, in November, Rodgers took a bond on the Nickel Plate, Bulldog, Sunnyside, and Copperfield Mineral claims, all of which were owned by Wollaston and Arundel.

The construction of a camp and the packing-in of supplies was at once commenced. The first supplies for the new camp at Nickel Plate were obtained from Fairview. In November, 1898, a pack-train of 35 horses laden with supplies left Fairview in the charge of George Cahill. Later, as things became better organized, supplies were shipped from the Coast cities to Penticton, then hauled by wagon to Keremeos, and from thence packed by horses to the Nickel Plate by the Camp Rest Trail. Permanent work on the claim was commenced on January 12, 1899, and within a year the bond was taken up. The consideration paid to Wollaston and Arundel was reported to have been $60,000, and a few years later the two partners sold other claims to Rodgers, and it was said to have been for a similar consideration.

In the early years of the Nickel Plate mine, Rodgers obtained a B.C. charter for the Yale Mining Company, and business was done through this company. Later on, when it was decided to build a mill, it was found that the original company's charter was not sufficiently broad to provide for the building of tramways, power flumes, and the like, or for the expropriation of land for rights-of-way. Consequently, a second company, the Daly Reduction Company, Ltd., was formed, and a charter obtained for it early in 1903, and from then on it became the operating company for both the mine and the mill.

Gomer P. Jones, who was to be connected with the Nickel Plate for so many years, was engaged by Rodgers as mine superintendent, and he arrived at the camp in August, 1900. Mrs. Jones and their daughter Avonia came in a month or so later and took up residence at the Nickel Plate. In the summer and early fall of 1900 a road about 15 miles in length was built over the mountains to the east of the mine to connect up with the Penticton-Keremeos Road, and from then on supplies were hauled direct from Penticton to the Nickel Plate. In the fall of 1900 work was also commenced on the building of a road between Keremeos and Princeton, and it was completed by mid-summer of 1901. Before the building of this road only the old Dewdney Trail had connected these two points.

In the fall of 1899, Thomas Bradshaw came over from Greenwood and bought the newly-built log hotel located near the mouth of Fifteen Mile Creek from a man by the name of Johnson. Shortly afterwards Mrs. Bradshaw and family came over to make their home on Fifteen Mile Creek. Bradshaw's stopping-place soon became well known to prospectors and others of Camp Hedley as a place where they could always be assured of a warm welcome, a good meal, and a comfortable bed. In course of time the establishment was expanded and, in addition, the Bradshaws had a thriving young orchard and alfalfa growing on their place and had also acquired a small herd of dairy and range cattle.

The land where the town of Hedley now stands was acquired by the Hedley City Townsite Company, and in the summer and fall of 1900 R.H. Parkinson, P.L.S., surveyed the town-site, and almost immediately building was commenced, judging by the Similkameen *Star*, which reported:

"Dave Hackney has a force of men busy constructing a large hotel. An assay office is also being built and will be occupied when completed by Messrs. Oliver and Fetherstonhaugh. Several other buildings will be started in the course of a few days, and as soon as the work on the road begins application will be made for a post office and mail service. Mr. R.H. Parkinson, P.L.S., will be manager for the townsite company and will be glad to furnish information regarding prices of lots, etc."

The Hedley Hotel, being erected by Hackney on Haynes Street, was a neat, two-story, hewed-log building which was opened early in March, 1901. Messrs. Kirby and Hine also erected a two-story log store building near the spot where later the Daly Reduction Company's office building was erected, and opened for business early the following spring under the management of F.M. Gillespie. Two small log cabins were also built on the town-site that same winter. During the summer of 1901 I.A. Deardorf, of Fairview, built a livery-barn, and C.E. Oliver put up a two-story frame building for an assay office and residence. The lumber for both of these buildings was hauled in from Penticton, but later that summer Messrs. Tillman, McDonald, and McRae hauled over their sawmill and planer from Phoenix and set it up on the riverbank across from the mouth of Sterling Creek and commenced cutting lumber. This mill was later to cut all the lumber required in the construction of the Daly Reduction Company's mill, the Twenty Mile flume, and other buildings, as well as the lumber needed in the town.

In 1901 F.M. Wells took a bond on the Kingston and Warhorse claims owned by Peter Scott, and development of the Kingston was commenced in the fall of the year. Later the Metropolitan claim was also acquired by Wells. Development work on the group continued more or less intermittently for a number of years until about 1936, when the Kelowna Exploration Company acquired the Kingston group.

The winter of 1901-1902 was a very quiet one for the new town, but in the summer of 1902 it was decided to build a mill for the Nickel Plate, and Hedley was selected as its site. Preliminary surveys were then made for the tramways, the power flume up Twenty Mile Creek, and for the mill-site by Wesley Rodgers, brother of M.K. Rodgers, and construction started that fall. Surveys were also sufficiently advanced so that contracts were let for the grading of the mill-site and for the building of the stone walls for the foundations of the mill, and this work was about completed by the spring of 1903.

In the late summer and fall of 1902, McDermott and Marks built the Grand Union Hotel, but sold it a few months later to Robert Herron and Anton Winkler. A few years later Herron sold out his interest to his partner, and under the management of Winkler it was in continuous operation until it was destroyed by fire on December 31, 1918. In the fall of 1902, C.E. Oliver and his associates began construction of the Commercial Hotel, which opened in the late spring of the following year under the management of Neil Huston and W.A. McLean. Within a few months McLean became the sole proprietor, and the Commercial Hotel still stands. In August, 1902, James A. Schubert, well known in the Okanagan, bought out the Kirby and Hine store and moved it down into the town near the bridge, and the log building thus vacated was later used by the Daly Reduction Company for temporary offices in the early construction days at the mill. Later that year Charles Richter, of Keremeos, built a two-story building as a butcher's shop and residence, and he supplied the town with its meat until he sold out the business to Cawston and Edmond. Shortly after this, John Mairhofer became associated with the business, first as

store manager and later as owner. His connection with the business continued until 1931, when he sold out to Eugene Quaedvlieg.

In the fall of 1902, W.E. Welby commenced running a stage line between Penticton and Hedley. Initially, the stage left and arrived on alternate days, but the following year a daily service each way went into effect, Sunday excepted. The trip usually took about 12 hours, which included a stop at the old town of Keremeos for dinner and a change of horses. Open stages, which carried six to eight passengers, were used, and the mail and travellers had to take the weather as it came, be it sunshine, rain, or snow. Later Welby acquired a Concord covered stagecoach, but this was reserved for special trips and occasions. Fred Revely, who had bought out Deardorf's liverybarn, ran a daily stage to Princeton in conjunction with the Welby stages, but travellers from or to upper valley points had to stop overnight in Hedley.

Up to this time one of the principal complaints of the residents was the absence of mail service. However, in June, 1903, this was remedied when F.M. Gillespie was appointed the town's first postmaster. He combined these duties with those of manager of Schubert's general store, and at first the post office was in that store. A little later an annex was built on the east side of the store

(Left) The three gentlemen are: left, Mr. Dickson, director, centre, J.L. Merrill, president; right, G.P. Jones, general superintendent.

(Below) The Nickel Plate mine's stamp mill and cyanide plant at Hedley.

(Above) Part of the historic Hedley Cemetery in August, 1985.
(Below) A breath-taking view of the Similkameen Valley, showing the main highway and the Similkameen River. The winding gravel road in the foreground leads up Nickel Plate Mountain. This photograph was taken from about halfway up the mountain.

building for the exclusive use of the post office business, and boxes were installed for rental to the public. This continued to be the town's post office until 1908, when Gillespie bought out Love's drugstore, and there it remained for the next 27 years. In the early part of 1903 L.W. Shatford put up a one-story building on Scott Avenue and opened a general store with F.H. French as manager. Two or three years later the store building was greatly enlarged and the firm's name changed to Shatfords Limited. In 1903 Dr. F. Rolls opened a drugstore and office.

In the early spring of 1903, work was commenced simultaneously on the construction of the mill and the grading and building of the flume which was to furnish the power for the mill. Four-horse freight teams, loaded with machinery, steel rails, and general supplies of all kinds, now became a familiar sight on the roads. About this time S.L. Smith resigned as agent for the Canadian Pacific Railway (CPR) at Penticton and accepted the position of accountant for the Daly Reduction Company, a position he held with this and the two succeeding companies until about 1937. Hedley became his home for 41 years. In August, 1903, Dr. H.A. Whillans accepted the position of company doctor, and he and his family moved down from Princeton to take up residence in Hedley. Later that year A.H. Brown, of London, Ontario, was engaged as mill superintendent, and shortly afterwards took charge of the mill. Brown was well liked by the men serving under him and also was held in high regard by the people of the town.

In September, 1903, Hedley held its first Labour Day celebration, which was rather a modest affair even although "some two or three coach loads of merrymakers came from Loomis, Wash., to join in the festivities and fraternize with the good people of Hedley." The main event was a baseball game between the Hedley team and one from Nighthawk and, although the visiting team was the better, due mainly to Wesley Rodger's pitching, Hedley won the game, on which a good deal of money had been bet by the backers of the respective teams. In addition, there was two days of horse-racing, and a grand ball marked the climax to the event, with the music furnished by "that famous knight of the bow" Joseph Brent, of Okanagan Falls. Later Labour Day celebrations were on a much larger scale. From a $1,000 to $1,200 would be given in prize money, and rock-drilling contests, baseball, and horse-racing were featured. Rock-drilling teams would quite often come from places as far away as Rossland to compete in these contests. Many visitors would come to the celebrations from both upper and lower valley points. The visitors would begin to arrive on Sunday evening, and by Monday morning the town would be full and travel in those days was by democrat, buggy, or horseback. The big Labour Day dance was the outstanding social event of the year for Hedley, and the best orchestra available was secured for the occasion. Sports would be resumed on the following Tuesday, but by early evening the visitors would have all departed to their various homes, and by nightfall the town had a tired, deserted look about it, with scarcely a soul to be seen on the

The W.T. Shatford General Store, Hedley, in 1903. Frank French, the store manager, is standing in the doorway. The man on far right, with suspenders, is George Cahil, who staked the Mascot Fraction for Duncan Woods.

streets as Hedley retired early to bed.

By the late fall of 1903 the mill building was about completed, and a good start had been made on the installation of the machinery. The tramways were all graded and most of the track laid, and also good progress had been made in the building of the Twenty Mile flume. It might be interesting to note that the ore crushers and stamp batteries were made in Eastern Canada, as was also the large air compressor for the new powerhouse. But the ore conveyers, Frue vanners, waterwheels, pumps for the cyanide plant, electric locomotives for the tramway, and most of the electrical equipment came from the United States, as did also the 20 large tanks for the cyanide plant. Twelve of these tanks were 34 feet in diameter by six feet in depth, and the remaining eight were 30 feet in diameter by 10 feet in depth. All were made from California redwood, knocked down and shipped from San Francisco by boat to Vancouver, thence by CPR to Okanagan Landing. From there they were transferred to the lake steamer and delivered at Penticton and hauled by freight teams the 50 miles to Hedley.

The first stamps of the new mill were dropped on May 4, 1904, and after a short period for making necessary adjustments, all 40 stamps commenced to drop, and their muffled roar became a familiar sound in the town. For the first few years of the mill's operation a considerable proportion of the values recovered was in the form of free gold caught on the plates. Each month two gold bricks, one from the free gold off the plates and the other from the gold recovered in the cyanide plant, were taken out under special escort to Penticton, and from there shipped by Dominion Express to the United States assay office in Seattle. The concentrates from the 24 Frue vanners, rich in gold, were pulled daily and dumped into the bin below, and after a period allowed for drying, the concentrates were then put into double sacks — a heavy cotton sack on the inside and a strong jute one on the outside — and the sacks well sewn. The sacked concentrates, weighing around 100 pounds or better each, were hauled to Penticton, and from there were shipped to the Tacoma smelter. The four-horse teams which hauled in supplies also hauled out the sacked concentrates on their return trip to Penticton. Dougal Gillespie, of Okanagan Falls, who then held the contract for hauling the company's freight, was paid $20 per ton on incoming freight and $9 per ton for the back-haul of concentrates. The round trip usually took about a week to complete.

During the years 1903-1906 the town grew rapidly and many new buildings were erected. "Hedley City is the liveliest town of its size in the interior," reported the *Star*. "Its hotels are always full, and, as in the case of the Commercial, an annex has been found hardly adequate for the demands upon this popular hostelry. There are two excellent general stores, in one of which, Mr. Schubert's, is the post office. There is a first class butcher shop conducted by Messrs. Edmonds & Cawston, and a livery and feed stable run by Fred Revely; a drug store and all the other businesses usually found in a bustling mining camp.

"Good sidewalks have been laid and a lot of street improvements made by the townsite company of which C. Oliver is the energetic resident manager.

"A fine hotel is now under construction at a cost of $15,000 and a large residence for M.K. Rodgers has been completed."

In the summer of 1903, Grace Methodist Church was built. This was the first, and for many years the only, permanent church building in the town. It was built mostly by volunteer labour under the enthusiastic direction of Rev. J.W. Hedley. For many years it played a prominent role in the life of the community, serving as headquarters for the school, the Twentieth Century Club, and the library. Other early ministers were the Revs. J.E. Fleming, C.E. Docksteader, L. Thomas, R.W. Hibbert, J.J. Jones, and George Kinney. As was to be expected, Hedley was but one of the many churches served by these ministers in connection with their work elsewhere in the district. The Presbyterian Church soon began to conduct services, at first with Rev. G.L. Mason in charge and later under Revs. J.C. Stewart, A.J. Fowlie, E. Hardwick, D.F. Smith, J.T. Conn, and A.H. Cameron. The latter, a pioneer of Western Canada at the time of the building of the CPR, was probably one of the best remembered of the early ministers. Presbyterian services were usually held in Fraser's Hall (or Fraternity Hall, as it came to be called), which after 1905 was shared on alternate Sundays with the Anglican Church. In May, 1905, the Archdeacon of Columbia, Ven. Edwyn S.W. Pentreath, visited Hedley, and as a result the congregation of St. Mary's was organized, complete with Ladies' Guild. Rev. E.P. Flewelling became the first resident Anglican clergyman, and the following year he was succeeded by Rev. E.R. Bartlett. Rev. Henry Irwin — Father Pat — so well known in Rossland in the early days of the camp, and remembered for his many kindly acts, was an occasional visitor to Hedley in the early days of the town, and when here would conduct services in one or other of the hotels' dining-rooms. An Anglican Church, however, was not built until the early years of World War I.

The first school for the children of the town was opened in September, 1903, in a room at the rear of the Methodist Church. Miss M.L. Whillans, a sister of Dr. H.A. Whillans, was Hedley's first school teacher. Under the terms of the "Public Schools Act" this was known as an "assisted school," and it was administered by a board consisting of S.L. Smith (secretary), W.A. McLean, and J. Brass. When inspected on May 5, 1904, it was reported that 19 pupils had attended irregularly throughout the year but that good work had been done. Miss Whillans resigned in June, 1904, and was replaced by Mrs. A.J. Colbeck. In September of that year the Hedley School District was created.

From the outset the major problem facing the School Board was that of finding suitable accommodation for its school. For a time a site on Ellis Street was occupied, then the Gazette Hall was used for a few months in 1905, after which the Ellis Street property again came into use. It is not to be wondered that the Inspector's report contained this comment: "The teacher is working under difficulties — room too small and poorly equipped." When school reopened on August 21, 1905, Mrs. Colbeck had been replaced by her daughter, Alice, and the house of W.A. McLean had been leased as a school. Plans had, however, been drawn for a new schoolhouse, but the tenders received were too high. The School Board, having secured a promise that the provincial government would pay the rent until a proper building was built, soon embarked on a novel plan. Several businessmen in the town, S.L. Smith and G.B. Lyon amongst others, were consulted, and they "secured a lot, built a house on it and moved the school into it before the last day of January, 1906," at a cost of $756.38. In the meantime, Miss Marion Lamont had become the teacher. In February, 1906, the plan to build a two-room school was announced, but further delays ensued and the school was not completed until July, 1907. Miss H.J. Blake was the first teacher in this new school.

In passing, it should also be noted that a school was started at the Nickel Plate mine early in 1905 under Miss K. Johnson. Elected to the provisional School Board were G.P. Jones, Charles Joyner, and E. Mills. Miss M.R. Ford taught at this school during the 1905-06 term, and thereafter the school was discontinued.

In the summer of 1904, C.A.R. Lamby, government agent at Fairview, held an auction sale of the lots held at Hedley by the government, and many of the lots were sold at good prices. About that time, too, M.K. Rodgers was successful in his negotiations with the Department of Indian Affairs at Ottawa for the purchase of the flat on Indian Reserve No. 2, which adjoined the company's millsite. With the acquisition of this land the company had ample room for buildings for its staff, and also for sites for tailings dams, limekiln, and lumber and wood yards. In the spring of 1904 the company announced its intention of laying pipelines to supply water from their Twenty Mile flume to the houses in the town, but evidently difficulties were encountered, for in August the *Star* announced:

". . . the town now depends almost entirely upon two wells and a water wagon for its supply of water. All the water in the creek is now diverted for mill purposes. In the meantime until a permanent system is completed, preparations are being made to give a temporary service through pipes laid on the surface of the ground."

This system was none too satisfactory and gave rise to the peculiar statement in the *Star:* "Hedley can boast of having the most unique water supply in B.C. It furnishes warm water during the day and cold at night." In due course pipes were laid underground and a normal service was instituted.

During this year, too, electric power became available. As early as December, 1903, it was reported that "Electric light was used at Hedley on Saturday night (December 5) last, the dynamo being driven by steam power." Its use became more general the following spring, for in April the poles were in place, ready to receive the wire, and that month electric lights were used for the first time in the Methodist Church. By the fall the houses were being wired for electric light.

In the fall of 1904, the Similkameen Hotel opened for business. A modern, well-built, and comfortable hotel, it soon became a popular stopping-place for travellers.

Unfortunately for the town, it was burned down in February, 1916. For some time, too, it had been rumoured that a newspaper was to be published in the town. This became a reality on January 19, 1905, with the appearance of the first issue of the Hedley *Gazette,* with Ainsley Megraw, formerly of the Vernon *News* and Midway *Advance,* as editor and manager. The *Gazette* was, under his management, a clean, well-printed, weekly paper. This newspaper suspended publication on August 16, 1917, at which time James W. Grier, a veteran newspaperman of the Kootenay and Boundary country, was owner and editor.

Hedley had the distinction of having the first bank in the Similkameen Valley, and for a short time the only bank in the valley. On April 20, 1905, the Bank of British Columbia opened a branch, with G.H. Winters as manager and L.G. MacHaffie as teller. Winters was shortly afterwards transferred elsewhere, and MacHaffie was promoted to manager and J.J. Irwin became the new teller.

It was also in the summer of 1905 that John Jackson built the New Zealand Hotel, but this hotel was destroyed by fire in the early morning hours of November 6, 1911. That fall G.H. Sproule leased a building he owned to John Lind and the Peterson brothers which, when reconstructed by them, was opened in 1906 as the Great Northern Hotel. Hedley now had six hotels, and for a few years there was business for them all. As was common in mining towns of the day, the hotel bars were kept open 24 hours a day and seven days a week.

In the summer of 1905, Finlay Fraser built Fraternity Hall, thus giving to the town its first hall for meetings, dances, and other social events. It was also used as a lodge-room by the Masonic Lodge and other fraternal organizations. When the hall was under construction, a freak wind-squall struck with such force that the building was toppled over and badly wrecked, but fortunately the men at work on it escaped with only minor injuries. Business houses were also increasing. John Love was now well established as the town's druggist, and James Clarke cleaned and repaired the watches and clocks for the camp. In September, 1905, Campbell and Shier opened their "gents furnishing and clothing store."

Hedley was very definitely growing up, as is indicated by the number of community projects and organizations undertaken. No sketch of the early days of the town would be complete without some mention of the Twentieth Century Club, which had its birth on New Year's Eve, 1903, at a social evening held in the Methodist Church. During 1904 it held weekly meetings in the Methodist Church and reached a membership of over 100. Its career was, unfortunately, a short one, for it disbanded on September 7, 1906.

By 1905, too, the Hedley Athletic Association was flourishing under the presidency of Dr. H.A. Whillans, and plans were afoot to establish a gymnasium. In August of that year the Hedley Orchestra came into being, with H.A. Wright as conductor, and the following month the first concert was performed for the public. Fraternal organizations were also not neglected. Early in March, 1905, the first steps were taken towards the organization of a Masonic Lodge. The moving spirits in this effort were

A. Megraw, Arthur Clare, Finlay Fraser, and A.H. Brown. The probationary stage of the lodge's existence came to an end in July, 1906, when full standing was granted to Hedley Lodge, No. 43. A few years later an Orange Lodge was also organized.

One of the first campaigns undertaken by the editor of the newly established *Gazette* was the organization of a Board of Trade. Early in January, 1905, a preliminary meeting was held, with A. Megraw as chairman and John Love as secretary, and formal organization was soon completed. While there was temporarily much enthusiasm, the interest began to wane, but later, in 1907, the organization was reorganized and continued to function with greater success.

In September, 1905, a change was made in the management of the Daly Reduction Company. M.K. Rodgers was succeeded as manager by R.B. Lamb, A.H. Brown was succeeded as mill superintendent by W.H. Brule, and Arthur Clare ceased to be mill foreman. However, Gomer Jones continued on as mine superintendent. Employees and residents of the camp alike were sorry to have to say "good-bye" to Rodgers and the members of his staff who were leaving with him. For the year that Lamb was manager, the Nickel Plate was a steady producer, and it might be noted that it was under his management that the machine and carpentry shops were built and equipped with all the necessary machines and tools for making any needed repairs to the plant. In the fall of 1906, Lamb was replaced by F.A. Ross as manager and E.A. Holbrook replaced Brule as mill superintendent, and a few months later Clare returned to take up his former position as mill foreman. During the three years that Ross was manager, the mine continued to make steady shipments of ore to the mill at Hedley, which was also supplemented by ore from Sunnyside No.'s 2, 3, and 4, where important ore bodies had been developed while Rodgers was still man-

ager. During the early years of the mill's operation many were the visitors who came from far and near to see the plant and to have explained to them the various processes used to extract the gold and also, if possible, to ride up the tramways to the mine. In the spring of 1907 the Geological Survey of Canada sent in Charles Camsell to make a survey of Hedley Camp, and the fieldwork was completed the following summer. Camsell's very comprehensive report on the geology of the camp was printed by the Department of Mines at Ottawa in 1910.

These changes in company management naturally affected the town, which was almost entirely dependent upon the mine and the mill. An indication of this dependence is reflected in the history of the Hedley Hospital. In February, 1905, employees of the Daly Reduction Company discussed the possibility of establishing a hospital. Many meetings were held, and a public subscription raised which, together with a grant of $1,000 from the provincial government, assured the funds for the construction of the building. In September, the General Hospital Society, with a provisional board comprising G.P.

(Right) The Great Northern Railway trestle spanning Twenty Mile Creek. The Daly Co.'s dam can be seen below the trestle, and the reduction plant is on the right.
(Inset) The first GNR train into Hedley, Dec. 23, 1900. The "station" was a converted boxcar.
(Below) The Similkameen Hotel in 1906.

Jones and John McKinnon from the mill, and Finlay Fraser, F.H. French, and L.G. MacHaffie from the town, was organized. In addition, deeds of two town lots were transferred to the society by Hedlund and Thomas. The following month a temporary hospital of two beds was opened in the building on Ellis Street vacated by the school. The following year the hospital was incorporated, and in the spring of 1907 the new building was erected by Messrs. Boeing and Brass.

"The building is a three storey structure 24x40 feet with a wing 16x26," reported the *Gazette.* "The lowest floor or basement contains kitchen and laundry and the main floor, entrance to which from the outside is made from the hillside, comprises the hallway, one large five-bed ward, two private wards, operating room and bathroom. The third-storey is yet unfinished but could supply two comfortable bedrooms for nurses."

However, the hospital was not opened until the early spring of 1910, at which time the *Gazette* made the following explanation of the delay. "Although young in years it has experienced the rigors of adversity, and that

at a very early period of its existence, for the scheme was scarcely launched until a staggering blow was administered to it by accession to power of unsympathetic management of the leading industry of the place, and without the active sympathetic interest and co-operation of that industry the institution could not drag out an existence. That blow was administered when Lamb became manager and the weight of it was not lifted until his successor, F.A. Ross had taken his departure. But it is pleasing to note that as it was the attitude of indifferent aloofness on the part of the management of the D.R. Co. which left the institution practically stranded and unable to open its doors when the building was completed, it was from the same institution that succor came under the new ownership, for it was the generous vote of $500.00 by the directors of the present company in New York which put fresh life in the people here and encouraged others to help until the $500 has grown to $1300 and a sufficient sum was in hand to enable the institution to be opened for the reception of patients, while a contribution of 50 cents per month from each employee is an important lift for the

board in providing funds for running expenses."

The first operation was performed in the hospital on February 23, 1910. Dr. M.D. McEwen was the surgeon-in-chief, and Miss Bond and Miss Fraser, both of Vancouver, were the first two nurses. The hospital was closed down in the fall of 1930 and never reopened, and finally in 1945 the affairs of the society were wound up and it passed out of existence. During the 20 years the hospital was in operation, it gave good service to the community and district, but, like many other small hospitals, receipts seldom, if ever, kept up with expenses, and at the end of the year there was usually a deficit which had to be met in order to keep the hospital in operation.

In the years 1906-08, building operations had slackened off somewhat, although T.H. Rotheram built and opened his pool-room and store on Scott Avenue in the summer of 1907. Shortly after his arrival, Rotheram organized a volunteer fire brigade, which later gave valuable

(Above) Gen. Supt. G.P. Jones in 1915. (Opposite page) The Hedley Gold Mining Co's tramway up Nickel Plate Mountain. Said to have been one of the longest in the world, hundreds of horses and mules were gathered from around the countryside to haul the heavy cables into position.
(Below) An excursion to the Nickel Plate mine in 1909. This photo shows a group posing beside one of the tramway locomotives and ore cars.

service to the community in fighting the fires which occurred from time to time. As early as 1903 the possibility of telephone connection with other parts of the province had been discussed. However, two years were to pass before the Dominion government built a line from Kamloops to Penticton by way of Merritt, Princeton, Hedley, and Keremeos. By February, 1905, the valley had direct wire connection with the outside world, for a telephone had been installed in Love's drugstore. Later an exchange was installed at the rear of this store, and Love received the appointment as agent. Originally the wires had been strung on trees, but by July, 1907, it was announced that they had been put on poles from Hedley to Vernon. Still further evidence of the town's growth was the organization of the Hedley Golf Club in April, 1909, with the links laid out on Pinto Flat.

In 1909, the Daly Estate gave an option on all its holdings in the Hedley Camp to a New York syndicate headed by I.L. Merrill. That spring

ORE TRAIN
NICKLE PLATE MINE
HEDLEY B.C.

the syndicate sent in a party of five or six people to sample and make an examination of the mine. The examination took a good part of the summer to make, and, when completed, the decision was reached to take up the option. A new company, the Hedley Gold Mining Company, Limited, now came into being and took over the former company. In the reorganization which followed, Gomer Jones became general superintendent and Roscoe Wheeler, of Oakland, California, was engaged as mill superintendent. B.W. Knowles, one of the original examining party, became the mine engineer and William Sampson, who had been a shift-boss, was promoted to mine foreman. F.A. Ross and E.A. Holbrook, after a residence of three years at Hedley, left the camp, taking with them the good wishes of employees and residents of the town.

For years one of the great needs of the valley had been proper railroad connection with the outside. The agitation for such a line was prolonged and, with the advent of rival proposals, at times, heated. Principal contenders were the Vancouver, Victoria and Eastern Railway and the Great Northern Railway. In 1908 the latter company, having acquired the charter of its rival, commenced the grading of their line from Keremeos to Brookmere, and steel was laid during the following summer and fall. Regular train service was commenced on December 23, 1909, and the first train from Oroville, Washington, to Princeton arrived at Hedley Station at 11 A.M.

"The station at Hedley has not yet been built," announced the *Gazette* "but a box car has been provided on a siding with steps leading up to it, a stove placed therein and shelves around the sides for parcels and luggage."

With the coming of the railroad the four-horse freight teams and stages disappeared from the roads, and a new era was entered upon. Of all the many prospectors who once had climbed the steep slopes of Nickel Plate Mountain and of nearby Apex, Northey, and Riordan Mountains, and had there trenched, dug open-cuts, sunk shafts, and driven tunnels in their search for gold, how very few now remain. Some had left early for distant, greener fields; others, with more faith, stayed on until no longer able to do the assessment work on their claims; most are now dead. A few attained wealth, others made a smaller stake, but the majority gained experience only as the recompense for their labour. With their passing went much of the romance and glamour of those early days of Camp Hedley, the memories of which still linger on in the hearts of the few.

STEVESTON
A SPLENDID OPENING FOR CAPITALISTS

From a mud flat on the Fraser River to a spirited boom town, this community struggled packing the finest Sockeye that would showcase its heritage to world prominence by 1890.

NEW Brunswick native Manoah Steves, now living in Baltimore, Maryland, considered his next move carefully. Before returning to Canada, he studied maps and geography. Impressed by British Columbia, he wrote to the postmaster of Victoria and New Westminster. As a result, he received the name of William Ladner on the lower mainland and an invitation to visit the area.

In 1877, Manoah landed near Point Garry on Lulu Island, a delta on the Fraser River in southwestern B.C. Finding a heath of 400 acres free of rocks and boulders, so unlike his native province, Manoah bought some property and began a modest homestead. He built dykes on his land and started a dairy farm. To New Westminster residents, these island pioneers were known as "mudflatters," a pejorative for the tidal marsh plain on which they lived. With few other settlers, the land was exactly that: a mud flat of lush and lusty grass. But to this pioneer it was a new life for his wife and six children. In 1878, they bid farewell to Maryland and rejoined their father on the homestead.

In the wake of Manoah's ambitions, William Herbert Steves, his oldest son, imagined the area becoming an energetic metropolis. William laid out the town of "Steves," envisioning a major seaport terminal competing with Vancouver. He mortgaged himself with land purchases and speculative business deals. In 1889, at age 29, William instilled the family name in Steveston. He also started the town's first newspaper. On January 31, 1891, the Steveston *Enterprise* made this bold, though now sentimental prediction: "Vancouver will be a future suburb of the city of Steveston."

Steveston truly possessed its founder's ambition. In the 1890s, the construction of waterfront wharves, fish camps, and boat yards created a boom for the salmon canning companies and fishermen. In the 1891 edition of the *British Columbia Directory*, the following promotion appeared on the inside cover: "Steveston is the Coming Town of B.C...this place has been designed by nature for a large town. . . . Splendid Opening for Capitalists who wish to reap big profits." Although pretentious by today's standards, such advertisements were not uncommon.

It was indeed a splendid opening for capitalists. In 1882, only the Phoenix Cannery occupied the wharf. Then in 1889, Henry Bell-Irving, a civil engineer from Scotland, purchased nine canneries in Steveston and formed the Anglo-British Columbia Packing Company Limited. By 1893, four more canneries started on the three mile waterfront strip known as Cannery Channel. In total, 14 canneries packed nearly 200,000 cases of salmon, at 48 pounds per case, that year. By 1897, the 23 canneries that competed for shoreline space, packed over 500,000 cases, mostly for overseas markets. With the construction of hotels, saloons, stores, an opera house, and a post office, Steveston became a pioneer boom town.

(Above) A coloured postcard depicting the salmon fisheries at Steveston, B.C. (Right) A typical salmon cannery, this coloured postcard shows Ewen's Cannery. (Below) An 1895 salmon label from the Gulf of Georgia Cannery at Steveston. The Sockeye depicted on every label was the symbol of prosperity for the canneries and the community.

Sockeye salmon overwhelmed the Fraser River before the commercial fishing and canning industry expanded. Not surprisingly, the lore of Steveston's "unlimited" bonanza attracted many immigrants from Japan, the United States, and Europe. Various ethnic groups established fish camps near the canneries; language barriers generally divided them and kept the peace.

As word of Steveston reached Japan, the Japanese government permitted and, even encouraged, its citizens to emigrate to Canada. For these Japanese capitalists, the Sockeye were better than gold. They had already established a herring fishery in B.C. With the influx of Japanese fishermen to Steveston, they formed the Japanese Fishermen's Benevolent Society, a trade union with a membership of 1,800. At the turn of the century, about 4,000 Japanese men, mostly single, lived in Steveston.

By this time the canneries had combined to form the Fraser River Canners' Association. They were determined to keep raw fish prices down. Native Indians were the first fishermen on the Fraser River. They harvested salmon primarily for subsistence, but as canners moved in and promoted competition, they switched to commercial fishing. The Indians and whites organized several times and were known as the British Columbia Fishermen's Union in 1899. Their membership, almost equalling the Japanese, was often at odds with them over fish prices.

The fishermen toiled for days at a time in small, two-man skiffs on the Fraser. Only the weekly fishing closure, a conservation measure, permitted them and the salmon a respite from the drudgery. On Friday midnight, a cannon boom signalled the start of the closure. Hungry and sodden after five days of fishing, the weary fishermen pulled in their gill nets and started for home. In complete darkness, hundreds of boats probed and clamoured their way in, using only kerosene lanterns for light. Much bad language could be heard on shore when boats and nets became entangled.

Back on land, time was scarce. Nets had to be cleaned and mended; boats repaired and restocked. Yet somehow they found time on Saturday nights for excitement in the saloons and gambling houses. But by Sunday afternoon, throngs of masts and oars once again cluttered the channel. Before six in the evening, these gentlemen manned their paddles and charged out to sea. Many curious visitors arrived from Vancouver to witness this summertime ritual. Once in position, the fishermen pause in anticipation. . . . Suddenly, the cannon booms and hundreds of gill nets sail over the gunwales and thrash up the Fraser. Imagine the commotion as the fishermen scrambled to have the first net in the water.

Within 20 minutes, the nets would be brimming with salmons and humpbacks. The fishermen pitched the six pound Sockeye into the storage wells, and sometimes in the spirit of fun, the humpbacks into an adjacent net. As the wells filled up, the canneries would send out a tug to remove the catch. If the canners felt generous and the demand was high, they paid the fishermen 20¢ per fish; however, more often than not, it was only 10¢ or 15¢.

Spontaneous is the word that best describes Steveston weekends. By 1900, thousands of excited fishermen, cannery workers, and residents crowded the rustic boardwalks. During the fishing season, the population swelled from 400 to 6,000. The sockeye rush was a splendid opening for capitalists but, also, a splendid occasion for gambling, drunkenness, and brawling.

The scene was rather chaotic as hundreds of single men, without the calming influence of women, guzzled 5¢ beer in crowded bars. These were the sure ingredients for disorderly conduct, and Chief Const. Thomas Calbrick had his hands full. In 1895, he requested a new jail for Steveston when he realized that too many people had keys for the old one.

The Steveston police had other troubles as well. In 1900 the Crown seized all police records looking for evidence of bribery paid by Chinese businessmen who sold liquor illegally. The Crown suspended the police chief and replaced him with the reform-minded John McAllister. He rounded up the gamblers and bunco men, some from as far away as Seattle, and told them to get out of town. But that still did not reduce the gambling houses and brothels. By 1906, three more chief constables would succeed him. Apparently the provincial government refused to finance a new courthouse and jail for Steveston. A sardonic note in a 1906 police report berated the government's decision: ". . .the resident municipal population is just as morally clean as any to be found in the civilized world."

Those less boisterous joined the Salvation Army temperance parades held on Saturday nights. Marching down Moncton Street, the paraders encouraged the "fallen" in the gambling houses, saloons, and brothels to repent. Yes, "sporting women," too, capitalized on the occasion. No one knows how successful the paraders were, though many people did hurry to witness this spectacle.

There were not many operas in the Opera House, just some union meetings. But Charlie Windsor, owner of the Garry Point Cannery, once used it to stage an old-time Indian dance for 700 natives. For decorations he made streamers of salmon can labels and covered the dance floor with tin stamping scraps from the cannery.

Steveston became the salmon capital of the world because it canned the finest Sockeye at a reasonable cost. Its favourable location near Point Garry, a well-known navigation landmark, courted tall-mast sailing ships from around the world. They could cruise in to Cannery Channel and dock at the canning plants directly. After loading up with canned salmon, they sailed back to Australia and Europe and sold the product for half the cost of fresh meat.

The cannery workers made up the other half of Steveston's transient population. Originally, native Indians and whites cut the fish and packed the cans. The whites spent the whole winter and spring making cans by hand. The companies also employed Indian and Japanese women and, even their children, to fill cans, paying them all $1 to $1.25 per day. Interestingly, child daycare was not a problem in the canneries. The companies set up a house where the working mothers took turns babysitting the children. If a house was not available, the children stood nearby or were carried on their mothers' backs as they worked.

Labour shortages in the 1890s brought the Chinese to Steveston from the railway construction camps, or other canneries in the United States. They were experts at butchering fish. Because fish is highly perishable, their speed and accuracy was essential if it was to be canned immediately. The white workers then shifted to minor supervisory roles or moved elsewhere to mining and logging. By 1895, Chinese labourers made up the majority work force, earning 1¢ per can.

The need to can everything within a 10 to 12 week period imposed a frantic pace on everyone. The Chinese labourers worked nonstop gutting 2,000 fish in 10 hours. By 1900, they worked on a contract basis arranged by an English speaking Chinese boss. The language barrier still existed and contributed to a misunderstanding in one case. On August 1, 1901, the Vancouver *Province* reported an incident that lead to an "Insurrection of Chinese in a Cannery in Steveston This Morning." Foreman R. Williams apparently used poor judgement when he tried to discipline two employees for "doing their work carelessly." According to the article, Williams tried "to put the refractory Chinese forcibly out of the cannery, when they refused to leave at his command." Perhaps, because of the language barrier, they could not understand what he was trying to accomplish. But as he persisted, "all the Chinese in the place left their work, and, with their knives raised above their heads started threateningly for the white foreman." Cooler heads prevailed, however, and following a brief delay, work continued as usual.

Working conditions inside the canneries were brutal. The Chinese workers canned the fish by heating filled cans in a large open vat, steaming with hot water. They added salt to make it hotter. In the early days, they stayed in the "Bathhouse" and kept it closed to retain the heat, mistakenly believing that a draft or outside air would harm the product.

By the turn of the century, the canners considered the production bottleneck of manual labour. Because there was no way to increase the butchering or canning process when fish were plentiful, the canners rejected the surplus and would not pay the fishermen for their catch. During the peak year of 1897, thousands of salmon lay dead, fermenting in the channel, among the reeds and the rushes, because the canneries lacked the processing capacity. With prolonged low tides, the air soured over neighbouring Richmond. Ironically, the farmers downwind of the source objected and petitioned the Richmond council for action. These grievances reached the Health Department in Victoria and prompted Dr. Davie to

(Left) The Smith Butchering Machine of 1906 was dubbed the "Iron Chink" because it gutted and cleaned a whole salmon faster than any of the Chinese workers. The serrated wheels simultaneously cut and gorged the fish before another set sliced it for canning.

(Below) Steveston's Moncton Street in 1899, looking east from Third Ave. The great fire of 1918 razed the buildings on the south side of the street. The fire started behind the Star Cannery one block due south and, spread north by high winds, caused over $500,000 in damage.

Two coloured postcards depicting the salmon industry. The top view shows salmon being unloaded at a New Westminster Cannery. The bottom view shows the interior of an unidentified cannery with the salmon about to be processed.

visit the area. However, after a swift inspection and brief lunch in Steveston with the council, he soon returned to his office bewildered and dumbfounded. Eventually, the stench and the complaints abated after high tides and nature took its course.

However, as necessity is the mother of invention, a Canadian entrepreneur would develop a butchering machine to change the industry. In 1901, Mr. E.A. Smith from London, Ontario, formed the Smith Cannery Machines Company in Seattle, Washington. With a capital investment of $21,000, he built the Smith Butchering Machine two years later and installed one for testing in Bellingham, Washington. After some minor improvements, the machine proved so reliable and efficient that it became known as the "Iron Chink," quite an hon-

(Top) The Britannia Cannery's Native Indian bunkhouse is one of the few remaining company bunkhouses still intact. As many as 50 workers bunked in this house across from Britannia Cannery.
(Left) The Britannia Cannery shipbuilder's workshop in 1992. Built in 1890, it has seen fires, flood, and windstorms; it not sits abandoned partially surrounded by the wetland forest.
(Below) The Gulf of Georgia Cannery Plant in 1992. Built in 1894, this cannery became the single most productive B.C. cannery in 1902, earning the nickname "Steveston's Monster Cannery." Tall-mast sailing ships berthed directly at the plant's shipping doors to load canned salmon for world markets. Situated beside the Star Cannery, it narrowly escaped the great fire of 1918 and continued production until 1946.

ourable mention knowing that it replaced some of the indispensable Chinese labourers.

However, on this side of the border, the canners dismissed the idea of a machine equalling or surpassing the Chinese workers. Inevitably though, they installed five machines in the Fraser River canneries in 1906. Before long, production increased and so did employment, to keep up with the butchering machine. Today, after many decades, Smith Butchering Machines still operate on the same principle.

Despite the boom time in Steveston, not all canners and fishermen prospered. By 1900, about 30 canneries and thousands of fishermen operated on the Fraser River. Competition engaged the companies and unions in a classic struggle over prices. The B.C. Fishermen's Union demanded a firm 25¢ per fish; the Fraser River Canners' Association offered a sliding scale of 20¢ and 15¢ through the season. Previous strikes failed because of union disorder. This struggle, though, would pit union against union and spotlight the town.

By custom, the Japanese and other immigrants boarded in company bunkhouses. With a strike looming on July 1, 1900, the companies threatened to cut off food and support for the Japanese. To strengthen their position, the Japanese and B.C. Union pledged mutual support, then called for a strike on July 8.

After 10 days, the Fraser was fat with Sockeye. The unions' solidarity crumbled as the Japanese grew impatient with the strike. Confrontations occurred on the Fraser between B.C. Union boat patrols and Japanese strike breakers. The Canners' Association exaggerated minor clashes and used its influence with the local judiciary to persuade the Attorney-General to send in troops. So on July 24, 1900, 200 soldiers from the Sixth Regiment, Duke of Connaught's Own Rifles (D.C.O.R.), commanded by Lt.-Col. Charles C. Worsnop, assembled on shore at 6:30 A.M. Steveston was under the grip of martial law.

Before long, 2,000 wearied Japanese fishermen slipped out in their skiffs and cast nets in the Fraser. They had remained loyal to the B.C. Union until hunger and intimidation won out. "They had seen strikers parade and wax eloquent, but without practical result," said a report in the Richmond *Review*. The Japanese settled for the Canners' original offer. The B.C. Union, however, maintained its vigil as the strike polarized the community.

The Canners' Association then started rumours that the Japanese were importing vast quantities of arms. Believing the strikers would riot, the troops dispersed to guard the Gulf of Georgia Cannery, the Phoenix Cannery and the Scottish-Canadian Cannery, furthest on the flat.

The situation was not really as tense as it seemed, however. In fact, Colonel Worsnop had sympathy for the strikers. The most serious incident occurred when the fishermen surrounded the soldiers bivouacked behind the Gulf of Georgia Cannery, taunting and jeering them as "Soldiers of the Queen" and "Sockeye Fusiliers." Henry Bell-Irving demanded that Colonel Worsnop read the Riot Act, but the stoic commander declined, content to watch the strikers wear down and disperse.

The great strike of 1900 ended with a compromise on July 30 when the B.C. Union accepted a fixed price of 19¢ per fish. The D.C.O.R. went home, and the canneries resumed full production. More strikes would occur in

Canneries provided bunkhouses for transient fishermen and cannery workers with separate quarters for whites, Japanese, Chinese and Native Indians. This row was part of the Scottish-Canadian Cannery complex on Point Garry. The company sounded a whistle for its employees whenever fish were brought in. Living conditions were primitive with disease sometimes affecting the whole house.

Steveston, but without military action. A later provincial inquiry vindicated the B.C. Union, as the local justices who issued the order for the military's presence could not substantiate their claims.

The move into the twentieth century brought misfortune to Steveston. With a population of 10,000 in 1906, devastating fires, floods, and a decline in fish stocks curtailed the fishing and canning industry. A spring flood in 1905, the Chinatown fire in 1908, and five years later, the Hell's Gate slide, 95 miles away in the Fraser Canyon, are but three examples.

The fires and floods upset the residents, but the slide crippled the economy. It disrupted the salmon spawning cycle enough to reduce the 1917 run by more than 80 percent. Many canners either abandoned the business or consolidated into shipbuilding. The people who depended on the salmon runs either went into farming or quit entirely. However, the following year would test the mettle of the community as never before.

The Star, Steveston, and Lighthouse canneries, three hotels, the post office, 15 to 20 dwellings, and most of the wharves all went up in smoke on May 14, 1918. Frustrated by strong west winds, the fire fighters dynamited several houses around the canneries in a futile attempt to create a fire break. When the fire gutted the Lighthouse Cannery, 22,000 cases of salmon sat ready for shipment. Thousands of cans popped like gunfire or plunged into the channel. Precious fishing nets and boats disappeared.

Fire engines from Vancouver, New Westminster, and Point Grey rushed to Steveston. One Vancouver engine broke down en route; a second engine ran into trouble at the scene. The retired Harold Steves, Senior, son of W.H. Steves, described it best for a Steveston history project 20 years ago: "The fire of 1918, that was the one where the fire engine from Vancouver broke down before it got here, and when they did get here — some of the Japanese had stores along there in the part where I said Chinatown used to be, one of them packed his safe out in the middle of the road, and in the thick smoke, the fire engine hit it! That finished it. The only place left on that side of the street was the brick building."

Damage exceeded half a million dollars, and 600 people became homeless. While the canneries had insurance, the small businessmen and fishermen lost their livelihood. However, Steveston's misfortune was a boom to other canneries in B.C. and the U.S.A. After two consecutive bad years, business shifted elsewhere as canners and fishermen tried to recover. Demand for net twine inflated the price beyond what the fishermen could afford. The salmon run would start within six weeks and many fishermen had nothing. Despite the calamity, Steveston redeemed itself to dispel the legacy of misfortune. When the fishing industry did recover, it was in a league that was never the same.

From a mud flat to an industrious community was the dream of an ambitious pioneer. W.H. Steves passed away in 1899 before Vancouver surpassed his visionary seaport terminal. Steveston never did incorporate, but it propelled the westcoast fishing industry into the twentieth century. Entrepreneurs made fortunes and pioneers built lives on the bounty of the Fraser River. Now approaching the twenty-first century, Steveston is the largest commercial fishing harbour in Canada.

The Salvation Army temperance parade marching down Second Ave. from the wharf on Saturday night, passing all the bars and gaming houses. To the left of the Misfit Clothing Store is a sign advertising "Temperance Beer" for 5¢ a glass.

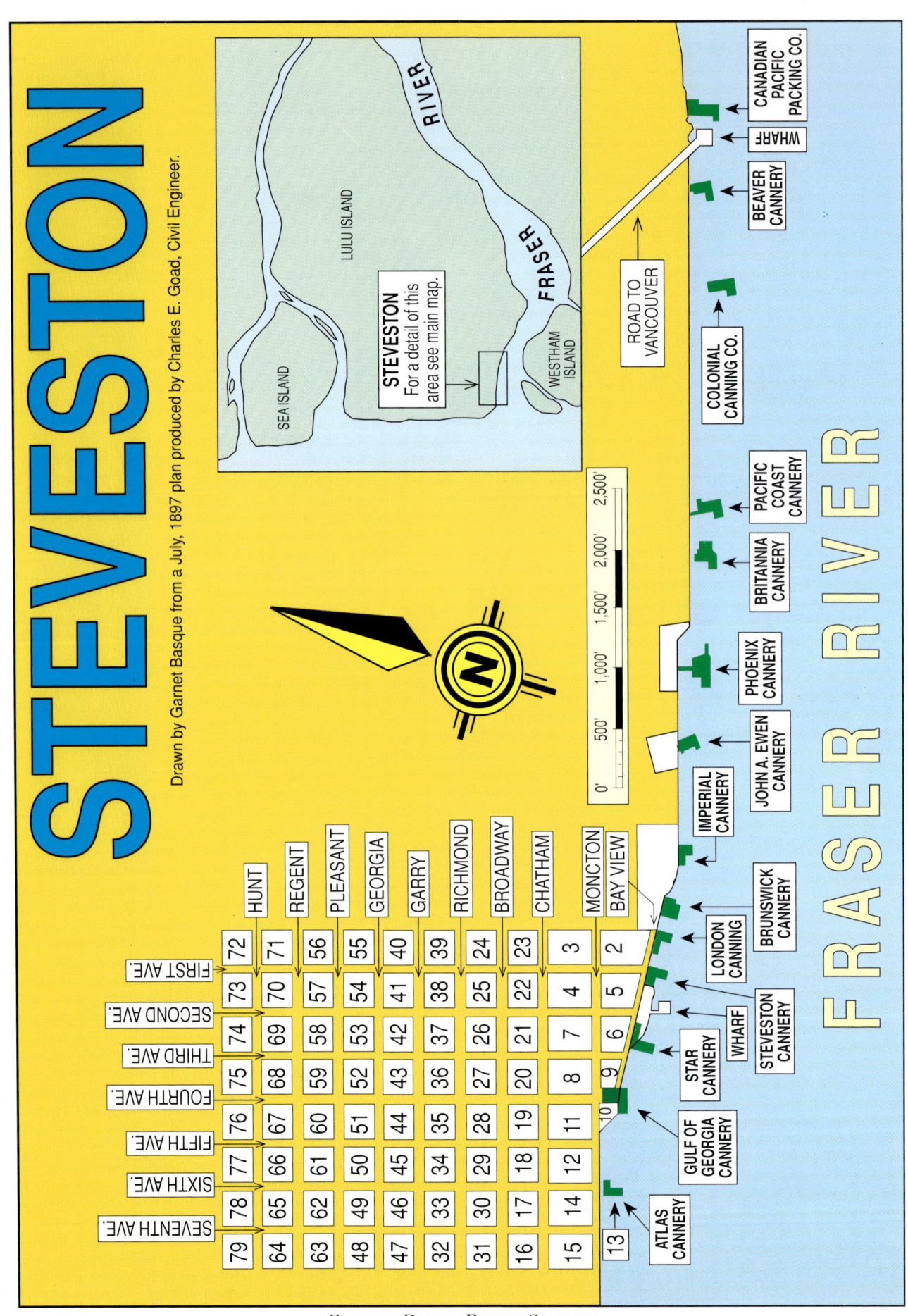

STEVESTON

Drawn by Garnet Basque from a July, 1897 plan produced by Charles E. Goad, Civil Engineer.

LULU ISLAND

RIVER

FRASER

SEA ISLAND

STEVESTON
For a detail of this area see main map.

WESTHAM ISLAND

ROAD TO VANCOUVER

0' 500' 1,000' 1,500' 2,000' 2,500'

CANADIAN PACIFIC PACKING CO.

WHARF

BEAVER CANNERY

COLONIAL CANNING CO.

PACIFIC COAST CANNERY

BRITANNIA CANNERY

PHOENIX CANNERY

JOHN A. EWEN CANNERY

IMPERIAL CANNERY

BRUNSWICK CANNERY

LONDON CANNING

STEVESTON CANNERY

WHARF

STAR CANNERY

GULF OF GEORGIA CANNERY

ATLAS CANNERY

FRASER RIVER

HUNT — 72 73 74 75 76 77 78 79
REGENT — 71 70 69 68 67 66 65 64
PLEASANT — 56 57 58 59 60 61 62 63
GEORGIA — 55 54 53 52 51 50 49 48
GARRY — 40 41 42 43 44 45 46 47
RICHMOND — 39 38 37 36 35 34 33 32
BROADWAY — 24 25 26 27 28 29 30 31
CHATHAM — 23 22 21 20 19 18 17 16
MONCTON — 3 4 7 8 11 12 14 15
BAY VIEW — 2 5 6 9 10 13

FIRST AVE. SECOND AVE. THIRD AVE. FOURTH AVE. FIFTH AVE. SIXTH AVE. SEVENTH AVE.

(Left) Built in 1890, the Britannia Cannery now sits hauntingly quiet. Converted to a shipyard because of reduced salmon stocks, it repaired and maintained fleet boats until 1979. The 1890 salmon pack that shipped directly to overseas markets, bypassing Victoria and San Francisco, drew world attention to Steveston's canneries. (Opposite page) A plan of the town of Steveston and the waterfront showing the location of the various canneries. (Below) The heart of Steveston, the waterfront today is home for almost 1,000 fishing boats, making it the largest commercial fishing industry in Canada. In the background are restaurants and marine supply stores that cater to both tourists and fishermen.

INDEX